# MORE FRANCE PLEASE

# MORE FRANCE PLEASE, We're British

## *15 LESSONS ON LIFE IN FRANCE*

Helena Frith Powell

GIBSON SQUARE BOOKS

*For Julia, without whose ability to perform one-handed cartwheels this might never have happened.*

This edition published for the first time in 2005 in the UK by

Gibson Square Books Ltd
15 Gibson Square, London N1 0RD
Tel: +44 (0)20 7689 4790; Fax: +44 (0)20 7689 7395
info@gibsonsquare.com
www.gibsonsquare.com

© 2005 by Helena Frith Powell

ISBN 1-903933-56-0

Sales by Signature
Castlegate 20, York YO1 9RP
Tel 01904 633 633; Fax 01904 675 445
sales@signaturebooks.co.uk
www.signaturebooks.co.uk

UK distribution by Central Books Ltd
99 Wallis Road, UK London E9 5LN
Tel +44 (0)845 458 9911; Fax +44 (0)845 458 9912
info@centralbooks.com
www.centralbooks.com

Printed by WS Bookwell Ltd

# Contents

*Swot Notes on France*

# Acknowledgements

A huge thank you to John Witherow and Carey Scott at the *Sunday Times* for giving the go-ahead for the French Mistress column, which was the catalyst for this book. Also to Karen Robinson for coming up with the name. Masses of thanks to all the people that feature in the book. I have been hugely impressed and touched by the amount of time people have been prepared to give to me and how open they have been with their stories. Thank you to Jaqcues Kuhnlé for reading through it all and correcting both my French and my English. Thanks to my friend Jonathan Miller for his brilliant editing and ceaseless enthusiasm. Also many thanks to the witty and wonderful Carla McKay for coming up with hundreds of titles and listening to me drone on for hours, something that is unlikely to change. I am eternally indebted to Peter and Dominique Glynn-Smith for bringing us to France in the first place. I dread to think how dull our lives might have been if it hadn't been for that chance meeting with you. Thanks also to Martin Rynja, my publisher, for coming up with the idea for the book and his exceptional support throughout the process. I am indebted to Dawn Alderson at Russell-Cooke Solicitors, Bill Blevins at Blevins Franks International and John Siddall Financial Services for all their invaluable professional help. Finally a huge thank you to my lovely husband Rupert who always was, and always will be, my favourite editor.

# Preface

This is the book I wish I could have read before I moved to France. I hardly knew the country at all, and knew nothing of how to live there. I was carried away by the whole adventure of it. Going to a new place, a strange language, a different culture. I was fed up with living in a small village in Sussex where the pub was the focal point of life. I was tired of getting on smelly trains up to London most mornings and horrified at the prospect of spending everything I ever earned on school fees. Even if France wasn't the answer, it had to be better than where we were.

But why did we pick France? France is the country that has everything: the most romantic city in the world, great food, fine wines, two skiing areas, great beaches, endless countryside, trains that run and roads that let you drive. But above all, it is as far south as you can go before things get strange. Even though I am half Italian, I would not dream of living full-time in Italy. I remember too vividly the hassle my Italian aunt endured when she owned a house on the Amalfi coast. And even though the weather is better in the south of Spain, I just don't feel comfortable there; neither in the British enclaves, nor in the parts reserved for the Spanish. Spain has the air of having been half-built by a Moroccan in a hurry. France feels solid.

British buyers are considering buying houses in more exotic locations—Morocco, Croatia, Thailand. Yet what would I do if anything went wrong? How happy would I feel with this culture? How would I understand the language, laws and customs?

Britain has had a relationship with France for more than a thousand years, even if most of the time we have been enemies. But we are more like members of a family who always argue at Christmas. When I lived in Germany, *that* felt really strange. People would stop me when I was driving and tell me to turn on my lights. At street crossings, nobody moves until the little green man tells them to. All this felt very alien. In contrast, France feels familiar. Many of the words are similar; the people are courteous, even if sometimes difficult. There is a bad bureaucracy, but it is a bureaucracy that works. France is both familiar and foreign, I thought.

In retrospect I was naïve. We showed up in an isolated house, with a water system supplied by a spring, an electricity current that kept going off, all the while speaking only a few words of the language. In addition, I was about to give birth to our second child. It is only through good luck that things didn't go horribly wrong for us.

What I have tried to do here is to cover the topics that are essential if you are to make a success of living in France. I have had the help of many others who have been very kind in sharing their success and failure with me. Things that I wish I had known before we moved and things I found out through (sometimes) bitter experience.

If a second house or new life in France isn't yet an option for you, I hope this book will give an idea of the exhilaration and challenges that are involved in moving abroad. There is nothing wrong with a bit of armchair emigration—there are certainly fewer forms to fill in!

Helena Frith Powell
Sainte Cécile
Languedoc

# Languewhat?

I had never thought about living in France until my husband came back from a press trip to Thailand. Before he had unpacked the suitcases, he told me we were moving there. I ignored him.

'I met a couple on a boat,' he said. 'I want to go there and write a book.'

'Don't be ridiculous,' I said. 'Things aren't that bad.'

'They live in the Languedoc. It's in the south.'

'The what-e-doc?' I said. 'Never heard of it.'

To me the south of France was Cap d'Antibes, Juan-les-Pins, Monte Carlo. Beautiful people, vast yachts and rocky beaches. Good for a holiday, but not a place to live and bring up children.

At the time we were living in Sussex in a converted printing press. We had just finished doing it up, a job that had taken almost two years. Rupert, my husband, worked for the *European* newspaper. I was working freelance as a journalist, as well as headhunting for media companies. Although my mother is Swedish and my father is Italian, after their divorce when I was two years old she had married an Englishman. I had been living in England almost all my life and felt totally at home there. I couldn't imagine a life without Marks & Spencer, thatched cottages or muddy country walks.

Nothing more was said about moving until a letter arrived three months later. It contained a hand-drawn card showing a lovely house on a hill, surrounded by olive trees and vineyards.

I read the contents of the card and looked at the photo the couple had taken of my husband lying in a hammock on a cruise ship. Obviously another tough assignment for him.

'It was such fun meeting you on the Star Clipper,' read the card. 'Do come and stay if you're ever in the region, we would love to introduce you to the Languedoc.'

I looked at the drawing of the house again and compared it with the view from our front door. The French house had palm trees, sunshine and a swimming-pool.

Idyllic though the village of Mayfield is, we looked out over a car park and constant drizzle. Next door was the pub, which I had grown to hate. Not so much because it was next door, but because Rupert wasted too much time and money there.

'That idea of yours about moving to France,' I said. 'Let's go and have a look.'

Within a week we were planning a trip to Pézenas, a medieval town twenty minutes away from the Mediterranean. Olivia, our daughter, was then around three months old. We left her with Rupert's parents and drove to Stansted. Just the drive to the airport was enough to make you want to leave the country. Despite allowing for more than two hours to get there we almost didn't make it. We ran on to the plane and arrived at Carcassonne in blazing sunshine an hour and a half later. It was early October.

Peter Glynn-Smith, an attractive man of around 70 with more energy and wit than all the 30 year olds hanging around the Mayfield pub, met us at the airport. It was him Rupert had met in Thailand. Married to Dominique, a French woman, Peter had lived in the Languedoc for 12 years and had grown to adore the region.

'This is a wine growing area, the biggest vineyard in the world,' he said, as we drove from the airport. 'There are a couple of great cities, Montpellier and Nîmes, we are close to Spain—we often pop down there for lunch—there are large sandy beaches, flamingos and oyster beds, and mountains to the north, which funnel the wind in another direction. They say we get more than 300 days of sunshine a year, but when it rains, it really rains. I have lived all over the world, but I like it best here.' The best news for house hunters was that the house prices were a third to a quarter of what you pay in England, helped by the strong pound. We were sold.

The housing market in the Languedoc, when we first started looking, had agents, but they seemed reluctant to give us any information about houses for sale. A former Buddhist monk turned estate agent drove us long distances to look at unsuitable properties. He was deaf in one ear and overtook cars on corners. Another agent, an Englishwoman, was reluctant to sell anything. Rupert explained to her that this was her job.

'Oh no,' she said. 'I don't want the place overrun with foreigners. I liked it best a few years ago, when it was quieter.'

We wanted an old property in the middle of nowhere, ideally with five bedrooms and a swimming-pool. We looked within a 30 kilometre radius of Pézenas for over a year.

Every time we came out we would stay with Peter and Dominique. The problem was that, because Peter is an interior designer, their house is one of the most elegant in the region. We would trawl around wrecks all day and come back to the tranquillity of St Siméon, and wonder if we had started on a mad mission.

To make matters worse, Peter introduced us to all his friends, most of whom he had designed houses for. For example, Norman and Stephanie, who live in one of the most beautifully converted mills in the world. We would go for long lunches on their terrace, which is in between their pool and the vineyards next door. It was the ultimate in luxury picnicking. You felt you were in the middle of the countryside, while sitting at a marble table drinking local wines.

In all we must have made seven or eight trips, some with

Olivia, some without. I'll never forget her taking her first bath in the Languedoc, in Peter's beautiful round marble sink. The trips were great fun. Peter and Dominique looked after us splendidly, organising dinners and showing us the region. As soon as we found a house with any potential at all, we would call Peter in to take a look. 'This could be the most exquisite house in the south of France,' he would invariably announce, tape measure in hand. I would stare at three rotting walls and a hole in the roof and try to share his vision and enthusiasm.

By now, of course, I was totally set on moving. I had come to love the way of life I had seen so far. I imagined my children (I was pregnant again) running around Peter's pool with his daughter Laura. I envisaged daily trips to the Pézenas delicatessen to stock up on marvellous cheeses and local goodies. I thought more and more about a life in the sun.

But by now we had also given up all hope of ever finding the perfect place. The isolated house with swimming-pool and five bedrooms didn't seem to exist. We would have to try to rent somewhere and try to find a house once we were installed.

On the final afternoon on what we had decided would be our last house-hunting trip we ended up near Clermont l'Hérault, a small town to the west of Montpellier. Another English agent showed us a couple of properties. He had been a plasterer and came to the south of France ten years ago on holiday. After a week in the sun, he decided not to go back to Bolton. The most impressive thing about him was the amount he drank.

'I start off with beer,' he explained. 'And move on to a bottle of wine and half a bottle of Ricard every night.'

His shape and colour confirmed this.

We told him that we were visiting one more place before returning to England. We were about to give up on the whole thing or try to find somewhere to rent.

'Well, you'll buy it,' he said.

'How do you know that?' we asked.

'I just do,' he grinned, tapping his red nose.

We drove away resolving never to drink as much as he did. But the strange thing was, the minute we turned off the main road to follow the small track to the final property, we knew it was right. The tiny country road ran through vineyards and *garrigue*, the scrubland made up of stunted oak trees, broom, rosemary and thyme.

I was expecting something disappointing around every corner, but instead, three kilometres after we had turned off the main road, we saw the house on top of the hill. Old stones, blue shutters, swimming-pool, roses and olive trees in the garden, and not another house in sight. As we turned up the drive, my nipples stood on end. Historically this has always been a good sign.

I found it hard not to smile as we were taken round. The lady who owned the house insisted on showing me every cupboard in it. I felt like jumping up and down shrieking: 'I don't care if there isn't a single bloody cupboard within a ten-mile radius.'

'Will you stop grinning,' hissed Rupert as we looked round the garden. It was stunning, filled with yellow, pink and red roses. There were palm trees by the pool and olive trees dotted around.

'I can't,' I replied, almost in tears.

The couple suggested we walk up to the vineyard behind the house to get a feeling for the countryside it stood in.

'Just make an offer now,' I said to Rupert. Both he and Peter glared at me.

'I love it,' I said.

'Well of course you do,' said Peter, trying to look patient.

We walked back to the house and I tried to look nonchalant. Downstairs the whole vast room was lined with books. One of our main concerns about moving had been where to put our books. It was a sign. I had to concentrate on not throwing my arms around the owners. Could it possibly get any better?

'The house is called Sainte Cécile,' said Madame Millière. 'She is the patron saint of music.'

I envisaged opera blaring from the house as we swam naked in the pool on balmy summer evenings. Did I imagine it, or did Bea, then in my tummy, do a somersault?

After about an hour we said goodbye to Monsieur and Madame Millière and went back to plan our strategy. There was no question we wanted the house. We could just about afford it, although it would mean re-mortgaging in Sussex. How easy would it be to close the deal?

We spent a night dreaming of life at Sainte Cécile, how the children would learn to swim there, the walks we would take, the dinner parties we would give, repaying the hospitality we'd been shown on our visits to the region.

At the estate agent's the next morning we resolved to play it cool. But we were due to fly out that day and there was no way I wanted to leave without signing something. We were instantly shown in to the boss's office. When I started telling him that there were cracks in the walls, he said that we could arrange a survey if we wished, but the property was sound. Besides, a Swiss couple had already made an offer. Just then, his phone rang. I caught my husband's eye. I thought it was important that he realised how crucial his next move would be.

'If we don't get this house I will never recover,' I whispered.

When the agent came off the phone, Rupert asked him how much the Swiss had offered. What about if we offer a sum £10,000 higher? I will ask them, he replied. We had to sign a formal offer, then the agent drove off to see the vendors in person. We were told to go for a walk and a cup of coffee.

We walked around in the sunshine for an hour, worried to go into any shops in case we lost the signal on our mobile phones. I kept telling my husband to call back and offer the asking price immediately. After an age, the phone rang.

'Please come back to my office,' said a voice.

They had accepted!

We all drove to the house, went on another tour and were shown all the cupboards again. Then we were offered a glass of champagne and some canapés. It all seemed terribly civilised.

'It's a bit less than we had hoped for,' said Madame Millière, patting my pregnant tummy. 'But I wanted the house to go to a young family.'

We sat down and went through all the things they would leave in the house and decided on a date for us to move in. They wanted one final summer there with their grandchildren so September the first was agreed on. This was six months away.

'And you must come and have lunch next time you're down,' said Madame Millière. 'I want to introduce you to my gardener.'

We went back to England with a photograph of the house, which I put on the fridge as I counted the days until the move. It showed the French windows downstairs, framed with roses. You could see the strong sun lighting up the glass.

From then on my life was taken over with 'the move'. I began to arrange the mortgage, the French bank account, how to give birth in France, childcare, having telephone lines installed and so on, all issues I will be covering in this book. I didn't speak any French. I spent most of my later school years in Sweden, where the first foreign language in schools is English. I took this as an opportunity to bunk off instead of doing something useful like learning French verbs. We employed a local French friend, Isabelle, to give us lessons twice a week. But I found it incredibly hard to get my head round the language. With Isabelle's help I fired off faxes to the Post Office, the local mayor's office, the local GP and banks. By the time we moved in September I would be seven months pregnant and wanted to get as much organised as I could beforehand.

The last week in August Rupert left for the Languedoc with Hugo and Julia, his two older children, then aged six and eight. The idea was that he would be there to sign the final papers and sort things out for when we arrived. Olivia and I would travel down a week or so later with Donia, our nanny, who had agreed to come and live with us.

Once Rupert had gone we started putting the whole contents of the house in cardboard boxes. The removal van arrived

two days before we were due to leave and took everything out
of the house. I was going to spend my last two days in England
staying with a friend.

I locked up for the last time and handed the keys over to Pat,
our neighbour. Her dogs, Hector and Camber, came out and
started running around, barking madly. My appearance was
usually a sign that they were going for a walk. I wondered how
much I would miss the walk out of the back of the house over
the fields, and the views of Sussex I loved. Pat looked as if she
was going to start crying and I thought briefly about cancelling
the whole thing. What the hell was I doing going to give birth
somewhere I didn't even speak the language? What was the
French for epidural?

Instead I gave Pat a hug and told her to come and see us.
Hector and Camber looked glum as I opened the gate and
walked out without them.

Two days later at the Ryanair check-in at Stansted I was
thinking even more seriously about going back to the unfur-
nished house in Mayfield. My main worry was where Olivia
and I would sleep. The floor might have been an option for her,
but in my advanced stage of pregnancy no way was it for me.

'I'm sorry,' said a particularly po-faced member of the air-
line's staff. 'You're too pregnant to fly.' Rarely have I come
across such unpleasant people, and I am including experience
working for a headhunter in the city of London, as I have
whilst flying the dreaded Ryanair.

This sadistic member of staff was telling me I wasn't, in fact,
going to get on the plane to pursue my dream, that, no, I
wouldn't be pruning my roses by the pool that afternoon.
Instead I would be driving back to Sussex with Donia and
Olivia to Mayfield.

I thought briefly about leaning across the check-in counter,
grabbing her polyester necktie and slowly strangling her.

'You're not serious?' I asked, hoping it was all a nightmare.

'I am,' she replied. I could see the beginnings of a smile form
under her fourteen layers of cheap foundation.

'But I have flown all over the world while pregnant. I even called BA to check how many weeks pregnant you can be and still fly.'

'Ah, well, they have different rules than us. With us, anyone over seven months pregnant has to have a certificate from their doctor.'

'And if I have that I can fly?'

'Yes.'

'How do you suggest I get you one now? I mean can I call my doctor and get her to fax it?'

'Oh no, I shouldn't think so.'

Olivia started to cry.

I picked her up and looked around me pleadingly. Was there a doctor in the check-in queue?

A colleague of Miss Sadistic came to my rescue.

'If your doctor could fax us something now, on this number, we could let you on,' she said, handing me a piece of paper.

I didn't dare explain to them that my doctor had recently committed suicide and that the lady who had taken over hardly knew me, so it was unlikely she would be able to say whether I could fly or not. I gloomily took the piece of paper and headed for the back of the queue.

Donia, who had been looking for some last-minute supplies of Calpol, joined us.

'You haven't got very far, have you?'

'We're not going,' I said.

She laughed and picked up Olivia who was falling asleep on the luggage trolley.

'No, I'm serious.' I explained what had happened.

I've always found a pregnant woman weeping hysterically is pretty effective in any situation. So when I got through to the secretary at the surgery (thank God it was the grumpy one's day off) I wept and told her what had happened.

She reacted like Moneypenny when James Bond is in a crisis.

'Don't you worry my lovey, we'll send it through straight away. Leave it all to me.'

Less than an hour later we were airborne, heading to our new home. I have never been so relieved to be on a Ryanair plane.

We landed in Carcassonne an hour and half later. It was wonderful stepping out of the plane into what felt like a sauna. I stood at the top of the steps and breathed in the air of my new home: wonderful, if slightly tarnished with aviation fuel. Rupert was there to meet us. He told us that the furniture had finally arrived that morning and the men were busy unloading the truck. Max the cat had made it too but was refusing to come out of the cage he had travelled in from England.

The three kilometre drive from the village to the house was even more beautiful than I remembered. The vines, the olive trees, the huge pines close to our house were all swaying in the gentle breeze. I was desperate to get to my new home and float in the pool. In fact, that day was spent mainly arranging for the beds to be put up so that we all had somewhere to sleep that night—Rupert had so far been camping in the garden.

By early evening the beds were in place and I went for my first dip. It was one of those situations where the reality is better than the fantasy. I felt totally relaxed and happy, despite the fact that the house was a shambles and there were around 150 boxes still to unpack. Olivia ran around the pool with her plastic caterpillar. Donia was busy covering herself in baby oil to ensure optimum tanning.

After the swim we opened a bottle of wine on the terrace. I remembered a moment of doubt I had had a few months previously about moving. 'I bet you,' a friend of ours in Mayfield had said, 'that after six months you'll be wondering what on earth you've been worrying about.' He was right, but it happened on the first day.

# Lesson 1
# Where to Live?

We ended up in the Languedoc by chance. But there are probably those of you out there willing to do some research and come to a decision on where you want to end up based on facts, as opposed to some guy on a boat. There are many things to consider.

Of course, the first thing you need to decide before you pick a region is exactly what you are moving to France for. If you're going for sunshine, don't move to Brittany. If you love wine, you should probably look at one of the many wine regions. If you're an aeroplane fanatic, try Toulouse.

Do you need to commute back to England for work? If you do, it would be wise to move somewhere within easy reach of several airports and the TGV. Do you speak any French at all? If not, pick a region that is used to foreigners, where they have language courses and where some of the locals speak English.

There are whole books dedicated to Paris and Provence. Obviously they are totally wonderful places and should be considered by anyone looking to move to France. But as particularly the latter corner of France is well-tracked by people such as Peter Mayle, I have included below the new regions which you will most likely want to explore if you are looking to buy a second home or move permanently to France.

*Northern France*

Those of you who are not mad about the sun can look at the north of France. Northern France has long attracted Brits wanting holiday homes within easy reach. The most popular areas have traditionally been Pas-de-Calais, Normandy and Brittany. The downside here is that the climate is not so very different from England, albeit southern England, although the winters are probably a touch less severe and the summers more reliable. The prices up north are more affordable than down south and if you're looking for wreck to do up for a modest amount of money this is where to start.

In Britain, Normandy is renowned for its half-timbered houses, its Camembert cheese and its cider. In France, it is renowned as the home of Madame Bovary and the part of the country where the British live.

'Normandy is fabulous,' says Guillaume de Perthuis, whose family have had a *château* there since the time of William the Conqueror, 'but it is overrun with Britishers. They came in the Normandy landings in June 1944 and haven't gone home.' His mother, the Countess de Perthuis, says that she has fond memories of the Normandy landings, even though the English bombed much of her property. Nowadays she claims not to be bothered by the English buyers, but that is maybe because she spends most of her time in Paris. 'We seldom see English people in our part of Normandy,' says the Countess. 'Perhaps it is because we live in the plain of Caen and the English people stay closer to the coast.'

Normandy has traditionally been popular with the English because it is so near to England's shores. David and Imogen Gardener bought a house there two years ago for that very reason. 'We looked at houses in other parts of France,' says Imogen. 'But I guess psychologically we wanted to be near to England.'

Another major attraction in Normandy is the price of housing. Compared to the south of England, house prices in

Normandy are still at least five times cheaper. The area is so large and diverse that prices can vary, but, roughly, you can buy a small cottage in the country for around £25,000; a larger house for £45,000; and a farmhouse with some land for £65,000. Areas closer to Paris are more expensive because of the number of Parisians who want a weekend home. The same price hike applies near the ferry ports, pushed up by English buyers who are prepared to come over every weekend and will pay a premium for less travelling time.

The Gardeners were working for the Caravan Club in East Grinstead when they decided that they wanted a change in lifestyle. 'We thought there must be more to life than working in East Grinstead and living in Eastbourne,' says Imogen. 'Then our employer offered us language classes. To my surprise, I loved learning French. I nagged my husband that we should move to France, particularly when I looked on the internet and discovered that we could sell our four-bedroom estate house in Eastbourne for this fabulous Normandy long house.'

Their new house is set in two acres of land in la Ferté-Macé, a small village in Orne, one of the least populated *départements* in France. They sold the house in Eastbourne for £180,000. They paid £150,000 for the Normandy house, which includes two self-contained *gîtes* that they manage to rent out most of the year. 'We are never going to be rich, but we are very happy,' says Imogen. 'We are never going back.'

Like 70 per cent of the English buyers of property who are seeking a second home, Mary Davis and her husband James bought in Normandy simply because it is so easy to get backwards and forwards on the ferry. 'We can get from our home in Poole to our house just north of Granville in less than seven hours,' says Mary Davis. 'The longest part of the journey is the boat crossing from Poole to Cherbourg.'

She and her husband bought a farmhouse with another

couple over 12 years ago. Seven hours may have been a good journey time 12 years ago, but now you can get from London to the Languedoc in less time, and instead of a chill breeze and a glass of cider you can be enjoying a *pastis* and the Mediterranean sun on your arrival. Nowadays, Ryanair flies from Stansted to Dinard, which will cut some journey times in half.

Unfortunately, no one is able to do anything about the weather. It is a topic that many people try to avoid when talking about Normandy. On the area's official website it only gives the average temperatures and rainfall for the months of March through to October, presumably on the basis that nobody in their right mind would want to stay there any other time. 'It is a shame,' says Imogen Gardener. 'Maybe if we move again, we will go further south.'

Mary Davis says that she would like to spend some time in their house in the winter months, but so far has not managed to pluck up the courage. 'I think it would be difficult in winter,' she says. 'We are quite isolated.'

There are a few English eccentrics who buy in Normandy because of the weather. 'I used to live in the south of France,' says Duncan Green. 'But July and August are too hot for an Englishman.' Green also enjoys the accessibility to England. 'I can get back to my father's home in Somerset in five hours door to door.'

The real attraction here is the escapism. Normandy is very peaceful. Even though it has one of France's most visited tourist sites, Mont St Michel, the coastline is less busy than Brittany's. Older people say that Normandy reminds them of the England of their childhood. Even house prices are about the same as they were in England in the 1950s.

'We paid £30,000 for our farmhouse,' says Mary Davis. 'We immediately invested £10,000 on renovation. We think the value of the house may have gone up a bit, but prices have not gone up anything like they have in England.'

Property experts warn English buyers not to expect much in

the way of capital appreciation. There is so much property available that prices are increasing only very slowly. Duncan Green is in the process of selling a four-bedroom house with over an acre of garden with barns, for £80,000. 'Almost anywhere sensible in the south of England and the property would be worth £1 million,' he says.

He recommends the Manche as an area where there are still good reasonably priced houses for sale. If you go too far south-east you run into the large number of Parisians who are buying second homes. Most popular of all are the ritzy seaside resorts of Deauville and Trouville, where Parisians come to have fun at the weekend. Just a bit further west is Honfleur, built on the west bank of the Seine. The fishing boats may have gone but the town is full of charming five-storied houses, cobbled streets and the possibility of a cooked English breakfast at every café. 'The English discovered Honfleur a few years ago,' says de Perthuis. 'I feel a bit awkward speaking French there now.'

But you don't need to feel trapped in an English enclave. Even if you want to stay near the coast and have easy access to England, there is over 600 kilometres of coastline to choose from. Administratively Normandy is divided into two rather confusingly named regions: Upper and Lower Normandy. Upper Normandy is the eastern part of the county and not the top part. It includes the *départements* of Seine-Maritime, with its white chalk cliffs and flat fields and Eure, which is full of forests and rivers. Lower Normandy to the west includes Calvados, the scene of the Normandy landings; Orne, home to farms and cider drinkers; and Manche, which is shaped like a thumb with Cherbourg on the tip of the nail.

The area known as Suisse Normande is between southern Calvados and northern Orne. It bears about as much resemblance to Switzerland as Little Venice does to its Italian namesake, but is still perhaps the most charming area for quality houses. This is where you will find many of the half-timbered houses made from oak and plaster. They blend into the landscape along with the cows, the trees, and the clouds.

Head even further south and the prices drop dramatically. Here you can buy a cottage that needs renovating for around £15,000. Andy Barr, 44, gave up his job as a criminal lawyer in Tottenham, London four years ago. 'I'd had enough,' he says. 'The work was terrible. One of my friends committed suicide, another is in prison and a third is snowed under with legal aid work. Enough was enough. We came to Normandy for a bit of peace and quiet. And we found it. I reckon the nearest night life is in Portsmouth.'

Andy now runs a website which introduces English buyers to properties in Normandy and the *département* to the south, Mayenne. 'Mayenne is good because it is cheaper and more quiet than Normandy,' he says. 'The other bonus is that if you tell people you live in Normandy they want to come and stay with you in the summer. Tell them you live in Mayenne and you'll never hear from them again.' A word of warning about the Mayenne. Some people who settled there a few years ago have had a terrible time, as have several of their friends. In some areas they are not used to foreigners and don't want to get used to them either.

## Burgundy

The countryside in Burgundy is extremely reminiscent of England and this was another region we considered moving to early on in our French house search. I knew it quite well as my aunt and uncle have a house there. It is a place that most British people drive through, or at best, stop for a night on the way to somewhere else. You turn left off the A6 at Châlon Nord to go skiing in the Alps. You turn right at Châlon Sud to go west of Burgundy towards the centre of France. Or you head south on the A6, the Autoroute du Soleil, thundering to the fleshpots of the Mediterranean coast. Any turning to the right between Dijon and Beaune will lead you to a village familiar from a wine list.

Burgundy isn't so much a place as a name on a wine bottle. If you pull off the motorway you will be surprised to discover villages that you already know from the expensive shelf of your local wine merchant's: Fixin, Gevrey-Chambertin, Chambolle-Musigny, Nuits St Georges and Vosne-Romanée. Except for this small area, it is surprising how few vineyards you see, unless you go looking for them. Otherwise the countryside is reminiscent of parts of the Cotswolds, with hills, forests and large fields.

The price of properties varies according to their proximity to the wine regions. For example, around the Côte de Nuit—the hilly strip of land between Dijon and Beaune, where the best wines have been made for centuries, the houses are relatively expensive—but nothing like prices in the south of England. To the west, around the Parc de Morvan, houses are less expensive. Further south, where even the wines get cheaper and more cheerful, the housing is more keenly priced.

'We bought a house here because it is eight hours drive from Calais,' says Malcolm Hogan, a retired diplomat. 'This way our impoverished offspring can visit us with their children without having to spend a night in an hotel on the way.' The Hogans bought a pretty house near the village of Brionnet four years ago for less than £60,000. 'The countryside round here is rolling hills, full of Charolais cattle,' says Hogan. 'It is pretty unsmart. Not much English is spoken. But it suits us.'

For many years in the Middle Ages Burgundy had been a separate kingdom to France. But the ill-fated siege of Nancy (1477) by Charles the Rash emboldened no doubt by a few bottles of decent wine, was the beginning of the end. The lands became incorporated into France and its leaders enjoyed the spoils. Its rulers were crowned in Reims. They drank burgundy wine, leaving claret from Bordeaux for the English.

Burgundy only became a place on a map again in 1964, when the four departments of Côte d'Or, Saône et Loire, Yonne and Nièvre were grouped together by a bored bureaucrat. Its administrative heart is Dijon, a place better known as a producer of mustard. It is a pretty, bustling city, with multi-coloured roofs and a fascinating old town.

Christine Jacob was a litigation lawyer in Hong Kong until she met a French winemaker on a junk on the South China Sea. She abandoned the law for the vineyards of Echevronne. 'It's a fantastic life,' she says. 'We are doing something others dream of.' Her estate, Domaine Lucien Jacob, covers over 19 hectares of Burgundy's best wine growing areas. They make around 100,000 bottles of wine a year.

The house is in the middle of a small village, with their cave a short walk away. She took me on a tour of her vineyards, some on slopes that seemed almost impossible to walk up. All the picking and pruning is done by hand. The views are breathtaking.

'Burgundy is a fabulous place to live,' she says. 'We eat well, drink well, have lots of fun.' She says that you could buy a very nice village house in Echevronne for £100,000, and the *château*, if it were for sale, for around £400,000.

Richard Parsons has been living in Burgundy for nearly 40 years. He came for the canals, and claims to be the first person to navigate them all as a traveller. He set up Continental Waterways, which sends nearly 7,000 people down the rivers and canals every year. His partner Susie Hopwood runs Burgundy Villas, which has a network of properties for rent all over Burgundy. She arranged the accommodation for Juliette Binoche and her staff during the filming of Chocolat, which took place in the pretty village of Flavigny sur Ozerain.

Susie Hopwood says that she came to Burgundy in search of some good luck. Since then she has fallen in love with a man and the region. 'I love the food here so much,' she says. 'We are going to start setting up cookery courses, so that people can come here with something worthwhile to take home.'

But her partner Richard cautions that life in Burgundy is not for the faint-hearted. 'People shouldn't come and live here just because the price of property is cheap,' says Richard. 'People have to realise that moving here will mean a change of culture and you need to adapt. Even so, for £300,000 you can buy an amazing place.'

I looked at a few places in the region, including an old village house with four bedrooms and a large garden. It was priced at £275,000. There were cheaper properties on the market that needed more work doing to them. Those who like town life should consider Beaune, where you can buy a three-storey town house for £200,000. Nonetheless, according to local agents, prices in the region as a whole have gone up by over 30 per cent in the last three years.

Joff and Mary Williams, both still in their 30s, got to Burgundy before prices went up. They moved there over ten years ago to set up a pottery. 'We had been living in Wales,' says Mary. 'I thought anything must be better than that.' Joff agrees. 'We were about to become the fourth pottery in a little village in Wales. I had heard of Burgundy in the film Passport to Pimlico. I suggested it to my wife as a destination, then, a week later, we saw a cottage advertised in an estate agent's in Ipswich. So we called the number, and came out.'

They looked at four houses, one of which they bought. Their son Isaac was ten days old. Joff had studied O-level French. Mary did not speak the language at all.

'I didn't speak for a year,' she says. 'I just listened to the French people who came to our house.'

Four years ago they sold the original house and bought a former *épicerie*—grocer's shop—for £40,000 in the pretty village of Vandenesse-en-Auxois. It had been in the hands of the same family for eight generations, but was in need of considerable work. There was even a tree growing through the kitchen floor.

'It took about five months to make the place habitable,' says Joff. He turned the next door workshop into a pottery, where he works and runs courses in the winter.

'We are never going to be rich,' he says. 'But we have a lovely life. Of course, it is not always the idyll that people imagine. You are always going to be a stranger. And it gets quite cold in winter—colder than England, although it is hotter in the summer. But we love it here.'

*Limousin*

If you're moving to get away from the cold, you need to head south. The south of France has a great ring to it. You could never imagine a bad day living there. It sounds so perfect and in many ways it is. There is plenty of sunshine, amazing countryside; from the rolling meadows of the southwest to the dramatic coastlines of the Mediterranean, olive groves, medieval villages and endless glasses of wine. I hadn't really travelled much in France until we thought about moving to France, and Limousin, in the southwest of the country, was one of the first places I got to know.

Some friends had bought a place there for £20,000. It seemed like a dream. No more mortgage. And they said it looks just like England did 50 years ago. Rolling hills, tall hedges, few houses. There didn't seem to be a downside, so we set off with Olivia (who was then six weeks old) to discover the region.

We left from Burgundy where we had been staying with my aunt and uncle. My aunt is Italian and my uncle is French. They have a house which belonged to his family and was the childhood home of his uncle, the photographer Henri Cartier-Bresson. It is the sort of house you imagine when you think about the French upper classes, lots of high ceilings and old furniture. The kitchen is basic, obviously built with servants in mind. All the beds are antique French. The average height of a French aristocrat must have been not much more than 5 foot 5 inches. I have to sleep diagonally in them. The house is in a medieval village called Noyers-sur-Sereine. The river runs about 100 yards from the house and there is an underground passage linking the two. My uncle's great–great aunt had a long-standing affair with the cardinal of Paris. He used to arrive from Paris by boat and sneak into her bedroom via the secret tunnel. The villagers never understood why this beautiful woman remained single throughout her life.

*Location, location, location*

George and Tina bought a crumbling manor house in the middle of nowhere outside a village called Grazay in the Mayenne (Pays de la Loire). They picked it up for hardly any money and did it up themselves. George is a builder. They worked on it for almost two years, and spent their life savings on it. Once the work and their savings were finished, they decided to try and

find jobs. George went all over the region, dropping off leaflets and talking to people. No one wanted to employ him. Tina was a hairdresser in the UK, but as she speaks hardly any French she couldn't get work here. Finally, George went to Spain where he got work through a friend, and Tina went back to England, where she is living with her mother. The house is up for sale but they have had to drop the price dramatically. 'It's just not the sort of region where anyone is going to spend €350,000 on a house, even if it is beautifully done up and has ten bedrooms,' says George. 'We really didn't think it through. I never imagined I wouldn't be able to get work. I have to say I feel there is a certain amount of xenophobia involved.'

Although George is keen to stay abroad, Tina has no desire to leave England again. 'At least I know what's what here,' she says. 'It was all meant to be a bit of an adventure, but I felt terrified by the end of it. They all seemed to hate us and I'm sure our cat, which just disappeared one day, was picked up and thrown in a well.'

When he works, my uncle writes books about the history of

art. My aunt does something intellectual with films. I had mooted the Limousin idea with them over lunch. We were eating, I recall, asparagus risotto. My aunt is a brilliant cook, and always travels with Italian risotto rice and parmesan.

'It's *la morta civile*,' she said. 'Civil death. There is nothing to do there and the locals are all less intelligent than the cow breed it's named after.'

My uncle nodded in agreement. 'Besides, nothing good ever came of moving somewhere named after cows,' he said.

We had arranged to meet our friends who lived in Limousin in a bar near where they lived. We arrived early in the evening after a long drive through stunning countryside, rolling hills and oak trees. They were right; it looks just like England. We parked the car outside the bar and walked in. As the door opened, a wave of stale smoke hit me. I buried my face in my shawl and clutched the sleeping Olivia closer to my chest. About four rough-looking locals looked up as we walked in.

I suddenly felt very self-conscious. It was a bit like walking into one of those pubs in Yorkshire where nobody talks. Instead, they just stare at you as if they're about to sacrifice you. As soon as our friends arrived, we left the bar. I decided against Limousin without seeing a single house.

There are grants to be had for people wanting to set up farms in the region (you can get more information from www.cr-limousin.fr) as the French government is trying to encourage people to move there.

*Bordeaux*

Wine is obviously a big attraction for people wanting to move to France and the most famous of all the wine regions is Bordeaux. For centuries the region has been sending its bottles to London and the world, growing rich in the process. But there are many other facets to it. The Atlantic coast is easily accessible, as are the Pyrenees. It is the fifth biggest city in France with many cinemas, theatres and cultural events. It is a great transport hub, with a choice of several airlines and two airports, as well as the TGV. The climate is good and the food delicious, particularly if you like duck.

David Eley, an artist who moved to Bordeaux in January 2002 with his wife and two children, advises Brits thinking about moving to the region against falling for the classic rural idyll. 'Don't automatically go for the *château* in the country, you can get far more out of life by being in the city,' he says. He tells a story of a poodle parlour two minutes down the road where a parrot serenades poodles with the Marseillaise while they have their trim. 'You wouldn't get that in the middle of nowhere,' he continues. 'And, in fact, the countryside is only 15 minutes away.'

The Eleys moved from Hampshire, originally with the thought of buying a country property. 'I am very lucky in that I can work from anywhere so I thought why not? Also most of my work is related to the wine industry, so Bordeaux was a natural choice.' He explains that when they saw their apartment, it just seemed like the perfect place. 'It has three terraces, one of which looks out over the Roman amphitheatre. This really is a wonderful city.' None of the Eleys spoke French when they arrived and the girls, were sent straight into the French educational system. 'We're really proud of them,' says David. 'Within three months they spoke pretty good French and within six months they were, by my standards anyway, fluent. Nowadays I really don't know what's going on when they speak French among themselves.'

Townhouses in central Bordeaux start at around £200,000. 'For £300,000 you can get something really special,' says Karin Auriol-Andrews, who has been working as an estate agent in the region for eight years. 'There is no doubt that Bordeaux is

undervalued compared with other major cities in France.'
There may be a good reason for this. Bordeaux has a reputation
for being a very unfriendly place. David tells me that during a
recent heatwave his wife got stuck in the lift. After half an hour
she could hardly breathe. 'The agent's response was to tell me
to learn to speak better French'.

David has since had a series of other misfortunes and is close
to giving up on life in France altogether. 'I feel as if I've been
abducted and incarcerated in a torture chamber and that there
is no way out,' he says. 'It's curtains for us, our whole world
has crumbled.'

His disaster story began the day he asked France Telecom to
come and mend the back-up mechanism on his computer, a
problem they had created whilst installing an ADSL line. The
technician who arrived not only wiped out his whole hard
drive, but also all his back-ups. In a rare moment of bureaucratic brilliance, David made the technician sign a piece of
paper admitting liability. Without that he would have had no
recourse at all. What he lost was a new business he had been
working on for 18 months, as well as every bit of correspondence he had ever had. 'It was rather like arriving home to find
your house had burnt down and all that was left was a sock. But
rather than it happening in the security of England, it happened
in France where I didn't know any of the rules or what to do.'

David is still fighting to get compensation for his losses.
They haven't even agreed on a preliminary amount to pay him
while they decide. He and his family are completely destitute.
'I have had countless meetings with lawyers and so-called
experts,' he says. 'What is most galling is that they act as if I
don't exist, arguing and laughing around me in my own home
as they go through the finer details of my personal life. And all
in front of the idiot who messed up my life, who for some
reason has a right to be there. People keep telling me that it's
the Latin culture, but in my view there is still right and wrong.'

For those looking for a place outside the city of Bordeaux,
Mary Wakefield, a tourism consultant who has lived in the

region for eight years, recommends Entre-deux-Mers, a wine-growing region situated between the Garonne and the Dordogne rivers. 'There are extremely few new developments there,' she says. 'It is all vines or forests and beautiful old houses. It is a lovely hilly region with beautiful views and there is unlikely to be much development as the vineyards simply don't come up for sale.' A large family house in the Margaux or Entre-deux-Mers region will cost around £500,000.

Jill Joiner, an estate agent who has lived in France for 15 years, says she is astounded at the number of British people coming to the region. 'I suspect they are escaping the house prices in Britain and looking for a better way of life,' she says. 'But these Brits are not retirees, they are young professionals, mainly in the IT business, whose main criteria is to be within an hour's drive from an international airport.'

*The Pyrenees*

Head southeast from Bordeaux towards the Pyrenees and after three hours you arrive in what is almost a different country. Perpignan is often described as one of the most significant crossroads in France. It has an extraordinary mixture of cultures. It is Catalan, but in France and half an hour from Spain. It is close to the sea, but also to the Pyrenees, making it an ideal spot for ski enthusiasts. It is also only an hour from Toulouse, which gives it international access. There are also Ryanair flights to Rivesaltes, just outside the city.

It took 33-year old Alistair Norman just one weekend to decide to give up his job as a successful IT consultant for David Lloyd's Leisure group and his life in England. 'I saw the view from the terrace of the house,' he says. 'And just knew this was the place for me.'

He is talking about a four-bedroom village house in a village called Lapradelle Puilaurens, half an hour from Perpignan. He came across it by accident, literally. 'I was on a biking tour in the nearby mountains and one of the guys came off so we had to find somewhere to stop and have the bike mended. After I had got over the initial fear of how to explain things to his wife I looked around and realised I had landed in a small piece of paradise.'

Alistair looked at four properties and chose a village house with a magnificent terrace view for £47,000. The house is in the middle of a tiny village, opposite a river. To the right of his house is the old school building and, a little further along, a charming medieval church. Both buildings have bells—the school bell chimes before the church bell and the locals say the right time is somewhere in between the two.

Alistair has already started a company called Upright Tours, aimed at biking enthusiasts. He will organise biking holidays (motor and pushbike) in the region and sell them to clientele in the UK. 'I'll give it two years,' he says. 'If it doesn't work out, I'll come back. At least I will have learnt French and had a great two years away from a stressful job.' Alistair, originally from Exeter, has no worries about maintaining contact with the outside world. 'I'll do it all on the internet, we're just about to get ADSL here in the village. I can't even get that at home in Bradford.'

Margaret and James Hogan moved to Port Vendres on the coast outside Perpignan just over a year ago. Although Margaret is Scottish and James is Irish, they had spent most of their adult life living in London. 'The one thing we were worried about,' says Margaret, 'is that we would miss the theatre, concerts and cultural events. So we chose this region as it's close to Barcelona, Montpellier and other big cities where we could go and find that sort of thing. What's been extraordinary is that since we moved to France we just haven't wanted to go anywhere.' They bought their village house, a two-bedroom apartment on three floors for £150,000.

'It is hard to find properties here, but it doesn't have a sea view which makes it less attractive to a lot of people,' says

James, a writer. Margaret, who was an editor in London and is now taking some time out, says it's ideal for them. 'We have a floor each and one shared floor. There is a granny flat, which is still home to the previous owner's mother, but once she goes we have the option to buy that as well. If we do, it will be more of a house but as things stand, we are quite happy.'

They chose Port Vendres as opposed to the more known towns on the coast such as Collioure and Banyuls-sur-Mer because they wanted to live in a 'real place'. 'I hated the idea of somewhere that just came to life in the summer,' says James. 'Although we knew the region because we used to visit Collioure, it wasn't the sort of place we really wanted to live.' Margaret agrees. 'I really enjoy the day to day life here and even if it can sometimes get a bit much stopping and talking to everyone you meet, you can, if you need to, get the pleasantries over with very quickly. Actually, I'm rarely in a hurry, I am focusing on cultivating my pottering, and I don't mean making pots.'

Margaret and James say there is nothing they miss about England. 'I'm just sorry we weren't in a position to do this much sooner.'

Ian Scott is one person who made the move much earlier than the Hogans; he has been in the region for over 35 years. 'I had just finished art school and was working in an office. I had a house, a car and all that stuff. One day I just thought, hang on a minute; they want the rest of my life for all this. I decided to retire when I was 22. I thought the only people I see selling paintings successfully are old fools so I decided to leave it for a few years, although I kept painting.' He gave up his job as an assistant art editor at the Medici Society and hitchhiked around the world for two years. 'It was all going well until we hit the Sahara with just a tin of sardines and two hard-boiled eggs. It looked quite small on the map. Luckily the locals kept us alive and we managed to get across it.'

After that adventure there was no going back. 'I decided I wanted somewhere with a good climate and political stability.

Ian bought a house in a mountainous village outside Perpignan called Llauro for £30,000 in 1974. 'With all its land and out-buildings it's probably worth closer to £250,000 now,' he says. Scott also has two galleries where he exhibits and sells his work. 'Now I'm an old fool and selling paintings. And unknown in four continents.' Ian, who is Scottish, says there is really noth-ing about Scotland he misses. 'I tend to go back to bury people and that's all,' he says. 'I went back to bury my mother a couple of years ago and found the place totally dreary.'

According to figures from a local estate agent, around 40 per cent of Brits who come to the region decide to buy. Laurent Sillon, Sales Manager at JMB Immobilier in Perpignan, describes it as one of the most popular regions in France. 'They love it here,' he says. 'They love the fact that it is close to Spain, the mountains, the sea and that it is not too built up.' According to Sillon, prices have been rising dramatically but they are now stabilising. He says that for £75,000 you can still find a small village house in the villages outside the city itself and a three-bedroom apartment in Perpignan.

## The Midi-Pyrenees

The area around Toulouse has seen a dramatic rise in expat residents during the last ten years. When Jill Allcroft moved to a village there 12 years ago, there were only three British families within a 100 kilometre radius of her and she used to have to head home for her annual supply of Branston Pickle. Now there are four English families in her village alone, which only has a popula-tion of 300. 'In a way it was a good thing,' she says. 'It forced me to really integrate with the locals and learn French, there just weren't any English people to mix with. Now, that seems an odd thing to say, they're everywhere.'

Jill and her husband Richard stumbled across the area sur-rounding Toulouse by accident. They were living in Sheffield at the time, and Richard was working as an engineer in Buxton. 'There was an estate agent there who had links with a French agent in this region,' says Jill, who was working as a medical lab technician in a local hospital at the time. 'We came down, saw nine properties in a week and signed on the dotted line. We were in our 30s and decided that if we didn't do it then, we never would.'

Jill and Richard bought a 13th-century stone farmhouse with 45 acres of woodland and meadow near the village of Boussan in the Haute Garonne, south of Toulouse. They paid £55,000 and spent another £60,000 and four years doing it up. The original idea they had was to set up a caravan park, but they found the state restrictions too limiting. 'They seem to dictate everything,' she says. 'From the number of showers you have to have to how much you can charge. The figures just didn't add up.' Richard now has his own building business and Jill runs the farmhouse as a holiday let. She thinks there are several reasons the region has become so popular with the English.

'There are a lot of 50-somethings now who are inheriting money. They've paid off their mortgage and they don't see the point in putting it into stocks and shares. Toulouse is a very accessible city, as well as being very beautiful. It is also smaller than say Bordeaux, which I think is less imposing for people,' she says. 'For rentals it is very well placed for Spain and both coasts and there is no doubt the whole region has been boosted by the cheap airlines. We can now go straight from Newcastle to Toulouse. But I rarely go back. There's not really anything I miss and I can get Branston Pickle here now.'

Driving to Mike and Posy Fallowfield's house just outside Manent-Montané about an hour southwest of Toulouse is almost like driving around the Devon countryside they left behind. The hills are green and rolling. The Devon lanes have been replaced with straight, empty roads, but the skyline could be from Dulverton. Mike and Posy bought their deserted farmhouse in July 2002 for £83,000. They sold their farmhouse in Devon for £585,000. 'The original plan was to let the house and buy a ruin,' says Posy. 'But we couldn't make the money work.' They still ended up with what can only be described as just that, but on a grand scale. Their 17th-century farmhouse stands alone just outside the village. It has 360 degree uninterrupted views, to the south you can see the Pyrenees. The house is large and will eventually have four bedrooms, a study, two sitting rooms, kitchen and a dining room. The only hint of civilisation now among the rubble and dust is an Aga. 'When Mike said we were selling up and moving to France, I said over my dead body,' says Posy. 'In the end I gave in, but my one stipulation was that we had to have an Aga.'

They moved into a caravan next to the house in March 2003. 'We thought we would be in the caravan for two or three months,' says Mike. 'We're still here and at least another month or so away from being able to move into just one room of the house.'

As with a lot of major property projects, Posy and Mike have found it has taken them much longer than they expected and cost them much more. In addition, Mike fell seriously ill last year and spent three weeks in hospital with a heart problem. 'There was one stage when I was sitting in the caravan, looking at the wreck of a house we had bought, thinking about Mike in hospital and wondering what on earth we had done,' says Posy. 'But we're through the worst now and I have to say the French hospitals were marvellous.'

They chose the region because an old university friend of Mike's lives close by. 'We looked at a lot of rubbish,' says Mike. 'At first we only had a budget of around £30,000 and were shown endless heaps of stones with brambles growing through them.' Once they decided to sell in England, they looked at a few more realistic options and finally settled on the farmhouse. 'We picked this place over the twenty or so others we looked at because the roof was sound and the walls were almost vertical and reasonably intact and we fell for the area,' says Posy. 'You should see some of the others we saw: several shells of farmhouses with collapsed roofs, pretty derelict and depressing, and they all seemed to have a concrete electricity pole right outside the front door. This one was at least lived in at one end!'

The region is easily accessible via several airports. The main and most international one is Toulouse. Depending on where you are outside the city, you have the choice of Bordeaux, Pau, Rodez, Castres, Bergerac and Carcassonne. The TGV line to Paris was recently completed, bringing the journey time down to just under five hours.

According to Kris Misselbrook, an estate agent with Aurignac Immobilier, prices have risen dramatically over the last four years. 'To buy a classic farmhouse, set in a hectare of land, in need of some work and with a barn, you're looking at least at €250,000. Four years ago you could find the same thing for less than half that. It has just snow-balled and I don't see it changing until the economy does.' Misselbrook says he is seeing a trend for people demanding properties at the lower end of the market in the region. 'At least half my enquiries are for properties for under €100,000. My response is well, I've got some nice ruins. For those willing to totally rebuild a property, there are some stunning timber-framed wrecks for around €85,000, but you'd have to spend at least another €100,000 doing them up.'

Helen Goossens moved to Nérac in the Lot and Garonne, an hour west of Toulouse, in 1993. She left her job as European marketing communications manager for Apple Computers when she discovered she had skin cancer. 'In the end it was nothing too worrying,' she says. 'But it made me realise that it was time to start living life rather than postponing it until my career was over. At the time I was working between 60 and 80 hours a week. So here I am, in my lock keeper's cottage on its own island with my four dogs and six cats.'

Helen found the 19th-century cottage by chance. She travelled a lot in her job and was always reading property magazines. 'I loved reading about houses for sale. One day I stumbled across an advertisement saying 'Are you a fisherman? If so, you will enjoy this lock keeper's cottage on an island.' I'm not a fisherman, but it sounded wonderful, so I called them.' A week later she had seen the cottage and fallen in love with it. 'It was in bad state and the brambles in the garden were taller than me, but I figured I could fix all that,' she says. She bought the cottage for £33,000 and then spent over double that doing it up.

She advises anyone thinking of moving to France to learn to speak French properly. 'It is very nice being part of the expat community,' she says. 'But it is so much nicer being part of the whole community and finding out about the region and the people. Also having the time to make real friends is wonderful.'

A chance meeting with a local clairvoyant gave Helen a new career. 'When she first came to my house, this practically illiterate woman started talking to me in Dutch, Polish, English and German, all languages my late husband spoke,' says Helen. 'I found the story of her life, the struggle to take herself seriously in the beginning, so fascinating that I wrote a book about it.' My friend Carla and I both had a reading with the clairvoyant. It was fascinating, although Carla's reading was much more exciting than mine. She is about to meet a charismatic man from the world of international commerce, while I am, apparently, entering a very calm and tranquil period of my life.

# Lesson 2

# Integration, Integration, Integration

My father always tells me that the only way to learn a language properly is to have an affair with a native. He speaks nine languages. All, he maintains, the result of his hectic love life.

Interestingly, his English is appalling. I remember him telling me when I was a teenager that the only English woman he had ever had a vague desire to sleep with was the queen. I found this more shocking than his prolific taste in women. My mother, he told me, learnt Italian in about three weeks. She confirms this and says it was because she fell in love, which seems to confirm my father's theory.

If the love-affair option isn't available to you, this is rather a pity. It is essential that you learn to speak French if you intend to build a new life in France, and the alternative methods are by far inferior. I know a woman who claims to get around France letting her finger speak by pointing at what she wants. It would be ridiculous to live in England like this, speaking or making no effort to speak English. Yet there seem to be plenty of Brits who are convinced beforehand they'll get by without speaking a word of French.

I was determined never to be like this. Perhaps I had an advantage. I already spoke English, Swedish and Italian and had done a bit of German. It is said that when you already know more than one language, the next one is easier.

But French didn't strike me as easier. It is as far from Swedish as it is possible to imagine, and spoken as they do in the *Midi*, the south of France, incomprehensible even to most Parisians.

The price of failure is social isolation. I could already see the consequences: to live in an English-only ghetto of teas, bridge and golf that might as well be Surrey.

Learning French is vital but it is very very hard. Most of us learned it at school and arrive here perhaps even with a GCSE or A-level, yet completely unprepared to understand a single word. Although all French children are supposed to do English, it seems they have as much trouble with our language as we do with theirs. Indeed, there are surveys that the French themselves are finding it hard to master their own language.

I started lessons before we moved. I spoke almost no French, added to which, I don't have my mother's natural talent for languages. Learning French has proved to be one of the major challenges in making a success of my new life in France since moving here. Once we got here, I carried on having lessons for about a month, until my French teacher and her husband got divorced and she moved out of the region. It was only four years later that I found another teacher.

Marylene loves teaching me how to speak 'proper' French and delights in telling me how many mistakes the French make and how they can't use the subjunctive properly. She says her neighbour's French is worse than mine. Or rather, his vocabulary is more limited. However untrue, flattering me is guaranteed to keep her in a job for a long time.

Not everyone makes the effort to have lessons and to try to string sentences together in conversation. For me, life has become a lot easier and much more fun since I stopped having to plan everything I am going to say in advance.

There are a couple of things that have genuinely helped me to learn the language, and still do. The first is the radio. As we live in the middle of nowhere, I spend a lot of time driving around. I started listening to non-stop talk shows like *France Inter* and *France Culture* as soon as we got here.

To start with, it was appallingly depressing. I had no idea what they were talking about. Eventually, though, I worked out that the news comes on the hour and I made a point of listening for stories I knew were likely to run.

The second thing was finding a French friend and I was lucky to find one who comes from the north and so speaks the language comprehensibly.

I met Alex because I had become addicted to her husband's wine. He makes a fantastic Chardonnay-Viognier, Vignes de Nicole, which I first drank when we were house-hunting. Some women crave banana sandwiches when they're pregnant—I crave Chardonnay.

Once we had found a house, visitors started to arrive from England. Among these was a friend who had just landed a part-time job as wine buyer for the London Match bars. When he told us he was coming on a wine-buying mission, I was determined to find the maker of the Chardonnay-Viognier. Millions of pregnant women all over London would be eternally grateful, I argued. Jean-Claude Mas, as we found out the maker was called, is a young man with an MBA from Birmingham University and a vision for the wines of the region. We all became great friends, and Alex, his wife, became my most constant source of French.

I also met a lovely Frenchwoman called Caroline, whose daughter goes to school with my daughter Olivia. She and I meet once a week and speak in French and English. Although she is not a teacher, I find my time with her more useful than a lesson because I am just talking and, by doing that, constantly coming across things that I have always wanted to know, like the difference between *neuf* and *nouveau* (*nouveau* means new to the owner, *neuf* is brand new).

She also talks me through other cultural differences, such as saying thank you.

The French seem appallingly bad at it. You invite people for dinner and the next day you expect to be fielding calls from admiring friends and neighbours.

'The French say thank you on the evening,' says Caroline. 'And they tell you they have eaten well [only if the have eaten well— if not, they won't say anything about the food] and that's enough. You invited them and so you obviously wanted them to be there, so they have no reason to be overly grateful.' After dinner at my gynaecologist's house, I wrote a card to say

---

### When to *tu* and when to *vous*?

It's a nightmare, a very complicated issue to which there seems to be very few easily defined rules. I usually *vous* everyone and Rupert goes for the *tu*. As a foreigner it is easier to get away with using the wrong word, the French will just assume you're ignorant and not rude. Personally I find the conjugation of *vous* much easier, so am happy to carry on being ultra-polite. It seems it's OK to *tu* children, but once they get beyond 18 they have to be *vous*-ed. In fact, Jérôme, Peter and Dominique's son, tells me his teachers started *vous*-ing him from around 15. In terms of adults, the more famil- iar you are (and this is defined by social class, circum- stances in which you meet and so forth) the more likely it is you will be on *tu* terms. I would never dream of *tu*-ing Geneviève, my clean- ing lady. This keeps a distance between us which we're both happy with. Once, early on, I did *tu* her by mistake. She said she preferred *vous* as it was '*plus jolie.*'

There is a famous story of one of General de Gaulle's generals with whom he had worked for decades. The general suggested they had worked together for such a long time that to *tu* each other would be more natural. De Gaulle replied: '*Comme*

---

*vous voulez.*' A total snub.

My child minder Chantal and I still *vous* each other after four years. Although we are friends and we have a lot in common due to the children (who call her and her husband *maman* Chantal and *papa* Gilbert) I think we have gone beyond the stage where we can now comfortably change to *tu*. It would just seem wrong somehow.

If you are invited to someone's house and the hostess *tu*'s you, you should *tu* her back (assuming she is not 50 years older than you). It is apparently up to whoever's house it is. My friend Alex *vous* her parents-in-law and they *vous* her, even though they are now related and live in the same house. In fact, she calls them M and Mme Mas. I asked her once why she doesn't call them by their first names. 'They never said to do so,' she replied. 'I think it has to do with their age.'

Her husband, Jean-Claude, says *vous* to her parents, but they *tu* him. When I asked Alex why there was this difference, she couldn't explain. If the French don't know, what hope is there for the rest of us?

I remember a male French friend of mine, who shall remain nameless, once telling us that *vous*-ing your lovers was 'sexier' than *tu*-ing them. If you ever saw the film

thank you. His wife called this a 'charming habit' and told me it was only the English who ever wrote. The same seems to apply to presents. You never get a thank you note for a birthday present to a child.

I made friends with an old lady in the village who does what a lot of them seem to do, sit and watch the traffic go by. She is as broad as she is tall and I suppose about 70. Normally she wears slippers and a pinafore, the uniform of the elderly ladies here. Every time I drove past her, she would glare at me as if I'd

*Dangerous Liaisons* with John Malkovich and Michelle Pfeiffer you'll know how right he is. What struck me as strange about his comment was not that he *vous*-ed his lover, but that he thought it such a normal thing to have a lover and to discuss it openly. Especially as he is married to a friend of mine and she was there at the time.

Guillaume de Perthuis, my aristocratic friend from Normandy, once came home from school aged eight and *tu*-ed his mother. His father slapped him across the face and told him to stop being so insolent. His parents still *vous* each other (and of course he *vous* them). But I am happy to say people like the de Perthuis are in a small minority.

So, in summary, *tu* people you like and want to be friends with and who are of a similar age and social background, as long as you meet them in a friendly setting. If you meet them in a formal environment, you may have to wait to *tu* them. *Vous* those you want to keep a distance from or you are required (possibly due to their age) to show respect to. I tend to take my lead from the French, and so far have not messed up too badly. But if I ever take a French lover, I will insist on being *vous*-ed.

pushed in front of her in the bread queue. I couldn't understand what her problem was. It wasn't even as if I had foreign licence plates on the car, so it couldn't be that she hated the English. I decided to smile broadly every time she glared and see what happened. One day, after about a month of waving and smiling at her, she finally gave in. She smiled back. Now she even stands up and waves, especially if the children are with me.

Rupert has taken up the national sport, cycling, which has endeared him enormously to the locals. At first, I thought it was rather sweet. He went off three times a week with a bunch of old codgers dressed in skin-tight lycra, cycled up and down a few hills, and that was it. Recently the whole thing has taken on a rather more serious turn. I found a copy of *Vélo Magazine* under the bed. Instead of poetry, now he talks about gears, heart-rate monitors and some guy called Lance.

But Rupert's cycling obsession has been a very useful introduction to the village and has had something of the effect of a love affair, as his French has improved remarkably—especially when he's talking about gears and inner tubes. Since we invited the cycling team for an English breakfast, they view us with renewed respect. 'Anyone who can eat that stuff is a stronger man than me,' said his French cycling mate Charlie, pointing at a pot of Marmite. The bacon sandwiches, specially imported for the occasion and served with HP sauce, were an instant hit.

We were subsequently invited to the retirement party of one of Rupert's cycling gang. Everyone he cycles with is retired. Except Lilian who is female and one of the fittest (and thinnest) women I know. In between running the local toy shop in Pézenas, she also runs the London and Paris marathons and triathlons throughout France. Cycling with retired old men may seem like a cop-out, but these sexagenarians can whiz up a vertical incline in no time.

The cyclist retirement party started at lunchtime and was held in our neighbour's garden, which is about 500 metres from our house. There were about 70 people there, including the cycling team and their wives. Between midday and 2pm a lot of pastis was drunk. Then it was time for lunch. Oysters and mussels were followed by plates of ham, *saucisson* and *pâtés*, then spit-roast wild boar (ideal for me, a semi-vegetarian who doesn't like seafood). The children all ran around playing, the guests sat at long trestle tables eating and drinking. There were speeches and a small cabaret—mainly Charlie dressing up like a woman. At around 5pm we thought we could politely leave. We said our good-byes and went home for a cup of tea. At around midnight we went for a walk. There seemed to be a lot of noise coming from our neighbour's garden. At first we thought we were imagining it, but as we got closer we noticed that many of the cars that had been there at lunchtime were still there. We bumped into one reveller who told us this was perfectly normal. 'We party all day and all night and then the women drive us home,' he told us. In the background we could hear Charlie singing.

One of our first social events in the region was an invitation for dinner at the home of Jean-Luc and Prune Clerc. They were childhood sweethearts and one of the happiest couples I have ever met. He runs the most wonderful delicatessen in Pézenas, which used to be owned by Prune's father. Everyone loves the deli, mainly because of him. He is the human equivalent of a teddy bear. It was a great honour to be invited to their home. Our friend Peter told us he had lived here for several years before getting an invitation. It is the most stunning house, a Victorian building hidden away in the centre of town with a huge orangery and garden. The pool looks as if it was built 150 years ago and is surrounded by mysterious hanging plants. The whole house and garden looked to me like a tropical forest, plants and vivid colours everywhere. Inside the walls are covered with paintings painted by Prune, a talented artist as well as a dancer and gym instructor.

We were asked for 8 o'clock and arrived at 8.15. No one else was there yet. I had not yet got used to the *Midi* and the fact that everyone is appallingly late for everything. So we were shown around the garden and the house and then asked to sit down in the orangery. There was a bottle of Laurent Perrier Rosé in an ice bucket and eight champagne flutes on the table.

'Oh brilliant,' I said. 'My favourite.'

Jean-Luc and Prune smiled and carried on chatting. At a quarter to 9 we were still the only people there and the bottle remained firmly closed. The French attitude to drinking is very different from ours. They really do drink in moderation. And as we found out that night, you only open the bottle once everyone is there. During dinner I found the amounts of wine they poured into the glasses ridiculous. Why were they being so stingy? We do live in the biggest wine-producing region in the world. There is hardly a shortage of the stuff. Added to which, two of the guests were winemakers. I've got used to it now. And even if I still drink more than the average Frenchwoman, who will drive you mad by hanging on to the same glass all evening, I prefer my measures small. A glass filled to the brim now seems very gauche.

The dinner was fun. I had some idea of what was going on until about 10 o'clock when everyone got fed up with making an effort and launched into fast, furious French. But even then it felt good to be somewhere totally foreign, somewhere new—there was so much to learn and do. Prune and I became good friends that evening and started playing tennis together every week. We would give each other French and English lessons on court.

I soon discovered that there are also a good many traits which the French share with the British. My friend Beatrice left England around 25 years ago to marry into the French aristocracy. She is incredibly elegant, and it was at her house (I use the term lightly, it's about the size of Victoria train station), that I first learnt about French snobbery.

We had dinner in the cave. Luc, Beatrice's husband, makes very good wine which he sells mainly to English supermarkets. There was a roaring fire and about 35 people sitting down to dinner. I was seated next to Luc's cousin and asked him, out of curiosity, if there were words or phrases in French that one should avoid.

'Of course!' He replied. 'Lots of them.'

I asked for an example. He told me about the time his son came home with a girl he wanted to marry.

'When we opened the door, she said *"Bonjour messieurs, dames."* It was appalling.'

'What was appalling?' Had I misheard this phrase I had thought of as totally inoffensive up until now?

'You can't say that, it is for shopkeepers, it is terrible, unforgivable.' He looked as if he was going to choke on his *foie gras*.

'What did you do?' I asked, feigning horror.

'We totally ignored her.'

'For the whole weekend?'

'Of course,' he delicately wiped some bread from the corner of his mouth, 'he's married to a perfectly nice girl now.'

The Mills & Boon tragedy of not being allowed to marry someone due to a careless phrase killed my appetite for the dinner but roused my curiosity. Had I really landed somewhere more class-ridden than the home-counties?

There are just as many things to avoid in the French language as in English—maybe more. Phrases and words that you thought were totally innocuous like *enchanté*, *manger* (only animals eat, humans breakfast, lunch or dine) sound terrible to the wrong ears. Of course, a local neighbour wouldn't be offended if I told him I was *enchantée* to meet him. But a lot of the more educated French would.

In fact, I don't know why I was surprised to find this. I remember my aunt Piera telling me off when I was about 12 years old for starting to clear the table before Bertrand, my uncle, had finished eating.

'It is terribly bad manners,' she told me. 'And it upsets your uncle.' I was amazed. At home, clearing the table was always seen as a good thing. Piera then went on to tell me that Bertrand had been brought up in an extremely bourgeois French family. Before anything was cleared from the table, everyone had to have finished. Otherwise the flow of the meal would be interrupted. His mother once fired a maid for saying '*Madame vous êtes servie*' instead of '*Madame est servie.*' The difference is minimal, but to a sensitive bourgeois lady the thought of being feasted on by her guests was obviously too much.

🚲 🚲 🚲

You will find when you move to France that a lot of family and friends will decide to visit you, so you may not need to make many French friends. With so many of ours arriving, our good taste in finding our new home has been rather too exuberantly affirmed—the flow of guests doesn't stop. My parents-in-law came to stay the first Christmas we were here, and never went back. Luckily they bought their own house, and, as one of the things I was worried about was depriving my children of their family, it has been good having them here.

*My friend Prune.* I started going to Prune's gym class, the most brilliant gym class I have ever been to. It started at 8 am when she would rock up in her black Jeep looking insanely cool and glamorous. She always wore great clothes and was beautifully turned out even at that time in the morning. She was a total fitness fanatic, but her classes weren't about jumping around. Her whole philosophy was centred on stretching. I still don't know, how, but I have never been so sweaty and out of breath as during those classes. And for two days afterwards I could barely move.

'You must stretch every day,' she told me. 'As soon as you get up, just do it, any time during the day you have a minute, stretch, hold your ankles and count to five.'

I will never forget the phone call from Beatrice who used to come to Prune's classes with me.

'I have some terrible news,' she said. 'Prune, our wonderful gym instructor, is dead.'

She had been out cycling with Jean-Luc on his day off and some lunatic, who was on medication for depression and shouldn't even have been driving, drove into her and killed her instantly. He also hit a 10-year old boy who lost a leg as a result.

The funeral was the following day. The speed at which it happened shocked me. I remember when our neighbour died in Sussex, it seemed an age before we gathered in a cold crematorium in Tunbridge Wells.

The whole town showed up to show its support and sorrow at the Pézenas church. Beatrice and I stood at the back. Her husband and son followed her coffin into the church, weeping openly and leaning on each other for support. School children she had taught could barely speak as they related how she had inspired them. A lady who I think was her mother also spoke. Everyone in the church was crying, including us. I felt devastated. After the service, the cortège walked slowly through town to the cemetery where she was interred in the family tomb. A funeral worker dressed in a sort of space suit was charged with pushing her new coffin in among the old, decaying ones. The whole thing was horribly macabre. I couldn't quite believe she was in there. The final part of the ceremony involved everyone lining up to pay their respects to Jean-Luc and Hugo, their son. It was the kind of line you have at a wedding in Britain. I watched people go before me and tried to work out words of comfort before I got to them. This would have been hard enough in English, but in French all I could come up with was 'I'm so sorry'.

The man who killed her got two years in prison and is probably out now, back behind the wheel of a car. As my cleaning lady Geneviève said: 'It just proves that in France you can commit murder, as long as it's with a car.' I still do Prune's stretches every day.

Jonathan Miller, another very good friend, came to stay about 17 times before we finally told him he had to buy his own place. He dutifully went off and spent a fortune on a house four times the size of ours and had it beautifully renovated by our designer friend Peter. He holds exquisite dinners in his garden but is otherwise rarely here. When he is, he still seems to prefer to hang out with us, so is often found on our terrace, plotting his latest crusade against the BBC or the Channel ferry operators. He is godfather to Olivia and I fear is instilling her with subversive ideals. She has already sent two au pairs packing back to Poland and Slovakia and caused havoc at school. Miller pronounces himself 'delighted' with her.

Of course, you will also find that you are invited by the local British simply because you are an expat.

There are several classes. There are those who have holiday homes and those who live here. Those who live permanently in France tend to look down upon the former. Then, within the living-here category there are those who have recently arrived and the long-timers. Long-timers have been here for 20 years or more and have gone totally native. In the south of France, some of them even speak with a local accent. You would never think they were English if you bumped into them in the street. They in turn look down upon the 'newcomers', i.e. anyone who has been here less than ten years.

One of my neighbours, Ray, is in this category. The first time I met him, he showed up at my house covered in blood. I was swimming in the pool when Donia, my nanny, popped her head over the terrace.

'There's a man covered in blood at the door,' she said, in the same voice you would use to announce the postman. Donia is used to drama. In one year she was taken hostage in the petrol station she was working in and hit over the head with a gun, she crashed her car into eleven others (during the same incident), and she was attacked by a psychotic heroin addict on the streets of Brighton.

Throwing on a sarong, I rushed upstairs. Ray had fallen off his horse while riding in the *garrigue* close to our house. A rabbit had popped out of a hole. His horse went one way and he went the other. Ray left England 25 years ago to escape borstal and Mrs. Thatcher. He married the daughter of the region's most celebrated folk singer and has made a life down here as a jazz musician. He is known as Ray Trop and has a reputation for being a bit of a madman, albeit an incredibly talented one. He is a brilliant guitarist and singer, and a total flirt.

The girls looked at him in total horror as I bandaged him up.

'You've got a big hurty,' my daughter Olivia said.

'No,' laughed Ray, looking dreadful. 'It's only pretend. Just a bit of paint.'

Despite the shared nationality, there is almost more antagonism between the Brits in France than there is between the French and the Brits. As journalists writing about France, my husband and I are always being blamed for 'bringing more Brits' over here. My mother-in-law was recently stopped in the street by a British estate agent who you would think would be delighted to have the place crawling with potential house buyers. 'It's your son's fault there are all these people coming over here,' she said, referring to a book he has written on the region. 'I preferred it when it was more quiet.'

The British, in fact, seem to antagonise each other easily. Another English friend recently bought a house in a village close by and told me that one of her British neighbours showed up on her doorstep soon after she moved in.

'I thought I would come and introduce myself,' she said. 'Us both being English and all that.'

'Of course I immediately loathed her,' my friend told me.

Another friend who wishes to remain nameless tells me she totally despises the habit the English have of using the odd French word in a sentence. 'They'll say, oh which *boulangerie* do you go to? The other thing I hate is people kissing me three times. Most of them I wouldn't even want to kiss once, but to adopt the local habit of three is unforgivable.'

I have asked people what it is about other expats that bothers them. 'I didn't come hear to hang out with other Brits,' is one common retort. 'They're all so boring. All they want to do is sit around drinking all day and getting red-faced,' is another. 'A lot of people probably move to France to reinvent themselves,' says a friend of mine who has lived here for 14 years. 'It is very easy to be exactly what you want to among the French, they don't know enough about England to place you.'

Despite our efforts, we have not done as well at integrating as I would have liked. I can count my French friends on one hand. I am under no illusion that we will ever be considered French. That much is obvious, however many French lessons (or lovers) we have. There seem to be two worlds which exist next to one another. A lot of dinners we are now invited to are either predominantly English or French, in other words people that speak French along with the French or just English.

But the question remains—how far do *you* want to integrate?

*False friends*

***Actuellement*** means 'at the present time,' and should be translated as currently or right now. *Je travaille actuellement*—I am currently working. A related word is *actuel*, which means present or current: *le problème actuel*—the current/present problem. 'Actually' means 'in fact' and should be translated as *en fait, en réalité* or *à vrai dire*. Actually, I don't know him—*En fait, je ne le connais pas*. 'Actual' means real or true, and depending on the context can be translated as *réel, véritable, positif*, or *concret*: The actual value—*la valeur réelle*.

***Affaire*** can mean business, matter, deal, transaction, or scandal. 'Affair' is the equivalent of *affaire* only in the sense of an event or concern. A love affair is *une liaison, une affaire d'amour*, or *une aventure amoureuse*.

***Une affluence*** is a crowd of people: *Il y avait une affluence attendant à la porte*—There were crowds waiting at the door. 'Affluence' indicates a lot or a profusion of something (usually wealth): the affluent society—*l'ère de l'opulence*. There is plenty of information—*Il y a une* *abondance d'information ici.*

**Agonie** refers to death pangs or mortal agony, while 'agony' means severe physical or mental pain, but not necessarily just this side of death: *angoisse, supplice.*

**Arroser** means to water or spray. 'Arose' is the past participle of arise: *survenir, se présenter, s'élever.*

**Assister à** nearly always means to attend something: *J'ai assisté à la conférence*—I attended (went to) the conference. 'Assist' means to help or aid someone or something: I assisted the woman into the building—*J'ai aidé la dame à entrer dans l'immeuble.*

**Avertissement** is a warning or caution, from the verb *avertir*—to warn. 'Advertisement' is *une publicité, une réclame,* or *un spot publicitaire.*

**Blesser** means to wound, injure, or offend. 'Bless' means *bénir.*

**Bras** is an arm. 'Bras' as the plural of 'bra'—*soutien-gorge.*

**Une bride** refers to a bridle. 'Bride' is *une mariée.*

**Candide** means naïve or ingenuous. 'Candid' means open or frank: *franc, sincère.*

**Car** is most often used as a conjunction: because or for. As a noun, it refers to a coach or bus. 'Car' is *une voiture.*

**Caractère** refers only to the character or temperament of a person or thing: *Cette maison a du caractère*—This house has character. 'Character' can mean both nature/temperament as well as a person in a play: education develops character—*l'éducation développe le caractère.* Romeo is a famous character—*Romeo est un personnage célèbre.*

**Caution** is a financial term; it can mean guarantee, security, bail, or backing. 'Caution' indicates *prudence, circonspection,* or *avertissement.*

**Célibataire** as a noun means a bachelor, as an adjective can mean celibate or simply single/unmarried. *Célibate* is the adjective of *célibataire.*

*Chaîne* can refer to a chain, a production line, a mountain range, a TV channel, or a stereo. Chain can be a
noun—*une chaîne*—or a verb—*enchaîner*.

*Chance* means luck. Chance refers to *un hasard, une
possibilité,* or *une occasion.*

*Façon* means way, as in *voilà la façon dont il procède*—
this is the way he does it. It can be translated by fashion
when it is synonymous with way or manner, as in *à ma
façon*—in my fashion or my way. 'Fashion' is a style or
custom, usually in clothing: *mode* or *vogue.*

*Facteur.* In addition to factor, it can mean postman,
mailman, or maker—*un facteur de pianos*—piano maker.
A 'factor' is *un facteur, un élément, un indice.*

*Figure* is the French word for face, but can also refer to
an illustrated or mathematical figure. 'Figure' refers to
numbers *chiffres* as well as to the form of a person's
body: *forme, silhouette.*

**Napkin** is correctly translated as *serviette*: I need a
napkin—*J'ai besoin d'une serviette de table. Une serviette*
on its own is a towel.

*Parcelle* means a bit or a fragment, or can refer to a
parcel of land. 'Parcel' refers to *un colis* or *un paquet.*

*Particulier* as an adjective has a range of meanings: particular, specific, characteristic, distinctive, special, peculiar,
or private. As a noun, it refers to a person or individual.

*Pays* refers to a certain territory, usually a country, but
can on occasion refer to a *village.* 'Pays' is the third
person singular of the verb to pay: he pays me cash—*il
me paie en liquide.*

*Personne* as a noun means person, but as a pronoun, it
can mean anyone or no one: *Elle le connait mieux que
personne*—She knows him better than anyone. *Personne
n'est ici*—No one is here.

*Phrase* means a sentence. A phrase is *une expression* or
*locution.*

*Pièce* means piece only in the sense of broken pieces. Otherwise, it indicates a room, a sheet of paper, coin, or play. Piece as a part of something is *un morceau* or *une tranche*.

*Préjudice* means loss, harm, or damage. 'Prejudice' refers to *préjugé(s)* or *prévention(s)*.

*Saler* means to salt. 'Sale' is the noun for *vente* or *solde*.

*Secret* can, in addition to the English sense of secret, mean reserved or reticent: *Il est secret*—He is reserved. 'Secret' refers to something that is not public knowledge.

*Sensible* means sensitive or even nervous, as in *pas recommandé aux sensibles*—not recommended for people of a nervous disposition. 'Sensible' means to show good sense, e.g., in making decisions: *sensé, raisonnable, sage*.

*Souvenir* is the French verb for 'to remember' as well as a noun for memory, recollection, and remembrance. *Un souvenir* is a keepsake or memento.

*Spectacle* refers to any sort of exhibition: *un spectacle de danse*—a dance performance or something that others can watch: *le spectacle de la rue*—the bustle on the street. *Spectacle* can mean an exhibition, but is usually used with a negative connotation: you made a spectacle of yourself—*tu t'es donné en spectacle*.

*Supporter* means to support or hold up, as well as to endure or put up with something. 'Support' means all of these things, but in the sense of enduring something, *soutenir* is the more common translation.

# Lesson 3

# One Egg Is *Un Oeuf*

One of my favourite beginnings to any book is 'There was no possibility of taking a walk that day' from *Jane Eyre*. If *Jane Eyre* had been written by a Frenchman, the first line would have been: 'There was no possibility of a baguette that day.' France is a nation obsessed with bread. No meal is complete without it. It melts the heart even of the toughest functionary. I once came back to my car to find a traffic warden about to write me a ticket. 'I was just getting some bread,' I gasped as I ran towards him and my illegally parked car, waving my baguette. 'Oh I see,' he responded, eyeing my loaf. 'That looks good, which baker did you get it from?'

All sorts of bread, not just the baguette, are central to the French way of life. The absence of it is fundamental to the country's history. Would there ever have been a revolution if Marie Antoinette hadn't suggested the peasants eat cake? There are still those in France who make the sign of the cross on their loaf before breaking into it. There are fierce arguments about the decline of bread, the addition of chemicals, the decline of the artisan bakery and its replacement by the bread factories attached to the supermarkets. The relationship between a French person and bread is more than one of food, it is emotional. There is a French expression: *Triste comme un jour sans pain*. As sad as a day without bread.

You will never go for a meal in France and not be given bread. Whatever the time of day or night, however lowly an establishment, there will be a basket of bread. If you are used to butter with your bread you will have to ask for it, as my father-in-law does. He often ends up with beer instead of *beurre*, but I don't think he minds too much.

This obsession with bread has now reached our household. And not just any bread. Bread with texture and with taste. There are certain bakeries that are to be visited just because of their *pain complet*. Or raisin and nut loaf.

We used to be perfectly capable of eating lunch without a baguette. Not so now. Every time I leave the house the phrase 'will you get some bread on your way back?' rings in my ears. Rupert seems lost without it. If I fail to get bread, he will grumpily search the freezer for some and then complain. 'Would have been nice with a bit of bread,' he'll say, prodding his pasta. How this happened to us, I don't know.

Bread dictates the rhythm of our life. The consequence of this mania for fresh bread daily does actually mean you go shopping every day and therefore end up eating a lot more fresh food. Forced to go into town to buy some bread, you may as well pop into the fishmongers (where you will often be given a recipe to go with your fillet of fish), the butcher or the *crémerie*, for the perfect cheeses to go with the bread.

This shopping, imposed by the necessity to always have fresh bread, presages what soon becomes a complete dietary transformation when you live in France. The seasons become much more important. We live quite near Bouzigues, which is famous for its oysters and other strange looking crustaceans. They produce 15 tons of oysters a year and 100 tons of mussels. In our local market town, these *coquillages* are sold from wooden cabins in the central square, conveniently between the best bakery, the best *crémerie* and an interesting wine shop. It is no coincidence that the town statue of Marianne, the bare-breasted revolutionary, is set into the small place separating these businesses. She holds aloft a sign with the rights of man, but she has obviously chosen to take up her position where there will be plenty of good bread, and accompaniments.

One declares loyalty to one shack or the other, and for some reason we have become the customers of Ludovic, who soon gets to know you and remembers what you order and how you wish it prepared.

For example, Rupert will always have the medium-sized oysters, opened. Ludovic sells a dozen for around £3. Although they're said to be the sexiest food going, oysters don't really turn me on. In fact, I find them slimy and faintly gross, which is a shame as they are otherwise a perfect food, no calories and loads of protein. I notice the French like to eat them with bread—but only brown bread.

What does excite me though is the asparagus season. In England asparagus was something we could rarely afford. And even when we could, it wasn't very good. In France, the asparagus is wonderful. You get the thinner or the thicker variety, both delicious. Green or white. Both varieties are better steamed, never boiled. A sage French woman told me an asparagus tip should never touch water. Because I am partly Italian I love them with a sprinkling of parmesan on top. They are also great roasted or grilled. When the season starts you see them everywhere, sold in a *botte*, which is a bunch about as big as both your hands can comfortably go around.

My favourite place for buying asparagus is in our neighbouring village. There is a young couple there who open their garage and set up a table outside it every day during the season between five and seven in the afternoon, lending another meaning to the famous French phrase *cinq à sept*. They are there for a total of about five weeks and during this time I have to eat asparagus every day.

I normally pull up by their stall and they hand me the asparagus without me having to get out of the car, a sort of asparagus drive-through service. One evening I was on my way home from collecting the children and had to stop for my asparagus fix. Rupert was away on some trip to Africa. I had had a very busy day and was keen to get back home to do some more work, so when I saw an old couple standing chatting by the stall I decided to turn the car around first to save time. We have a Toyota Landcruiser, a bigger more cumbersome vehicle you could not hope for—although something resembling a tank is necessary if one is going to survive the drivers in France. I found a side road and drove in, then started reversing.

I did, in fact, see the great tree behind me, and was just wondering why the reversing alarm hadn't gone off when *crash*, the whole back window collapsed.

'Oh,' said Olivia. 'I wonder when Daddy's coming home. He's a very good driver.'

Bea was by now mimicking me, but thankfully getting it wrong and saying 'oh duck'. The asparagus man and his old gossiping couple were looking on amazed.

Still determined to get my asparagus, I drove up to the stall. The oldies moved away pretty sharpish. 'Two *bottes*, please,' I said, trying to control my rage. 'No, make it three.'

Once you have become a serious foodie, it is no longer enough to visit the *crémerie* for the cheese for your bread, but you will want to make friends with someone who actually makes the stuff, so you can buy it at the farm gate. General de Gaulle famously complained: 'How can you be expected to govern a country that has 246 kinds of cheese?' What is curious about this statement is that the French have not stopped inventing new ones, and this may explain why the country continues to present governance problems. It now has 365 kinds.

One day we spotted goats close to us. In France, this can only mean one thing—cheese. The farm, Mas Roland, has a green and yellow *Bienvenue à la Ferme* sign on the gate—an indication that they welcome visitors and are proud to show them how they produce the products of their particular *terroir* (an almost untranslatable French word which reflects the almost mystical qualities of particular plots of land to produce particular distinctive flavours).

The family here has been producing goat's cheese for 23 years. After meeting the goats and watching some of them milked, you can buy from that day's batch, which is a lovely, white crumbly cheese, or semi-fresh (about two days old) or mature (about four days old). The longer it stands, the creamier and 'goatier' it becomes. Mas Roland is a hamlet perched on top of an imposing hill which is surmounted on a road of many zigs and zags. It's actually easier on a bicycle than in a car.

*Bienvenue à la Ferme* is proving a wonderful way of bringing the children closer to their food. The farm is open every day between 4.30 and 7.30pm, so we can go there, on the way to the bakery. Until they could say the word goat, my daughters called it the 'baaaa farm'. There is something intimate and satisfying about seeing exactly where your food is coming from.

We also get our eggs from a local farm. Olivia is obsessed with eggs and would eat them at every meal if she could. She can't, partly because too many eggs aren't good for you, but also because every time anyone in the house has an egg, Rupert comes up with his favourite joke:

Why do Frenchmen only have one egg for breakfast?

Because one egg is *un oeuf*.

The girls still don't get the joke but groan in sympathy with me.

In the early 1990s, a French scientist noted that despite the fact that the French eat masses of runny cheeses, kilos of *pâté* and *foie gras*, drink gallons of wine and smoke millions of cigarettes, they are 30 per cent less likely to die from heart disease than their counterparts on the US or northern Europe. He also noted that the southern French were 30 per cent less likely to suffer from heart conditions than the northern French. In addition, just 7 per cent of French people are obese, despite buttery croissants and pastries, compared with 22 per cent of Americans. This phenomenon has become known as the French Paradox.

The French diet is beneficial not just for the heart but also leads to less bowel cancer, fewer circulatory problems, less osteoporosis and other problems. In fact, a recent study showed that men who had already suffered a heart attack and switched to a more Mediterranean-style diet cut their chances of a second heart attack by 70 per cent. A Mediterranean diet is easy to follow wherever you are in France. Choose fish above red meat, olive oil at every given opportunity, and at least two glasses of red wine a day. If you're worried about wine being fattening, don't. A whole bottle of Bordeaux is 680 calories, the equivalent of a cheeseburger and chips, and probably better for you.

When we first decided to move I imagined myself pottering around markets, picking out the choicest peaches and apricots. This does happen, but there are also supermarkets, which are sometimes more convenient. Every Wednesday in our village there is a market which consists of a huge vegetable stall run by a round, jolly couple. There is also a little old lady selling whatever is in season, be it strawberries or asparagus, from the back of her Renault 5, and a van that sells horsemeat. I don't think I've eaten any yet, but Donia (who speaks no French) did once come back from a butcher I know sells horsemeat with something that looked very odd. When I tasted it, it was vaguely sweet. I gave it to the dog, just in case.

The French love nothing more than comparing recipes, they talk for hours about the benefits of vanilla essence versus vanilla pods and other essential topics. The round, jolly vegetable stall lady is a very keen cook and once gave me a fantastic recipe for chocolate mousse. It was incredibly complicated and involved about 12 eggs. At a dinner, once your cooking methods have been dissected, they will ask you where you got your ingredients from. If it was the supermarket, lie.

By far the biggest market in my region is in Pézenas every Saturday. Here you can buy anything from children's shoes to fresh ginger. In the winter it is blissfully local, in the summer every other voice is foreign and there is nowhere to park. On the upside, the stalls are more varied and you can find some real treats. You can find every kind of flavoured olive, ready-made paella, several cheese and meat stalls selling all sorts of things the English will probably never eat.

Proof that Olivia has become totally French came one day when she proudly showed Monika, our recently arrived Slovakian au pair, a big fat snail she had crawling on her arm. 'Ugh,' said Monika, reeling backwards. 'It's disgusting.' 'No, it's not,' replied Olivia. 'It's delicious.' I myself have never tried them, but then eating something that looks as if it may have come from somebody's nose has never really appealed to me.

Snails are big business in France. They eat two billion of them a year, one third imported from Turkey and Eastern Europe. In fact, I once saw someone advertising a ready-made

---

Food and language

*Tomber dans les pommes*—literally, to fall into the apples—meaning to faint

*Couper la poire en deux*—to cut the pear in two—to meet halfway

*Faire le poireau*—to act like a leek—to be kept waiting

*Tirer les marrons du feu*—to pull chestnuts out of the fire—to be used as a dupe or a tool

*Se fendre la pêche*—to split one's peach—to laugh uproariously, to split one's sides, to laugh one's head off

*Tondre des oeufs*—to shave eggs—to be a skinflint

*Pédaler dans la semoule*—to pedal in the semolina—to take leave of one's senses

*Cracher dans la soupe*—to spit in the soup—to spoil something so that it can only be enjoyed by you

*Casser du sucre sur le dos de quelqu'un*—to break sugar on someone's back—to talk about someone behind their back delectable dish he described as *escargots aux grenouilles*. Snails with frog's legs. As with everything essential to the French lifestyle, the government is in control of the situation. In 1982 it passed a law that snails could only enter France at designated spots where the customs officials have snail testing machines. These ensure that the snails destined for the French consumer are alive and healthy. The classic French snail is the Burgundy snail, which is light brown, and feeds on the vineyards. They are usually cooked in their shells with a dab of garlic butter in each one, although in Burgundy they are sometimes combined with chanterelle mushrooms.

As a consequence of all this shopping, the most dangerous time to be on the roads in France is just before noon. Frenchmen and women with low blood sugar levels, having just had a croissant for breakfast, are rushing home or out to lunch. For, unlike England, the midday meal in France is still a big deal. The whole country shuts down between 12 and 2pm. If you want to get somewhere quickly, that's the time to go out. It's as if a curfew has been imposed. It always reminds me of walking back from work as England was about to play in the semi-final of the 1990 World Cup. Although I lived in central London there was not a soul about. *Everyone* here has a proper lunch. There is no question of grabbing a sandwich on the run. I even read a story recently about two burglars who broke into a flat in Agde. As it was midday, they stopped stealing things and ate a baguette. The police found crumbs all over the floor.

When you go out for lunch in France you will notice that most places have a *menu du jour*. This is usually extremely reasonably priced at between €10 and €15. For this you get four courses, as well as coffee. It is again part of their socialist values. The man in the street should be able to eat well at midday, it's his right, no matter who he is or where he is. In fact, you will find that the price of a coffee, a beer and a baguette is more or less the same throughout France as well. According to Fiona Cantwell, a former chef who now runs the Château Marcenac, you should try the menu of the day when you go out. 'Even if there is some offal on it you would never normally eat. You might like it, and, anyway, with four courses there's plenty of other stuff you can eat if you don't.'

Eating out in France, however, is not always good. I have had some terrible meals. In fact, last time I was in London I was amazed at how well I ate and what good value it was. I suppose I did go for sushi and Italian, both things you are only likely to find in the big cities here. Maybe the quality in general is better in big cites, but I have found where I live you have to be really careful not to go out, eat badly and pay a lot for it.

Zoe Harris, a new friend of mine, told me a story recently of an experience they had in a restaurant called Rivarolle in Marseillan, a small port on the Etang de Thau, close to Bouzigues. Some very good friends of theirs had come to stay. They had been with them a week and this was their goodbye meal on the way to the airport.

They arrived at the restaurant at 1pm. By 2.15 they still hadn't had any service at all. 'It was mother's day,' says Zoe. 'And I think they were short-staffed, as well as very busy, but they could at least have given us a drink and a basket of bread.' When their food arrived another hour later, the monkfish two of them had ordered was so tough she couldn't cut it. 'I don't know what they could have done to get it to that state,' she says. 'I've never seen anything like it.' Her son had oysters which looked as if they had been left out for hours, and they probably had been. They made him so ill he threw up all the way back to England. 'The other food was barely edible,' says Zoe. 'But, being English, we didn't want to complain too much. It was a terrible end to the holiday for our friends. What really annoyed me most was that they refused to accept they were wrong or apologise. They were so arrogant.'

Restaurants here seem to be divided into categories. There are those where you eat well for a fair price, there are good restaurants, semi-gastronomic restaurants and, at the top, gastronomic restaurants. I have not been to many gastronomic restaurants here but the ones I have been to have been good, if pricey. There are some wonderful semi-gastronomic places on the beaches near Montpellier. There is something glorious about eating luxurious food on a beach, surrounded by teak furniture and fans. You almost feel as if you're in Morocco.

In France, the English have a terrible reputation as big drinkers. In fact, we are now known as the drunks of Europe. Even in my relatively unknown region there is a bar in the next village known as the 'English Bar.' Whatever time of day or night you go past, you can see the Brits with their glasses of beer and copies of some English paper they have just bought. Alex, my French friend and wife of the winemaker Jean-Claude, says the French would never drink like the English. 'They have one glass of wine with lunch and two with dinner. They may not even go that far', she says, 'the culture is changing and a lot of French now only drink when they go out or are entertaining.' There are a lot of Brits who really don't do much else. You see them at the bars, red-faced from the sun and the *pastis*. 'They don't help the reputation of the English in France,' says Alex.

When I asked my friend Caroline what she found most repulsive about the way the English eat, she told me it was the habit of mixing cucumbers and cheese. 'In France a cucumber is an *hors d'oeuvre*. And cheese is, well, cheese.' She remembers an exchange she went on, aged 16, to Coventry. She was with three other French teenagers and every day they were sent off for the day with a picnic lunch. 'Every day we would open our sandwiches and find cheddar and cucumber,' she says. '*C'est pas possible*! Disgusting. We all refused to eat it. The only thing we ate from the picnic were the crisps.'

There are ways the French do things that we find hard to cope with as well. For example, my friend Carla McKay has a house in a village nearby. She woke up one morning to chattering voices outside. Her neighbours were having a gossip. 'How nice,' I thought. 'I'll take my coffee to the terrace and see what's going on.' When she looked over towards the noise, she saw that one of them was holding up a dead hare, while another ripped its skin off. The blood was gushing down the street. 'Now, you don't get that in Lower Heyford,' says Carla.

When I first moved here, I was practically vegetarian. It is really since having the babies that I have started craving meat. But still some of the things they come up with are too much. Tripe, for example. That's what we feed our dog. And why do they insist on eating every part of an animal from its trotter to its brain? They really are not in the least squeamish. Fiona Cantwell told me that when they signed for their *château*, the local mayor came round to take a look. He found some *foie gras* and *pâté* in the cellar that had been there at least 10 years, which he proceeded to eat, declaring it delicious.

For the true difference in culture between the French and the English when it comes to food, you need only look at the word *gourmand*. Its literal translation is greedy, which in English is an insult. In French it means the same thing, but it is not an insult. People are always telling me Leonardo (our son, now one year old) is *gourmand* but it is said with a hint of admiration, as if to say he eats well, as opposed to too much. The word *gourmet* in French means you appreciate good food and good things. This is an enormous compliment.

In a country more recently renowned for critical theory than breakthrough-cuisine, there are agonies in the French culinary establishment over a perceived lack of cutting edge. Jamie Oliver has become an unlikely TV hit here—the irony that an Englishman is now teaching the French to cook is not lost on the French chattering classes.

It is, in fact, the case that if you want a choice of daring restaurants propelled by determination to advance to the very frontiers of culinary experience, you are better off in London than rural France. 'The discovery of a new dish does more for human happiness than the discovery of a new star,' declared the most eminent French philosopher of food, Anthelme Brillat-Savarin. Brillat-Savarin considered the French revolution also as a revolution in the kitchen, inaugurating an era of bourgeois culinary supremacy and the rise of the restaurant. But the new dishes are now mostly being discovered and invented else-where. France suffers in the kitchen as in so many other things because it is so bureaucratised. As it is so hard to start a business, there simply isn't the same capital going into catering as in Britain. Many of the professional French restaurateurs seem to have left for greener pastures abroad, running huge and profitable restaurants in places like New York and London.

Nevertheless, the cuisine of the country, the basics of bread, cheese, olives, salads, grills of meat and delicious fish, make the experience of daily eating superior here. Perhaps this is the trick. Expect to eat well, but not always when you eat out. Usually we eat at home. Nothing could be easier than a couple of rump steaks you have marinated in olive oil for 24 hours and some French beans. Finally some fresh goat's cheese. And don't forget the bread. And of course the wine. The food here is more wonderful.

The closeness to food means, too, that entertaining here is easier, and something that most people find themselves doing more of. Entertaining is easier partly because there is absolutely no shame in buying at least your pudding ready made, if not everything you put on the table. Why would you spend hours making a *tarte aux pommes* when your local bakery does it a million times better and for less than €10? The tradition of storing things like the *foie gras* and *pâté* mentioned above is so that the French housewife is able to produce a good meal at any given moment. I have often been invited to an impromptu lunch with Peter and Dominique and out of nowhere she has produced a spread that looks as if she had been planning it all week. If you analyse the ingredients, they are simple. Tomatoes, basil, melon, ham, lettuce, bread, cheese, *pâté*. But on a hot day with a glass of chilled rosé, looking out over their garden, it seems a feast fit for kings.

# Lesson 4
# Sleeping with the Enemy

When we first moved to France I had no fixed idea how I would make a living. So I invited the letting company Bowhills to come and see me in my new home to tell us if we could rent it out for the summer. My plan was that we would decamp to England or Sweden for two months.

'You'll have to change a lot of the fittings,' said a rather sniffy woman as she walked around the house grimacing. 'It's all a bit, well, shabby.'

She went on to tell me all the things I would have to provide prospective tenants with, from new linen to swimming-pool towels. 'The good thing about it though,' she looked at me and started to fill in some dreadful looking form, 'is that it's big enough for two families with several children between them to share.' The thought of someone else's children running around my house was enough to put me off the idea of renting forever. I told Mrs Sniffy that I would have to think about it.

A lot of people who move to France decide to make money by renting out their homes. The formula is simple. You sell up in England, buy somewhere here for a quarter of the price, and convert part of it into a *gîte*. If you have no mortgage, you don't need much of an income and so you can live off the rent from your *gîte*. Or you keep a smaller place in the UK and rent out

---

*Top rental tips*

1. Do think carefully about location if you're buying to rent. Easy access to the UK is essential.
2. Talk to an agent before you buy and find out what you could realistically get for your house.
3. Get legal advice on the rental contract, or at least run your contract by an experienced agent.
4. If you're not going to be there, make sure you have someone on-site who can look after the property and guests for you.
5. Don't be tempted to overcharge. Guests will take it out on your house.
6. Get a hefty deposit.
7. Remove the phone, unless you have discussed it with the tenants beforehand.
8. Don't go for a cream colour scheme.
9. Do use a local, reputable agent, at least if you're not going to be there.

---

your house in France during the peak summer months when you can get literally thousands of pounds a week. This pattern has become so widespread here that it is now known as *la maladie anglaise*.

The formula may be simple, but it is an area full of unexpected pitfalls. Penny and Alan, friends from Sussex, for example, have a house nearby and rent out a cottage attached to it. Their first tenants came from Birmingham and were due to stay for two weeks. 'We rushed around like mad getting the whole place ready for them,' says Penny. 'We had done a lot of work to the cottage and were really pleased with the results. We had always planned to buy somewhere where there was the possibility of an income,' continues Penny. 'Our idea was that once Alan retired completely we could downsize at home and live here almost all the time.'

The guests arrived a sunny Wednesday morning and Penny

showed them around the newly converted cottage. 'I felt proud and happy showing them around,' she said. 'It was like the beginning of a new era for us.' Everything seemed to be fine until they found their tenants outside the following morning with their bags packed. 'They had been kept awake all night by scratching and scrabbling in the attic, and they were convinced the place was infested with rats,' says Penny. 'I was horrified and tried to calm them down, but they were having none of it. They upped and left, leaving us an address to send the refund to.'

In fact, their cottage isn't rat-infested, it is home to a small mouse-like creature indigenous to the south of France called a *loir*. It is translated as a dormouse in the dictionary but it has small circles round its eyes, rather like a raccoon. The next day, the Hastings-Jones called in the pest control people. 'This man arrived with a box of carrots and a bag of poison,' says Penny. 'I couldn't believe it. And all he did was roll the carrots in the poison and shove them under the tiles in the roof where the *loir* go in and out. He charged us £100 and cluttered off, warning us not to tell the authorities we had done this as the *loir* is a protected species. I have to say, I rather liked the look of them and felt really miserable about the idea of killing them.'

The following day, Penny went outside expecting to see the garden littered with dead creatures. Instead she found a row of carrots that had been neatly pushed out. 'It was as if they'd been offended by this foreign object,' she says. 'They had just pushed them out, without so much as nibbling on them.'

Alan and Penny have decided to let them stay and now warn tenants about them with a description and picture in the information manual. 'We've tried to make it a positive thing,' Alan explains. 'To make it part of the whole experience of being here, as opposed to just a pest.' So far, they have had no more complaints.

Not many people let strangers rampage through their home for their own enjoyment. It is only driven by necessity. Another of my friends who rents out her house over the hill from us calls her tenants 'the enemy'. She arrives at the beginning of every letting season with bags of supplies. 'I've just got to get the place ready for them,' she says. 'God knows what state it will be in once they've all gone.'

When Selina Howard decided to build a £1 million house on the French Riviera, the future rental income she could get was very much part of the equation. 'I figured that if I could get £3,500 per week for the whole of the summer, the house would at least run itself in terms of costs and any profit could be put towards the mortgage.' Her house was barely finished when her agent told her she had some tenants. They were a New York family with one small child. He was an investment banker, she a housewife. The fact that they had decided to rent the house for the full six weeks was a huge bonus. 'I was delighted,' she says. 'It seemed too good to be true, I hadn't even had to go looking for anyone.'

Pat Bellis of Riviera Search International, the agent dealing with the property, said they should have seen the warning signs. 'I only had contact with the wife before they landed, and she seemed OK, if a little demanding. They wanted all sorts of child-safety equipment, and were very insistent on having a king-size bed.' The owner assured Bellis that the bed was king-size and left for England. When the couple arrived, they took one look at the bed (queen-size in the US) and threatened to sue. Bellis spent the rest of the day locating a king-size bed. 'The man was incredibly aggressive,' she says. 'He was furious at the inventory the owner had left, which was 10 pages long and listed everything in the house. The client threw all the papers up in the air and shouted: 'does she really think I've flown all the way from New York to steal a corkscrew?'

Bellis and the house manager managed to calm them down, but not a day passed during the six weeks when they didn't phone up to complain about something and threaten a lawsuit. In addition, they had demanded air-conditioning units in every room, at a cost of £250 a month each, as well as barriers around the swimming-pool, which cost another £1,000.

*Rates*

- You should make sure your rental rates are easy to understand and, although there will obviously be differences between seasons, try to keep them to a minimum.

- If getting your bookings early is important to you, you will need to quote lower rates. If you are prepared to take a bit of a risk and wait, you can go for higher ones.

- 'The pattern of holiday bookings has drastically changed over the last few years,' says Marcelle Speller from www.holidayrentals.com. 'People are no longer just booking four weeks in the summer. They book holidays over Easter, half term, they book long weekends. It is no longer the case that if you're not fully booked in January for the summer you should panic. People are more flexible now and will book much closer to the time of travel.'

- Bear in mind with weekend bookings that the changeover will cost you as much as it would if someone had stayed for a week, so you may want to factor in the cost of cleaning at least into the rent you quote for shorter periods.

- Make sure your contact details are correct. There is nothing more annoying than not getting through—people will rarely try more than once.

- When you get an enquiry, reply straight away. Some wonders even use instant messaging now and reply within minutes.

Howard was lucky she had appointed an agent to deal with it all and gone back home. 'I would strongly advise anyone

### Advertising

☙ You can just advertise the property on a holiday home website. The key to this is to make sure your advertisement is spot-on. The copy you write should be engaging and readable. Normally you have room for between 500 and 1000 words, but you must tell potential tenants the most important things first, as they often won't read the whole thing.

☙ 'Think of your advertisement as a pyramid,' says Speller. 'With the key points at the top and more details as you go down. The headline should give a short well-crafted summary including the type of property and its most important selling features.' The sentences should be clear and concise. Remember that some people reading the advertisement may not be English so don't use colloquialisms or abbreviations.

☙ The Internet is a visual medium and your choice of photograph is absolutely crucial. It is the most important selling tool in the whole advertisement. Only use clear, well-lit, bright photographs taken on a sunny day. Try to include both interior and exterior shots, people like to have an idea of the décor and style of a place.

thinking of renting to get professional help,' says Bellis. 'If at all possible, go for a local British agent and stay away from the whole rental process, let the professionals handle it.' This could either be an agent, or someone living locally who does this kind of thing for a living. An agent is likely to be more expensive, charging up to 25 per cent of the rent. The going rate for an individual is around 15 per cent of rental income.

When we'd been in our house for about six months, I met a

charming man who lived in the nearest village to us. He wasn't here during the summer months and suggested that I take on the renting of his house. He would pay for all the advertisements, I would take the bookings and see people in and out, making sure the place was clean and so on. It seemed like an easy job. He was charging £1,300 a week and the house was quickly booked up for July and August. Six weeks before the tenants descended, the whole of their rent had arrived in my bank account. I would have to think about giving it back to the owner when the time came.

We had agreed that he would give me 30 per cent of the rental income, which was a very good deal. The first visitors came from Israel. There were two families with teenage children. The men were all huge and the women tiny and beautiful. I showed them around while silently cursing the lunatic nextdoor neighbour who had chosen that moment to move his collection of tractors around his rather unsightly plot.

'It's wonderful,' they all said. 'And so peaceful compared with Tel Aviv.' Their stay was marvellous, except for one of the huge men going through a sun-lounger. I was particularly struck by how much one of the mothers appreciated getting up in the morning and just going for a walk in the countryside. Something I do every day and had started to take for granted.

The problems started with the arrival of the next guests, some rather grumpy types from the north of England. Suicide bombers did not frequent their daily lives so they found the neighbour irritating and noisy. In addition, the sanitation system collapsed on their second day and the downstairs bath filled with sewage. I was telephoned at 11pm and told to do something about it. I explained that French plumbers only work 35 hours a week (at best) and that they were unlikely to come and see to a sewer at that time of night. I promised I would have one there the next morning. That night I lay awake trying to work out how to keep my promise. One of the worst things about living here is getting anything done. Plumbers, electricians and so on, are horribly unreliable.

The first two plumbers I called at 8am couldn't do anything for a week. The third one said he would be there at midday. I called the house and told them I would send the cleaning lady in to clean the sewage-filled bath and see them there at 12pm. They seemed to have calmed down and I thought the worst was over.

At noon, I was there, as were seven rather hot and irritable people waiting to have a bath. The plumber, of course, failed to show up. And by then it was too late to do anything until at least 2pm as France shuts for lunch. I offered bribes of wine and baths at my house but my suggestions were met with stony silence. I couldn't really blame them. As Marcelle Speller, of Holiday-Rentals.com says: 'People who come on holiday just want it all to be perfect, they don't want to deal with things they have to deal with at home, they just want to relax.'

The sewage saga continued throughout the summer. It would be fixed by some mad plumber only to break down again. Finally it was concluded that the fault lay with the person who originally converted the place for putting in a pump that was too weak to do its job properly. But I had eight weeks of disgruntled guests, which was hellish. And not an experience I am keen to repeat.

Luckily my friend has decided to stop letting out the house. He says the damage caused by the tenants, such as a tear in the swimming-pool lining and breaking the automatically closing gates, negates the profit.

'People on holiday will behave in a manner they wouldn't even think of at home,' says Alexandra Wills. She bought her house on the outskirts of a small village close to Toulouse for £150,000. She put down £50,000 and has a mortgage for £700 a month. She lets the house for £1,300 a week during July and August. 'I realised that I could work from anywhere and thought it would be great to be able to come on extended holidays with my daughter but not feel like I was wasting time. Also, prices in this region were still relatively affordable when

*Agents*

Agents can earn up to 25 per cent of the rental income in France, depending on how long the rental period is and how much they do. At the most basic level, there are companies which simply advertise your property and take the money for it. The fee for this service is normally 15 per cent. A good agent should see tenants in and out and arrange for cleaning staff. It may be well worth the cost but you should be clear from the outset exactly what the agent will do for his or her commission. The following questions should be asked:

☞  Will they pay to advertise the property?
☞  Will they guarantee a minimum level of bookings?
☞  Will they vet potential guests?
☞  Will they inspect the property before and after each booking and check the inventory?
☞  Will they welcome guests and show them around the property?
☞  Will they organise repairs and maintenance?
☞  Are they available 24 hours in case of emergencies?

To find agents or local property-management people the best thing is to talk to other property owners in the area. Whatever else, though, make sure they speak English as a lot of guests won't speak French.

I bought this. I think it was a very good investment.'

Alexandra tells stories of cream sofas covered in chocolate stains and horrendous telephone bills. 'It got to a stage where I almost said no children. Get a hefty deposit, that's my advice, and throw the phone out. Everyone has mobiles these days.' She says she will carry on letting her house. 'It gets easier as the years go on, and you learn what not to put in it, like cream carpets that need to be steam cleaned. The sad thing is, you end up furnishing it for eventual disasters and not for yourself. And the thought of other people trashing your house is awful. It is very hard to tell what they're like over the internet.'

### Self management

If you are planning to advertise your house yourself, you will need a house manager, someone on-site who can deal with the plumbing if it breaks down, who can see the clients in and out, and arrange for the cleaning staff to come in once they've left. A house manager will cost anywhere between €100 and €400 per month.

Leaving the keys with a neighbour is really not an option. It won't make you popular and if anything goes wrong, there is no one there to deal with it.

According to Tony Tidswell, who runs www.rentalsfrance.com, you should be ploughing at least half your turnover into marketing the property. 'There is such a lot of competition now,' he says. 'If you don't have your house on several sites and come up with a nice-looking brochure chances are it won't get rented out.'

According to Bellis, who deals mainly with up-market properties, no amount of deposit, however, will safeguard you from some tenants. 'In some of the real luxury homes, even a £10,000 deposit won't cover the damage. It is mainly caused by Russians, who have that kind of money, along with a complete lack of respect for other people's property. In fact, a lot of clients, not only Russians, have an 'I've paid a lot of money, so I'll do what I want attitude.' Bellis tells of a collection of several precious antique vases being smashed as they were thrown at the husband of a family who rented a house in St Tropez. 'He was a British peer, with his own manservant and two wives. I don't know which of the wives did the damage, maybe both of them. I think they got fed up with him going out partying all night with his mates from Monaco, really not the kind of behaviour one would expect!'

Jeffrey Quirk of JQ International, a tax and law firm based in southwest France, maintains that most unpleasant rental experiences are the fault of the owners and their desire to save money. 'Nine times out of ten it's the owners who create the problems,' he explains. 'Most expats leave their brains behind on the airplane. They come out here and expect to do it all on their own. They forget how they would do it at home and try to do it all under the table as cheaply as possible.'

Quirk's advice is not to cut corners. 'Declare everything and get a proper contract drawn up, otherwise you have no recourse. And get a reputable agent involved, decide on the commission and all the terms before you start.' He also advises vetting your potential tenants. 'Some are a higher risk than others. The jet-setter hooray-Henry types tend to want to get wrecked and then wreck your house.'

Anyone looking to rent should take into account all costs and taxes before they think about making a profit. 'There is not only income tax but wealth tax, property tax and residential tax,' Bellis says.

The *taxe foncière* (property tax) is calculated according to how much land you own, how many buildings you have and so forth. It is payable even if your property is empty, providing it is habitable. Bellis quotes a client with a house of 400 m² with 2000 m² of land. They pay around £2900 a year in property tax.

The residential tax (*taxe d'habitation*) is payable by anyone living in the property and is levied by the town where the property is situated. The amount is calculated by the land registry and based on the average rental value of the property in the previous year. They will take into account the living area of the property, including outbuildings located less than one kilometre from the main house. If the property is the main family home there are reductions for dependants, which are calculated as a percentage of the rental value. This tax is not paid by those exempt from income and wealth tax. According to Bellis, it is normally around the same figure as the *taxe foncière*. It is worth noting that even if you don't live there full-time, if you occupy the building on January 1st, you are liable to pay the residential tax for the full year.

In terms of declaring your rental income, if you are not a French resident you must still declare it in France. You can declare the income and French tax paid on your tax return to the UK authorities. But there may be some additional tax to pay if you have not paid as much in France as you would at home.

If you are a French resident, *any* income has to be declared in France. You have to declare the amount you made on your annual French tax return. The authorities will deduct 72 per cent of that income and tax you on the remainder on a sliding scale according to how much you earn.

There may not be much left to declare once you've paid all the costs of running a house. 'Cleaning staff will charge you around £6-10 an hour—that's if you can find any,' says Bellis. Even if you can find staff, they are not always reliable. One agent tells the story of a cleaning lady near Avignon who cleaned three houses one season and they were all burgled during the winter. She was never seen again. 'And if you pay a cleaner or a gardener legally, you have to pay 40 per cent social security costs on top of their salary.'

Homeowners who go by the books are not likely even to cover their costs. Bellis continues, 'There are also all the other costs such as insurance, water, electricity and gas, which are all very expensive. In addition there is the general maintenance of the house. We specialise in the Côte d'Azur and there might be floods one day and scorching sun the next, and when there's not enough water, concrete structures can crack. Talking of swimming-pools, there's the cost of that.'

The issue of swimming-pools has been worrying renters in France ever since the Prime Minister's nephew drowned in one. The so-called Raffarin Law declares that any pool, rented or not, must have a barrier of some sort to prevent people falling into it. In typical French fashion, the law was announced and a

### Pool tips

🏠 New pools should come with a 10-year guarantee. Make sure your installer provides you with this. If it is a big name company, get something in writing from head office before signing or paying.

🏠 Be careful in rocky or mountainous regions that might have porous or seismic ground. Pools can move and leak, which can cost a fortune in water and repair bills. Installers are not obliged to check this. Get an engineer involved if you're at all unsure.

🏠 A pool maintenance man will cost around £50 per week.

🏠 Don't put too much chlorine in or your hair will turn green.

🏠 When buying a property without a pool, do make sure you have the required minimum amount of land to build one.

🏠 Check out the law regarding fences and nets.

deadline set before they had even decided on the details of it. For those with rental properties, the deadline for putting in place a security measure was January 1st 2004. But, even as the deadline passed, the government had not announced what was acceptable under the new law. Finally, they have since issued further rules, and it seems that those rushing to put up expensive fences (which can cost thousands of pounds) may have been wasting their money. A simple alarm, available for around £500, is enough to meet the legal requirements. However, it is worth checking with your insurance company what sort of security device they will accept, as some of them will only take on liability if there is a fence. This could leave landlords in a very awkward situation should an accident occur. Also you should remember to turn your alarm off at night if it's very windy. I have been woken up at night several times by it going off due to a violent gust. This is obviously only safe providing your children don't sleepwalk in the garden and you remember to turn it back on in the morning.

Quirk, who runs *chambres d'hôtes* (bed and breakfast) himself, says he has between 30 and 40 people a year coming to stay who are looking to-buy-to-rent. According to a survey carried out by www.holiday-rentals.com, 80 per cent of owners are not

---

### Get off my lounger!

If you have just bought a home in France, this is what you should do. Take a picture of the ugliest house you can find and send it to everybody you know with the following message: 'This is our new house. We are so hoping you will visit. For some reason the swimming pool is a bit green at the moment, and the neighbour's 12-year-old son's clarinet practice gets a bit tiresome, but they have a lovely dog, although he does seem to bark at any opportunity, particularly before dawn.'

It is certainly what we should have done. Instead,

renting out their properties to make money. 'They do it to keep their dreams,' says Speller. 'They rent out the properties so they can use them and enjoy them, it is not a money-making scheme. This fact is further reinforced by the statistic we came up with when we asked what their future plans for the property were. One hundred per cent said they planned to keep it or leave it to their children.' Paul Beaufils, who runs a website called www.buyahouseinfrance.com, agrees. 'Everyone I have come across looking

with each summer the wasps and the guests arrive. It's hard to know which are the more irritating. People we haven't seen since university call to tell us they just happen to be passing and would love to come and stay. This is odd, because our house is on the way to nowhere. Others are even more blatant: 'I know we haven't really kept in touch, but we thought you must be getting bored with life out there all on your own, so thought we would come and stay for a week, with our three children,' reads one email.

The upside to guests is, in my view, minimal. Some of them are very good fun, but for most of the time you are an unpaid cook, waitress, hostess and provider of sun loungers. Is there anything more irritating than watching someone else laze around on a sun lounger that has hardly had the pleasure of your bottom's presence in the last four years? Is there anything more depressing than watching someone else's children wreck your house?

I have started putting guests up with friends. There are people who do this for a living (God knows why). But it is a good solution.

to rent out their place is doing it to cover the mortgage,' he says.

Despite all the downsides, Ruth de Latude, who lets out four converted barns on her estate, loves it. 'We get to meet people from all over the world,' she says. 'Last Christmas we had eight Californians staying when the gas in their barn ran out. They had no hot water or heating for seven days, and it was freezing. They ended up practically living with us, became our best friends and even came to our wedding.'

# Lesson 5
# Dreaming Spires

When we were looking for our house, we were briefly tempted by a crumbling *château* for sale about five kilometres away, for the same price. Even we could see this was reckless. It is a most striking building, with a stunning façade that looks down the valley towards the village of Gabian. There is an 11<sup>th</sup>-century Romanesque church attached, very useful for weddings and christenings, and when we looked at it, there was even a camel in the courtyard, extremely good for keeping the lawn looking neat. But the upkeep would have been impossible. My stepson, Hugo, is still mad about the place. 'I can't believe we could have been living there,' he says whenever we drive past (which is most days). 'It's so cool.'

Cool? Try bloody freezing. A *château* in the winter has to be one of the most inhospitable places in the world. We once stayed with Lucy Archer and Colin Winter at their *château*, which they were restoring slowly, bit by bit. A warmer welcome you couldn't have hoped for, but the temperature in their bedrooms was probably hovering around zero. I have never before or since seen Rupert sleep with his socks on. The huge pile of our great friends Beatrice and Luc does have central heating, but it's too expensive to use. In the winter, you go to dinner there dressed in your duvet.

It was not only the cold that put me off buying Château de Cassan. The scale is just too vast. It's rather like having a Ferrari, every time something goes wrong it costs you more than it would to buy a normal car. Also there are about 200 windows. By the time you'd have cleaned the last one, it would be time to start again.

Still, the phrase 'a *château* in France' has a particularly nice ring to it. You immediately imagine dreaming spires, large grounds, marble staircases, fine wines.

However, the French seem to classify much that does not live up to that description as *châteaux*. Cynics say that a more literal translation of *château* is 'cow-shed'.

Sarah and John Colvin, a couple I met from London, said when they were house hunting in Bordeaux they had told the agent they wanted a *château*. 'By that we meant somewhere with spires,' says John. 'They showed us everything from farm-houses to glorious wine estates. I'm sure in England if you ask to see a castle you don't get shown a two-up, two-down ter-raced house.'

This could be because there are so many castles in France. According to Stéphane Gondoin, editor-in-chief of the website www.casteland.com, there are over 30,000 *châteaux* and medieval fortifications here. 'Many of these sites offer no or little interest for the general public,' says Stéphane. 'Or they are difficult to get access to (private property, wooded or rough ter-rain, under water even) and only a few thousand are open to visitors. I personally visited about 1,000 of the more inaccessi-ble sites, most of the time with rubber boots, heavy-duty clothes and not forgetting a compass to find my way around.'

At least in part, the French have the English to thank for their abundance of *châteaux*. During The Hundred Years' War (1337–1453) the French were forced to build thousands to defend the northern coastline. Further south in the Dordogne, the English and the French both built castles to defend their land. At one stage, Edward III had possession of one third of France. All along the Dordogne River are the monuments to the struggle for territory between the two countries. Some joke that the Brits have finally won the war, as they own so much of the land.

The *châteaux* in the Loire date from the 15<sup>th</sup> and 16<sup>th</sup> centuries and were built by the French royalty. The Loire was their playground and the hundreds of *châteaux* there were built as statements of power and wealth. The ultimate statement is of course further north, at Versailles. 'Louis XIV took the royal power to its ultimate conclusion,' says Colin Winter, who has been fascinated by castles since he was a little boy. 'Versailles is the epitome of the power of the French monarchy.'

Further south, mainly in the Languedoc-Roussillon region, are the Albigensian *châteaux*, built by the Cathars in the 13<sup>th</sup> century to defend themselves against the Catholic crusaders out to destroy them. Among these are some of the most impressive castles in France, built on top of huge rocks in stark landscapes. Along the Pyrenees are the relatively small 'commanderies', big box castles, built by the Templar monks to defend themselves against invasion from the Moors in the 11<sup>th</sup> and 12<sup>th</sup> centuries.

According to Colin you have to be 'mad and impassioned' to go through with buying a French *château*. 'It is not necessarily a rational decision,' he says. 'Unless you have masses of money, they have to be in some way commercial. We run *chambres d'hôtes* which is never going to make us rich, but the hope is that it will generate enough of an income to look after the building for you.'

In fact, the castellated *châteaux* that are the glory of so much of France still contain, remarkably, a wondrous and almost surreal cast of penniless aristocrats living in poverty on a huge scale. It can be argued that this verifies the theory that you would have to be mad to live in one. These are the houses where the *Marseillaise* is actually banned, as at Château Bourgade, between Pézenas and Béziers, where the count (and his English wife Ruth de Latude) are holding out for a restoration of the Bourbons.

Some English people end up in a *château* without even looking for one. When Fiona De Wulf started looking for a place to live, she was thinking about a cosy cottage somewhere in the Dordogne, Normandy or even the Loire Valley. She was 30, newly married to a Frenchman, and keen to settle in the country. One rainy day, driving through Burgundy, she stopped to look in the window of an estate agent's office. What she saw would lead to nine years of heartache, interspersed with fleeting moments of elation. A picture of a crumbling *château* covered in ivy caught her eye. She did not know then that there were great holes in the roof, and that the place had been largely uninhabited for over 70 years.

'The agent suggested we go and look at the place,' says Fiona. 'It was raining, and there wasn't much else to do. We looked through the gates and drove away laughing. I asked my husband who would be mad enough to buy a place like that?'

However, over lunch they found they kept talking about the *château*. Bruno, her husband, was bored of farming and wanted to do something different. She was looking for a challenge, and liked the Burgundy countryside.

'It reminds me of Surrey and Sussex where I grew up,' she says. They finished their wine, paid the bill and went back to look around the derelict property. They were horrified by what they saw. The ceilings had fallen in. There were pigeons and squirrels living in the roof. However, the original floors and doors were still there, even though the latter were hanging off their hinges.

The *château* had been built in 1650 by Antoine Comeau, Lord of Créancey. It had been passed down through his family for generations. During the Second World War the Germans used it as a local command post. After that it was abandoned, until some locals bought it in 1959 for use as a wine store. They lived in two rooms, without hot water or central heating.

Fiona and Bruno knew that years of neglect meant that it would be a monumental undertaking to restore it. But at least it had not been spoilt by tasteless renovations. So they made an offer for the *château* and five acres of garden. For £250,000 it was theirs.

On May 31 1994 contracts were exchanged and they were given the keys, even though you could walk into the *château* through holes where the windows had been. 'It was so daunting that we did not know where to start,' says Fiona. 'We started by pulling the ivy off the walls. This should be practised on a regular basis by anyone trying to keep their sanity when a wild and devastating project is trying to get the better of you. However, once that was finished, we had to decide what to do next.'

Finally they settled on doing up the cottage in the garden, which would give them a place to live while they finished the rest of the work. 'I thought if we could make the place respectable it might keep my mother happy,' says Fiona. However, even in the cottage there were problems. The ceiling had caved in on the old furniture, the main beams were on the floor and water was pouring in all over the place.

Fiona employed a Paris-based architect, but found that nothing got done. 'The workers kept promising to finish things, but nothing ever happened,' she says, 'three months passed and all we got was stories of in-grown toe-nails and stone masons' wives expecting babies. Eventually we were asked if we had been in touch with *Monsieur* B, a local architect and great expert in renovations. We finally got the message, explained the situation to our Paris-based friend and hired *Monsieur*. B. That was Thursday morning. On Monday morning, a whole team of builders showed up and work got under way.'

*Monsieur* B soon moved on to other jobs, but by then Fiona had established a good relationship with the builders. From then on she ran the site herself. They spent two years working out how the *château* could function. Heating specialists came to make estimates of how to make the place warm. Then they had to sell Bruno's farm in France to pay for the work.

'Work on the *château* started in 1997,' says Fiona. 'We took all the doors off their hinges, numbered them and stored them in an outbuilding. Then we began at the worst end of the building,' she says. 'There were lorry loads of rubbish, with occasional jewels such as a missing piece of the staircase. Then we had to do structural work, to hide pipes and wires. We took the roof off to get pipes and drains in.'

After about a year, the sheer scale of the project suddenly hit Fiona. 'I remember collapsing one evening in despair. I really thought we would never complete it.' Then fate intervened. A local worker was called in to take down some trees in the garden. Fiona asked him if he knew anybody who could come and help run the site. After a month he returned, saying that he was the man for the job.

'We would never have managed it without Henri,' says Fiona. 'He worked from seven in the morning until seven at night. We would have to tell him to stop.'

Along with Henri, Fiona cooked lunch and dinner for six or seven workers every day. 'It was great fun,' she says. 'The people in Burgundy love to work hard, but also to play hard. Builders round here love working for the English because we make them cups of tea. In addition, Bruno's wine cellar got quite badly decimated.'

French bureaucracy turned out to be relatively easy to negotiate, at least in the beginning. The *château* is a listed building, so there were a couple of grants from *Bâtiments de France*. However, Fiona cautions that the language difficulties can be hard for people to overcome at the beginning.

Several years of hard work and £600,000 later, the *château* has been fully restored into an elegant home. During renovation Fiona and Bruno hardly had time for a holiday. 'It was very hard to get away,' says Fiona. 'We could escape for a day or two, but either nothing happened while we were gone, or something dreadful happened. The builders seemed keen to use their initiative, often with disastrous results. And besides, we got so interested in the work that we did not want to leave.'

There are still things to be done. Fiona wants to redo the garden, clean up the woods and renovate the greenhouse. There is a pigeon loft that needs sorting out. There is also a rumour that there is a buried treasure under a blackberry bush. 'The trouble is, the place was full of blackberry bushes,' says Fiona. 'We haven't found the treasure yet, but we plan to keep looking.'

To help offset the running costs, some of the bedrooms and the cottage where it all started can be rented out. Fiona says the whole project has been immensely rewarding but extremely tiring. Would she do it again?

'Only if Henri were 10 years younger,' she says. 'And fortunately he has just retired, so I'll just have to stay here.'

Bordeaux is another place famous for *châteaux*, built on the profits of the wine trade. It can be a dangerous place to visit, for it is easy to fall under the spell of these romantic buildings. Gavin Quinney had led a fairly unremarkable life until the age of 40. He was living in Wandsworth, married with two small children, working for a computer company. But in June 1999 he found himself at Vinexpo, the Bordeaux trade fair. Instead of coming away with a couple of cases of wine, he bought Château Bauduc, a beautiful property on the edge of a busy market town called Créon, 20 miles southeast of Bordeaux. So what brought on this moment of madness? Was it the wine?

'Don't ask,' he says. 'I guess I was looking for a new challenge. I'm sure if I had the decision again I might do things differently.' In one respect he was lucky. The computer company for whom he ran the sales side had gone public in 1998, leaving him with a windfall of shares. He cashed in his options, and headed to Bordeaux with his family for a new life as a winemaker. Bauduc was built in the 19th century in the style of the belle époque and is surrounded by woods and a park. It has a 75-acre vineyard and 125 acres of woods and fields, as well as an apartment for the vineyard manager and an old farmhouse. The whole property cost around £1.7 million, about twice the price of a decent place in the 'Toastrack' of Wandsworth.

Buying a *château* in Bordeaux often means buying a working vineyard, which is what the Quinneys ended up with. 'Wine actually was the driving force behind us coming out here,' explains Gavin. 'It wasn't an interest or a hobby, it was a passion.' Angela was aware of this passion but didn't give it much credence. 'He'd talked a lot about buying a vineyard,' she says. 'But I didn't for a minute think he'd actually do it. I thought he'd forget about it, but it didn't go away and here we are. It was quite stressful doing up the *château* at the same time as trying to organise the vineyard, winery and the harvest.'

'The *château* is not enormous, despite its grand symmetry,' says Gavin. 'But it needed totally restoring in places.' The Quinneys moved into the farmhouse on the estate with their two children, Georgia and Sophie, then aged four and two. They had both done up houses in London and knew the key was to get a good team together. 'But it is very different here,' says Gavin. 'In London you just get a builder to organise the whole thing and bring everyone in. Here each part of the project requires its own artisan.'

Through a series of enquiries they put together a team of plumbers, electricians, stonemasons, carpenters, roofers, painters and decorators. 'It is essential to find the right artisan for the job,' says Gavin. 'We were lucky, we had to do a lot of fundamental work like rewiring the place, if we'd had some cowboy involved he could have caused serious problems. I would advise anyone doing the same to live in the region for a while before starting the project and to find out who is good and who is not.' Gavin and Angela started with a team of an electrician and a carpenter whom they trusted. They then brought in other artisans, at any one time there were around 15 working on the project.

Even without involving cowboys, the project had its problems. While doing some earth moving in the garden they suddenly discovered a huge hole. As the days passed, the smell from the hole got worse and worse. Eventually they brought in professionals who told them that it was the old septic tank and it needed replacing. They ordered one to replace it and meanwhile applied for all the relevant permits with the local *mairie*.

*Tips when buying a château*

1. Do triple your budget

2. Do employ local architects and workmen, but keep an eye on them. Don't leave even the smallest decisions to someone else.

3. Spend the money where it is needed and not, like Gavin did, on laying down the cables for outdoor lighting in the future. He says it's unlikely he'll ever be able to afford the lights.

4. Remember that a big property has high running costs, long after the renovation costs.

5. Do check references of local builders and architects or look at work they've already done.

6. Before signing anything, check out any future building developments of the local town, and roads etc.

7. It used to take between 20 and 30 years to build a château. Don't underestimate the time it will take to restore one today.

8. Fiona recommends always being ready to open a bottle of wine at any time of day and have a drink with neighbours and workers.

9. Do introduce yourself to the mayor. He or she can be very useful.

10. You may be eligible for grants, check with the local mayor's office or talk to *Bâtiments de France*.

*My top tip is to ignore all the above advice and don't be so silly. Rather than buy a château, it's much cheaper to stay with those who have.*

'A septic tank specialist came from the town hall and told us we not only had to replace that one, but that there was another one on the other side that needed replacing too. By that stage we had already ordered the new tank with a capacity of 8,000 litres. We then doubled that, as well as the cost. £6,000 later we have enough capacity to last several lifetimes, even with all the friends we have staying in the summer.' Another big issue was the overall plumbing. The previous owner had used the cheapest possible materials, 20 years ago, so all the pipes needed replacing. In addition, the whole *château* needed rewiring. In the grounds, one of the biggest expenses was knocking down the 20 or so telegraph poles that lined the drive to the house and putting all the wiring underground. 'Luckily EDF (Electricité de France) were doing some work at the time,' says Gavin. 'So we just combined it with them, which cut a lot of the cost.'

In terms of the decorating, the whole place needed an overhaul too. 'When we first walked in as the owners, we got a bit of a shock,' says Gavin. 'It's one thing seeing a place with all the furniture in place and pictures on the walls, but when it's all been shipped out, you notice that bits of skirting are missing and a lot of work needs to be done.' They decided to start more or less from scratch. 'We gutted the whole place,' says Gavin. 'We kept the original floors and ceilings but everything in between had to either go or be rebuilt.' They were very keen to keep the original look of the *château* so they decided not to change any of the dimensions of the rooms and to replicate as many of the original features as possible. 'In the drawing room, for example, there was an old marble fireplace that was falling to bits. After much advice on the subject, we decided it was better to get rid of it and buy another one from the era to replace it. It took months, but I eventually found one that was exactly the same size and shape in an antique shop in Bordeaux.' They kept the original parquet floors and the bevelled glass doors. There are seven sets of doors, each of which had to be removed and treated for weather damage. '*Châteaux* can sometimes be quite gloomy places,' says Gavin. 'But these doors create the most amazing amount of light. They are incredibly heavy though and, as well as being weather damaged, some of them were actually sagging in the middle and needed their balance redressing.'

In the kitchen they found that the fixtures and fittings they had thought were part of the sale such as the fitted cupboards had been removed. 'This is not unusual for France,' says Angela, Gavin's wife. 'I've heard of plenty of cases where they even took the light bulbs.' They invested in a butcher's block from a Bordeaux antique market and then built an oak and marble island as the centrepiece of the kitchen area. They had ordered a cooker from Lacanche but when it arrived it looked swamped in the huge kitchen space. 'We sent it back and got the professional size, which fits beautifully,' says Gavin. The fireplace, although oak, was stained a dark, sombre mahogany colour. They removed it to have it stripped and repainted before putting it back. 'It meant living with a hole in the wall for the five months it took to do it, but to do the job properly took a lot of time,' says Angela. The dining room is an extension of the kitchen and looks out over the colonnaded terrace to the south. This was landscaped by a local *paysagiste* with whom Gavin worked very closely. The view is breathtaking, downhill towards a single walnut tree in the middle of a green sloping field. On either side there are oak trees and beyond them vineyards.

They also remodelled the entrance to the *château*. 'When we arrived, everyone would literally park with their bumpers up against the main steps of the house. I wanted to change this and create a proper entrance by removing the cars from the front door of the *château*,' says Gavin.

The *château* has nine bedrooms, three of them with en-suite bathrooms. 'The French don't seem to like showers,' says Gavin. The master bedroom has a bathroom in one of the turrets and another small bedroom off it, which Gavin and Angela now use as a dressing room. 'The sad thing is, we can't afford to put any cupboards in now we've done all the other work,' says Gavin. 'All our clothes are still on IKEA hanging rails.'

Gavin and Angela chose all the colours for the walls themselves. Gavin would pick up the paint stocks from England on his frequent trips over to see his football team Chelsea play. He is still a season-ticket holder at Stamford Bridge and goes over around 20 times a year. 'Paint is so much cheaper in England,' he explains. 'And the quality is so much better. Even so, I think we spent around £25,000 on the painting of the interior. But we're really pleased with the results.'

The restoration of the *château* took around nine months and cost the Quinneys an estimated £150,000. Gavin also says that anyone thinking of taking on a *château* should do the sums again and again and again. 'With a house in London you might at most double your budget. But here with a *château* there are several issues you might come across, like we did—the septic tanks, the damp, the ceiling caving in at the farmhouse—that will all cost you £10,000 each to fix. And then you've got four bathrooms at £10,000 each before you've even started on anything else, although we were lucky in that a couple of the original baths were in good enough condition to keep.'

Despite having spent his windfall and more, Gavin and Angela have no regrets. Their wine business is going well. Gordon Ramsay chose one of their whites as his house wine and Rick Stein recently added them to his wine list. They rent out the farmhouse they stayed in while doing up the *château* and it is fully booked for the summer months in advance. The pace of life in Bordeaux suits them. In London, Angela worked at Condé Nast and rarely had time for herself or the children. 'I would leave the house before they got up and get back home when they'd gone to bed, this is so much more fun. I also find it a much simpler place to live; it's less stressful, less materialistic. The French aren't fussed what kind of car you have, the focus here is very much on food and wine, which is a relief after London.' Gavin agrees. 'It's amazing, we have only just got a front-door key,' he says. 'For two and half years we couldn't lock the *château*. Imagine that in Wandsworth.'

# Lesson 6

# The Money Thing

There will be a moment in every business phone call you'll make from France when you know that you are going to have to admit where you live. You are probably sitting on the steps, overlooking the pool and the pine trees, with the blue sky in the distance. You have seen on the television that it is raining in London, but here in the south of France it is another perfect day. Then the question comes.

'But you are not in England, are you?'

'No, I live in France.'

'Paris?'

'No. The south.'

'Ah.'

In their mind this is no longer a work call. They visualise the blue sky, the bottle of rosé wine for lunch, the afternoon siesta in the hammock.

'Lucky bastard.'

Daily abuse from harassed and envious colleagues and business contacts in London is just one of the normal trials of escaping England for a life abroad. The idea of escaping when you are retired, and fifty something, is to do so after having paid off life's mortgages, cashed in on long-appreciating UK property, and resettled for a life of essentially retirement, albeit with a bit of light activity interspersed.

But when you are twenty years younger than that, have a huge mortgage, children to bring up, and must depend for future income on a business plan that is entirely untested, it is somewhat different.

It is a good thing we did not know how hard the move would be, or we might not have had the courage to move in the first place. Our self-confidence sprang mainly from ignorance.

While it seems, in theory, that in an era of ISDN and now broadband (though not yet in our village), it is possible to substitute telecommunications for travel, and carry on with the same jobs as before, reaping northern European income streams to sustain a life of bread, wine, cheese and olives, in practice it is not so easy.

We reckoned that as journalists, and with my own sideline in lucrative corporate headhunting, we would have no problem. And this was the extent of our business plan.

In fact, we very nearly came unstuck while one child followed another. We have a big house, which means enormous out-goings and when things get bad we are often forced to take out money from maxed-out credit cards to put in the bank to cover the mortgage.

So here is the brutal reality of moving to France and taking your jobs with you. It is not impossible. But you will have to have nerves of steel to see it through. We started in a kind of haze of enthusiasm and then travelled to the depths of despair before regaining some financial equilibrium.

Rupert is a great person to live with when things get bad because he always believes something will come up. Incredibly, it does. He also says one should spend one's way out of a crisis which is why, despite looming poverty, even at the worst of times we seemed not to lack for wood in the hearth and food on the table. (Still, there are times when it is scary.)

'But what will come up? From where?' I often ask while staring at horrible letters from the bank.

'Don't panic, it's all under control,' he replies.

For journalists, writers, designers, artists, financial professionals and others, the appeal of sunshine, cheaper housing and plentiful inexpensive red wine needs no further explanation. Cheap flights, mobile phones, the internet and satellite television makes it technically more feasible than ever to work from almost anywhere.

The trick is to organise your professional career. In practice, this means building some entirely new networks, and recognising that some of the older ones may wither away.

I was quickly made redundant by my firm of headhunters. The economy was down, business dragging, I was a long way away when it came to plotting the corporate cull around the West End water cooler. Besides, if anyone has to get the chop, it is bound to be the smug git in the south of France, while the rest are slogging their way to work on the Northern Line.

Despite the difficulties that can accompany getting professionally established in France, and I have not yet come to the bureaucratic madness, the tax system, many more people are trying it. We are not the only northern Europeans here. There are winemakers, shopkeepers, designers, artists, journalists, novelists, estate agents, restaurateurs, and many others, all making a go of it. I reckon that for us, servicing clients in northern Europe and America works best—it keeps you farther away from French officialdom. But it is also possible to make it on a local level. However, one difference in France is that, unlike in Britain, your growth is limited because you are unlikely ever to want to employ anyone due to the high social charges.

There at least 500,000 British people living in France. Although many of them are retired or rich, there is a growing number making a living here. Paul Vernon, for example, fled from England over twelve years ago. His first step was to open a restaurant on the Riviera, even though 'I did not speak

French and knew nothing about restaurants'. The California Republic was a raging success, so much so that he sold it to a Frenchman after a year. Then he lived for nearly ten years on a hillside, enacting his own French version of the 'Good Life'. With no running water or electricity, and relying on firewood for heating, it was hard work. Now he works for I2I Europe, an internet company that puts on special events for companies such as Microsoft, Gateway and AMD. Vernon organised the first live interactive pub quiz from a bar in Monaco, with Prince Albert as a competitor. His company also staged the first live web transmission from the Cannes film festival. Would he go back to England? 'Never,' he says. 'The quality of life is so much better here. I love everything about it.'

For those who choose to move to France and decide to work there as well, the most obvious form of income is *gîtes*. However, there are now so many Brits offering compatriots places to stay that they say there are five *gîtes* for every guest.

A more imaginative approach is *chambres et tables d'hôtes*, an upmarket bed and breakfast. This is what Fiona Cantwell and Tony Archibold have created at the Château de Marcenac, close to Rodez in the Aveyron.

Tony has been mesmerised by castles since the age of five. His parents were posted to Geneva and there he saw his first castle, the Château Chillon. 'From then on, they became an obsession,' he says. 'I would ask to visit the castle every week-end, to me it was such a magical place.' Tony studied architecture at Oxford and never stopped visiting castles. He met Fiona and they moved to a terraced house in Reading. He worked as an architect whilst teaching at Oxford. Fiona was flying around the world cooking for the Ferrari Formula 1 racing team. 'We really only saw each other about once a week,' says Tony. 'She was always travelling. It began to feel as if we were living to work and not the other way round.' Fiona agrees. 'Our hours were completely different to every-one else's, so we were not part of the community and not really involved in anything.'

They decided to sell up in Reading and fulfil Tony's life-long ambition to live in a *château*. 'We would spend the evenings searching on the internet for castles while everyone else was watching television,' says Fiona. 'Our plan was to buy something and run it as a bed-and-breakfast to be able to maintain it. We picked the Midi-Pyrenees because it still has a slight frontier feel to it.'

'And because of The Hundred Years' War, it is full of castles,' adds Tony.

They sold their house in Reading and moved to a half-built *gîte* in the

*Moving to France*

To move all our belongings to France seemed to me incredibly expensive. We were given quotes from removal companies that ran into thousands of pounds. A cheaper alternative is to find an antique dealer who is UK-based and goes to France regularly to buy furniture. They often travel to the Continent with empty lorries, which they then fill with French antiques to be sold in the UK.

In the end we found a couple of young lads willing to make the journey, along with Max the cat. They ended up staying for a few weeks, helping us to sort out the house. Rather brilliantly, I was able to change my mind about where things were to go about a million times and because I was feeding them and providing litres of local wine, they couldn't complain.

region. This was to become their search headquarters. 'We knew we had to save every penny we could, so we went for extremely basic accommodation,' says Fiona. 'And we just prayed things would go smoothly.'

After weeks of visiting castles and discussions, they made an offer of just over £500,000 on a fantastic property on the edge of a village. They had prepared a business plan in French, Abbey National France had agreed to lend the money, it was now just a question of signing. The day before the signing was due to happen, Abbey National France pulled the plug. 'It was terrible,' says Tony. 'You put everything on the line to buy something and then you find there's no back up. In my opinion, they say yes to too many buyers and then cherry pick, thereby letting a lot of people down. We heard from the agent

---

*Capital Gains*

If you are selling a house in the UK to move to France, the ideal thing is to become a resident first. You will then not have to pay capital gains tax in France on your UK property. In order to do this, you must establish residence in France in the tax year prior to the one you sell in. To establish residency you need to spend more than 183 days a year in France. And you must not spend more than 90 days in the UK. You have to be careful, though, that the Inland Revenue does not use your UK property to challenge your French tax status. However, if you rent out your property this can be avoided.

---

we were by no means the only people this had happened to.' Barclays eventually agreed to step in and lend the money but by then it was too late. They had lost the property.

'We were devastated,' says Fiona. 'It was such a dream place, and to make matters worse, the buyers have done nothing with it, I've been to look.'

On to the next castle. Another stunning property, just outside a village. They prepared all the paperwork and the business plan in French, a process that took almost two months. At the last minute, the regional council decided it wanted to buy the castle. In France, the council has first refusal over any property within its jurisdiction.

'We were still living out of a suitcase and watching our capital slowly dwindle,' says Fiona.

They had been in France for almost three months by the time they found Château de Marcenac, which was on the market for less than £500,000. Again they found it on the internet. The castle is further into the countryside than the other two they looked at—next door to a farm where they now buy a lot of their food. It had been owned by a family who had used it as a holiday home for two or three weeks a year for 30 years. It hadn't been lived in full-time for over 100 years. The sale went smoothly. 'We finally have our dream,' says Tony. 'But as we're doing everything ourselves, there's not much time to sit about and enjoy it.' They have repainted a lot of the main rooms, using the original method of mixing linseed oil, water and lime—partly to create an authentic effect, but also to save money as paint is very expensive in France. They are renovating the bedrooms they will rent out one by one. So far two are complete. The plan is to provide luxury bed and breakfast and fantastic food. Fiona is a professional chef.

'Our aim is to be able to make enough money to maintain our lifestyle and the castle,' says Tony. He has already registered with the local professional architects' association and will continue to work as an architect for private clients.

'We may never be rich,' says Fiona. 'But we're living in this fantastic place, eating beautiful food and meeting interesting people who pass through. And seeing each other more than once a week, which was really the whole idea behind the move.'

Making money from wine is another option which a lot of people moving to France consider. But unless you have the capital to buy a huge vineyard, your choices are limited. One option is to focus on selling it, which is what the creators of www.picwines.co.uk are doing. Helen Genevier and Julie Statham met on their first day at university over 20 years ago. In 1997, Helen, who married a Frenchman, moved to the Pic St-Loup region in the Languedoc. Julie was working as a stockbroker for Deutsche Bank in Frankfurt when she decided she needed a change of career. 'I was fed up with stock-broking and fed up with working for a political organisation,' she says. 'I looked for a house for a week and when I saw the one I bought I decided I didn't want to go back to Frankfurt.'

It was during a dinner with friends who were visiting from England in the summer of 2002 that they came up with the idea of Pic Wines. 'We were talking about it half-jokingly, about how everyone that comes here goes home with boxes of local wine. Our friends said we should go for it, that they would definitely buy the wine from the web rather than cart it home.'

They spent two years preparing to launch the business. This included going on wine-tasting courses, writing hundreds of letters to local domaines to see if they would be interested in them selling their product, and a horrendous amount of paperwork.

'The last six months before the launch we were working on it full-time,' says Helen. 'Mainly sorting out the administrative stuff—the SARL, French and UK customs and VAT, and delivery. French administration is quite baffling, complex and littered with unhelpful staff.'

'Actually all the bureaucracy was really long-winded and depressing. We just wanted to get on with the business but there was always some piece of paper missing,' adds Julie. 'We couldn't sell a bottle until we had the right piece of paper, which we had to wait six months for.'

They chose 25 domaines out of the hundreds they had written to. 'We have to be reasonable and keep the number limited so we can generate a certain amount of volume,' says

Julie. 'But there are still lots of vineyards out there we would like to work with. Our aim is to get a good spread of styles to reflect what the Languedoc has to offer.'

Their first sale was in October 2003. 'A magical moment,' says Helen. 'It was wonderful going round the various domaines collecting the wine to ship, that's definitely the best part of the job.'

When Teddy Hutton and Nicola Russell decided to move from Oxford to France at the beginning of the 1990s, they were fleeing from Margaret Thatcher and the British weather. Teddy was a teacher of problem children and blamed Thatcher for the cuts in funding. Nicola worked as a publicist for various theatres such as the Royal Shakespeare Company and the Watermill Theatre in Newbury.

'My French grandmother died and left me £50,000,' says Nicola. 'This acted as a catalyst. We thought we would create a place where actors could come and rehearse. However, no sooner had we done it than the tax rules were changed and companies found it cheaper to rehearse in London.'

To begin with, life was a struggle. When the actors failed to show up, Nicola was forced to attract other types of activity. She contacted hundreds of people to offer them a venue to run courses. Nobody was interested. Nicola discovered that the only thing that worked was actually getting them to the place and showing them how it worked and the facilities. Now she runs courses in yoga, jazz music, creative writing, script writing, choral singing and there are plans to run a series of gardening courses.

Their first course began on July 27, 1997, teaching people how to be pop singers. 'I remember it well because at the end all the women were clustered around the television, weeping at the death of Princess Diana. It was all rather surreal.'

One of their most popular courses has been a fertility course, where people gather to discuss methods in how to conceive. 'It was also to help childless couples come to terms their infertility,' says Teddy who, when he isn't busy helping to run the place, works as a wood sculptor.

In order to pay for their French adventure, they sold half their Georgian house in Oxford's St John Street to Teddy's sister for £100,000. 'It's probably now worth £800,000,' says Teddy wistfully. A few years later they sold the other half to Teddy's mother.

Like many people before them, they went first to Provence, which they found overcrowded and too expensive. Gradually moving west, they discovered the Languedoc. Here they found a *chambre d'hôte*, where they based themselves over the next three years while they looked for a suitable property. 'We wanted it to be large enough, but in a village, not isolated. Teddy was very clear about the fact that he wanted neighbours. And there needed to be facilities for running courses, and not for running a hotel.

'We did not want to be hoteliers. What we have is a venue that people can rent for £2,500 per week in high season. Then we try to leave everything else up to them, although it never works out like that. We have to be here all the time and be involved, otherwise things don't run smoothly.'

When they came to the Maison Verte, they found a well-proportioned bourgeois house built in the 1830s, together with a two acre garden, outbuildings and winemaking facilities. 'It was big enough to do something barking mad,' says Nicola. Having bought it for £140,000, they spent £40,000 on it immediately, which included putting in new bathrooms, converting some of the outbuildings into *gîtes* and building a pool. 'I told Teddy that a pool would help attract the clients, but really it was quite self-indulgent,' says Nicola. 'I wanted a house with a pool.'

Six years later, the courses are full. The business is registered in France as a *Micro Entreprise*, which, although it does not give them any grants, means there are low rates of tax, provided they don't earn over £50,000 per year. They say that they don't earn more than this, but they have a good life.

'It is hard work,' says Nicola. 'We tell the guests that we

employ a team of electricians, plumbers, gardeners, and cleaners. When they ask what they are called, we say they are all called Teddy and Nicola. Employing people in this part of France is expensive and difficult.'

However, the satisfaction comes from people returning year after year. 'It is interesting to watch the guests arrive stressed and finding everything foreign,' says Teddy, 'and to see the transformation after a few days of playing boules and sitting by the pool. Also you can watch them develop. I always say that here we grow people as well as plants.'

Lorna Macleod fell into giving courses almost by accident. In 2000 she bought a large house in Uzès in the Gard in the south of France. She carried on working at her job as head of communications at the London Business School, until one day she decided that there was more to life than sitting at a desk. Happily ensconced in her house with a swimming-pool for which she paid £300,000, but which is now worth considerably more, she was attending a photography course in the Lubéron hills in Provence when she was struck by an idea.

'As I was driving home, I suddenly realised that I could do exactly the same thing,' she says. She began gradually by converting a large room into an atelier, and doing up the small house in the garden so that it could accommodate guests. She experimented with a small course in May, during which four people stayed. In the day, a local artist taught them painting. In the evening, they either ate with Lorna or ate out at restaurants. 'The whole thing was such a success that I am playing a fuller programme in September, including creative writing courses, photography and possibly even silversmithing.'

She is running the business as *chambres d'hôtes*, which means that there is a minimum of paperwork and bureaucracy, as the rules are not too cumbersome. However, she is aware that she may have to look into planning restrictions if the courses increase dramatically in number.

'So far it has all been very good fun,' she says. 'Marketing is via word of mouth or a website. The bonus is that I meet lots of interesting people, who so far have not complained and appear perfectly satisfied. They all seem very pleasant.'

---

### Viagers

An interesting way to plan ahead is to buy a property in France is through a *viagers*. You pay a deposit of 30 or 40 per cent of the purchase price and an annual rent as an annuity until the seller dies. The annuity at the moment is 8.5 per cent of the agreed purchase price a year. 'The advantages for the buyer are that they can buy now before prices increase,' according to Guy Medd from Gascony Homes. 'In addition, the seller has to maintain the property to an agreed standard. Finally, it is like an interest-free loan once you have paid the capital up front.' The obvious disadvantage is that you're gambling on the seller's health. André-François Raffray probably thought he'd got the deal of the century when he signed a viagers with Jeanne Calment who was 80 at the time. He agreed to pay her FF500 a month for her apartment until she died. He ended up giving her twice the market value for it before he died in 1995. She died aged 122, two years after him, and still holds the record as the world's oldest known woman.

---

The guests either stay in the *gîte* in the garden or at a local *chambre d'hôte*. Lorna provides a light lunch of salads, *pâté*, cheese and bread, while in the evenings people are encouraged to sample the local restaurants. On the final night there is a dinner for the whole group in the house. Prices for tuition and food start from €250 per week. Accommodation is additional, around €300 for the week. She decided to leave people to make their own arrangements to either fly Ryanair to Nîmes or take the TGV to Avignon or Nîmes.

Some people with an extraordinary talent might find that they are able to take advantage of the teaching opportunities, without all the hassle. Simon Fletcher left England 21 years ago because he wanted to work in Europe. An established artist, painting in watercolour and pastel, he also runs seminars for people who already know how to paint, but who want to improve their technique. A five-day course costs around £600 including half board and tuition, but he leaves it to other people to organise the courses.

'I work on a number of different courses, the most popular of which are the three-day courses,' says Fletcher. 'I will meet the people, normally around ten of them, and then we will go on a little walk to find a suitable subject to paint. I start painting. The people on the course can either watch me do it, or paint themselves. Then we have lunch together, more painting in the afternoon, then *apéritifs*, during which they can ask questions. The people who come are baby boomers: architects, designers, professional people who don't want to lie on a beach. Recently, younger people are getting interested. I reckon I can show them more in a week than they would learn in six months at art school.'

Simon and his wife Julie sold a Victorian house in Oxford for £50,000 back in 1982. Simon spent two weeks looking in the south of France, before buying a *maison de maître* for £12,000 in the foothills of the Cévennes. It is a large house, with beautifully proportioned rooms, and two terraces with splendid views over the hills.

'We have been doing it up ever since we bought it,' says Simon. 'We spent the first six months working flat out, so the place was a building site. Once it became habitable, we carried on improving the house whenever we had some spare money. But it remains a work in progress. There is always something to do.'

When they moved to the village they were the only foreigners in the place. 'People used to ask us, why have you come to live in our village? But they couldn't have been more hospitable. The children fought to play with our two boys, and when my wife became ill with hepatitis, the villagers rallied round and looked after all of us. On a professional note, living in France has enabled me to have a more varied and interesting career than I could have enjoyed in England.'

It can be much harder. Michael Simon, a 37-year-old IT Consultant, moved to Montpellier in the south of France to make a new start after his business went bankrupt in the UK. Even though he knew France relatively well and spoke the language fluently, he found the first six months an administrative nightmare. 'They are quite rigid,' he said. 'If you don't have the right bit of paper it just doesn't work.'

Eventually he and his wife settled in, they had two children and he found work for a French IT company. After four years he lost his job. 'I started going to interviews and was told that I was competing with between 900 and 1,400 applicants for each job. All my qualifications are English and they just didn't want to know. They simply don't accept them over there. Either you have a qualification from their *Ecole de Commerce* or *Ecole d'Ingénieurs* or you're a nobody.'

Michael and his family lived off his unemployment cover for several months but when that ran out he decided to go back to England to find work. 'I got a job straight away at home,' he explains. 'But my wife and family stayed down there. So I started commuting. Obviously this put a strain on the marriage and we eventually got divorced.'

Susan Wyles, a qualified nursery nurse had a similar experience. She moved from Canterbury to the Dordogne to set up a bilingual nursery school. The authorities would not let her start her business and demanded a translation of her whole three-year course into French. This still wasn't enough, so Susan, a single parent with a teenage daughter, did a degree at the University of Toulouse. This also proved to be insufficient for the authorities and after three years of struggling she gave up and went back to England.

Starting a business in France is really tough. There is not only the bureaucracy to deal with, but the whole mindset of the French. One business woman said to me: 'France has been practically communist in its outlook for so long that I think small businesses are really frowned on and not supported at all.'

Tony Tidswell, who runs several websites offering advice and help to potential settlers, says there is no point in coming unless you have thought it all through very carefully. 'The realities of coming to France and working in France are not encouraging,' he says. 'Unemployment is officially 10 per cent (in the south it is up to 30 per cent), so for a non-French person the chances of getting a salaried job are slightly just above zero, even for a short contract. Without fluent French, which will take you over five years of total immersion, and an educational diploma or degree from France, the chances of getting a salaried job are zero. Part-time work also requires fluent French and is very hard to get. Just 'getting by' is difficult unless you have some invested capital generating some income. You cannot start any business here without being registered and/or licensed and many trades are restricted 'professions' such as real-estate, travel, legal, insurance, financial, medical etc. Anything else and you have to pay in advance for the right to work and the taxation/social costs start at 50 per cent of your turnover (yes turnover, not profits). Working illegally as a non-registered alien will get you into serious legal and financial trouble. A local "sport" is denouncing people working illegally as the "denouncer" gets a cut of the penalties.'

For my own career, however, moving to France proved the best thing I ever did. Thanks to a very good friend, I started writing for the *Sunday Times,* mainly about Brits living in

France which in turn led to a column. A publisher then contacted me after the first one was published and I wrote this book. Rupert's legendary optimism has paid off.

# Lesson 7
# Running a Vineyard

There aren't many jobs more demanding than running a vine-yard. First, you are a fruit farmer, tending the vines, pruning and picking the grapes. You are open to the vagaries of the weather, such as hailstorms during harvesting and attacks from beetles and bugs. Then you become a chemist, blending the pro-duce until it becomes drinkable. Then you become a marketeer and salesman, trying to persuade sceptical consumers that what you have bottled is nectar, not nettle juice.

If it is so demanding, why do so many people try it? To do so as a foreigner in France, still the world's most famous wine-producing country, is difficult and takes enormous guts. To succeed you need to be clever, as well as lucky.

One of the biggest costs in the wine business is the price of the land in the first place. The best way is to inherit a vineyard, but that mainly happens to lucky Frenchmen. Englishmen need to buy their way in.

Jonathan Maltus, an Englishman who grew up in Nigeria, together with his wife Lyn, had the good fortune to possess both the inclination and the money to buy a vineyard at a time when many growers in Bordeaux were desperate to sell. In 1991 heavy frosts in April devastated much of the crop in the region. By the following year, prices in St Emilion had almost halved.

Maltus had sold an engineering company and at the age of 36 was looking for a new challenge.

'My wife Lyn and I had just married,' he says. 'We decided to take a bit of time off, so moved to Cahors in France. One of my neighbours was having trouble selling his wine. So I helped him out by selling a large consignment to Oddbins. I thought, 'this wine business looks easy'. Gradually I became more interested in it. And I soon discovered that it was not as easy as I had thought.'

He bought Château Teyssier, an estate in St Emilion, for £1.2 million, and began restoring its fortunes. Both the *château* and the vineyard had been neglected. Serious work was needed on the five hectares (about 13 acres) of vines. What he hadn't bargained on was how long it would take.

'You forget that there is a long period of time before you can sell your wine,' he says. 'In the beginning you have a large outlay and the income of a small sweetshop. You need much more money than you think to tide you over these lean periods.'

Fortunately for Maltus, St Emilion suddenly became sexy in 1996. It was the beginning of the so-called *garagistes*, 'garage wines', in Bordeaux. Growers were cultivating small parcels of land, tending the grapes carefully, handpicking them, and making them into wine. The small quantities produced meant that there was more demand than supply. Prices of the best garage wines start at around £150 per bottle and keep going up. Hew Blair, the buyer for Justerini & Brooks, helped launch their wine. He tasted the vats, walked round the vineyard and agreed to take all the production on the spot. Maltus was made. His winery is now a mass of stainless steel tanks for the Château Teyssier wine, while the much sought after Le Dôme has its own micro-brewery, containing four oak vats. Elsewhere there is a barrel cellar that can hold up to six hundred barrels. The place is as neat and tidy as a Swiss post office. Even so, Maltus pushes a hose aside in disgust. 'I am sorry it is so untidy,' he says.

The price of land in St Emilion is ridiculously high. A hectare of good vineyard will set you back around £150,000-£300,000, depending on the location and the age of the vines. Over in the area known as Entre-Deux-Mers—the land between the Dordogne and Garonne rivers—land is much cheaper, more like £20,000 per hectare. What's the difference? Wine growers will tell you it is all in the *terroir*—a word that in the case of wine includes the soil, the subsoil, the climate and even the history of the place and its winemakers.

*Buying a Vineyard*

**Do**
- Have a bigger budget than you think you'll need.
- Know something about farming and the wine business.
- Have a clear idea of your market— who is going to buy your wine?
- Talk to people who have done it.
- Try some of Jean-Claude's wine.

**Don't**
- Spend all your money on the property. You will need to invest and upgrade the winery.
- Try and drink all your production.
- Expect to make a profit in the first few years.
- Imagine it will be easy.

In 1990, Esme Johnstone and his wife Sara bought Château de Sours, one of the prettiest estates in Bordeaux, for around £1 million. Their timing could hardly have been worse. Prices were high, but then the devastating frost of 1991 hit. Their yield for that year was tiny. The wine they produced was not much good. 'It was a disaster,' says Esme.

However, he and Sara persevered. Michel Rolland, Bordeaux's most celebrated winemaker, visited and advised them to make more rosé wine. Tell most producers this in the Entre-Deux-Mers and they will walk away or hit you. It is considered something of a failure to make rosé. But Johnstone's rosé caught the attention of a number of critics, including Auberon Waugh. 'Like the dozy apprentice who fell asleep and invented Guinness, Esme Johnstone has chanced upon possibly the best rosé in the world,' said Waugh.

As the man who helped create Majestic Warehouse in England, Johnstone understands the importance of marketing. 'It's quite good fun,' he says. 'But the job of winemaker is 365 days a year. It is hard work. It is all about attention to detail.' He does not recommend it as a life for somebody who is retiring from the city. 'It is a young man's game,' he says. 'You need money and you need energy.'

The Johnstones have also converted one of the houses on the estate into a guesthouse. At Domaine de Sours you can swim in the pool, sleep in one of the three bedrooms, and dream that you are making wine, without any of the effort.

The Bordeaux boys say that good wine can only be made in their region. But in the last ten years, the price of land and *châteaux* has risen by at least three to five times. This makes it prohibitively expensive for newcomers. It is also tempting some people to prove them wrong by creating great wines in other parts of France.

One person doing just that is Patricia Atkinson. Her remarkable story began in 1990 when she moved to France with her husband who had always wanted to live here. They bought a *château* close to the Dordogne with a small vineyard (four hectares), but had no plans to become winemakers. Instead they worked as financial consultants while restoring the property. Shortly after they moved, Patricia's husband was taken ill and went back to England. She was left alone, spoke hardly a word of French and had to work out a way to make a living. The small vineyard became her only hope of an income. She learnt how to become a viticulturist, winemaker and estate boss. A decade on, the small vineyard Patricia started with has grown to an estate of 21 hectares. She has won countless awards for her wine and is the author of a best-selling book which tells her story.

Another city person turned winemaker is Graham Nutter. After a successful career in banking he has bought a vineyard in the Minervois, together with his French wife Béatrice. The Minervois is a relatively new appellation in the Languedoc, making wines that would sell for about a fiver in a British supermarket. This is the place for people to go who are looking for a lifestyle as well as a place to make wine. The land and buildings are cheaper. The weather is better. The *terroir* is as yet unproven, although many good wines are beginning to be made there.

'I want to create something splendid here,' he says. He started looking for a place in 1999. 'I visited nearly 40 properties,' he says. 'They were either too big, too small or too near the road. My wish list was quite simple. The property needed to be isolated, and the vineyard needed to have the potential to make a good wine.'

He says that when he drove up the avenue of St Jacques d'Albas, they knew this was the right place. 'I strongly believe in the soul of a place,' says Béatrice. 'We fell in love with its soul.'

There was much work to be done. The 28-hectare estate has the capacity to produce up to 150,000 bottles of wine a year. Much of the production was sent to the local cooperative. The previous owner had not had the money to invest in either the land or in the cellar.

'I wanted to get some of the wine away from the Minervois co-op,' says Nutter. 'The president told me that it was all or nothing. I had a word with my local *notaire*, who knew the president from their school days. After another conversation, we managed to reach an agreement.'

As well as upgrading the house, building a new cellar, tasting room and storage facility, Nutter is also planning a five-year programme to improve the quality of the vineyard. 'You have to invest in the soil,' he says. 'We are trying to re-establish the mineral content of the property.'

*Classification*

The organisation of the French wine industry is based on a system of classifications, which guarantee the origin of a wine from a certain area. Its specific purpose is to guarantee authenticity however it is now thought to protect the producer more than the consumer. The system was developed by the Ministry of Agriculture in the 1930s after pressure from producers of high quality wine who were concerned with the over-production of low quality wine during this period. This pressure resulted in the establishment of the *Institut National des Appellations d'Origine des Vins et Eaux de Vie* (INAO). The INAO consists of twelve regional committees: Alsace and Eastern France, Champagne, Southwest France, Loire Valley, Burgundy, Languedoc-Roussillon, Rhône Valley, Provence-Corsica, Vins Doux Naturels, Cognac, Armagnac and Eaux-de-Vie de Cidre.

There is still much work to be done. Nor does he think that because he is in his 50s, he is too old.

'I have a lot of energy,' says Nutter. 'After living in New York, London and Paris, I still wanted to achieve something else. I think where a lot of people go wrong is they spend all their budget on the property. You need to put a third into the property, a third into improving things, and keep a third for marketing and contingencies. If it all goes wrong, at least we can say that we tried.'

Jean-Luc Colombo, a Rhône-based winemaker and consultant, applauds Nutter's choice of region. 'Without question, Languedoc Roussillon is the area to buy a vineyard in France,' he says. 'Buying anywhere else is prohibitively expensive, assuming you can get hold of a vineyard in the first place.' The regulated French wine business—particularly in Burgundy or Bordeaux—discourages foreign ownership. The price of land, due to the wine boom of the last five years, means that a decent hectare of vines could cost anywhere from £20,000 to £100,000. But a domain in the Languedoc, together with vineyards, can be bought from around £750,000.

However, the process is by no means straightforward. Many sales are handled privately, so it is very hard to know what is on the market until it is too late. The first step for many would-be buyers is to contact the *Société d'Aménagement Foncier et d'Etablissement Rural*, known as Safer. This bureaucratic body was set up 40 years ago to help young winegrowers find vineyards and finance. It has now moved more into the property business. There are also a number of estate agents who specialise in selling vineyards, such as *France Vignobles et Propriété* and *Jean-Pierre Rambier* in Montpellier.

But even if you manage to buy a vineyard for £750,000, it is important to bear in mind that this is just the entry cost. 'Once you have bought an estate, unless you are very lucky, you will need to spend £100,000 on the cellar, £50,000 on equipment, and there are annual running costs of around £3,000 per hectare,' says Jean-Claude Mas, one of the area's most celebrated winemakers and husband of my friend Alex.

While it is tempting to think that you can cover these costs from selling the wine or even just sell the grapes to a *négociant*, oversupply in the wine world has led to a glut of grapes on the

> *Appelations*
>
> **AOC** (*Appellation d'origine contrôlée*). Still seen as the
> highest level of French wine, used to be strictly con-
> trolled and regulated. There are over 40 *appellations* in
> France. In general, the laws of any AOC control the
> following: the area entitled to the name; permitted
> grape varieties; density of vine plants; minimum alcohol
> levels; and yields. Within many regions there can be a
> hierarchy of *appellations*. The AOC classification is
> however no longer a guarantee of quality. The AOC
> laws have come under increased criticism as being out-
> dated and anti-competitive, providing only a collective
> marketing facade behind which some mediocre wine
> producers can shelter. The limitations imposed by the
> system have meant that some producers choose specifi-
> cally not to classify their product as AOC in order to
> retain maximum flexibility in their viticultural and
> winemaking techniques and in order to compete with
> wines from the New World.
>
> **VDP** (*Vin de Pays*): Good quality drinking wine that
> has to come from a certain region. For example, Vin de
> Pays d'Oc must come from the Languedoc.
>
> **Vin de table**: The lowest classification of wine. Can be
> bought directly from co-operatives for around £1 a
> litre. Drinkable, but only just.

market. The bottom has fallen out of the *vin de table* market;
even *vin de pays*—wine that is not *appellation contrôlée*, has
declined in price by 25 per cent in the last few years.

Ruth de Latude came to the Languedoc 25 years ago from
Yorkshire. Together with her husband Gilles, she runs the
Domaine de Bourgade. With over twenty hectares under vine,
including Cabernet Sauvignon, Syrah, Grenache and
Mourvèdre, they have found themselves caught in the falling

price trap. With *négociants* offering them 10 per cent less for their grapes each year—around 25 pence per kilo—it is hard to make any money from the vineyard. 'We are making much more money from the cottages that I have converted on the estate,' says Ruth. Despite this, Ruth and Gilles have recently invested in a winery and are now producing their own wine, called *Les Trois Poules*, thereby bringing the winemaking tradition back to Bourgade. According to Ruth, they found remains of Roman pottery at the domain which showed wine was probably made there over 2,000 years ago. 'It was always a working farm,' explains Ruth. 'But we used to sell the grapes to local winemakers. The price they paid gradually went down until it wasn't really worth our while. We decided that it was time to take the whole operation under control. We started this year and did everything by hand that we could, partly for reasons of quality and partly to save on costs.' Their first vintage will be ready in time for next season's guests. 'There will also be plenty of picking to do,' says Ruth. 'So we will be putting the guests to work.'

The Languedoc has come a long way in the last ten years in the wine world. If it continues to develop—and winemakers like the talented Jean-Claude Mas continue to work from here—the price of a hectare of vineyard will soar. Ten years ago, Jean-Luc Colombo was buying land in Cornas on the Rhône for £2,000 a hectare. Now it is worth anywhere from £20,000 to £100,000.

Nerida Abbott, a Londoner of Australian origin, came to the Languedoc after completing a PhD in Australia on the Shiraz grape. Shiraz is called Syrah in France. 'It is a key component of many of the fine red wines made in the Rhône. She now runs one of the largest *négociants* in the Languedoc, selling over 900,000 bottles of wine worldwide to clients such as British Airways, Oddbins and Sainsbury's. Her firm, Abbotts Sneyd Anderson has over 28 growers in the Languedoc-Roussillon region supplying liquid grape juice that is then turned into wine. 'In 1996 we decided to take the New World

concept of producing and branding bottles of wine and introduce it to the old world,' she says. 'It is very difficult for consumers to remember all the names of the different *châteaux* or
domains. The customer needs all the help they can get.'

New World wine growers—mainly Australian but also those
in New Zealand, Chile and Argentina—discovered that an
attention to hygiene, cleanliness and detail would pay divi-
dends. Some critics argue that the wines they make lack character, but in Britain at least, the consumer is voting with his
wallet. Australia is now a bigger supplier of wine to the British
market than France. Nerida Abbott and her partners are proving that it is possible to take this formula anywhere and make
it work. 'There are a number of reasons why I think the
Languedoc is the best place for us to be,' she says. 'First, I speak
French. Second, my partners understand the way the locals
work. Finally, this area is less of a closed shop than Bordeaux
or Burgundy. Here they are very open to our ideas and way of
doing business.'

Her company produces a range of wines all named after
clouds. Her top wine, Abbotts Cumulo Nimbus is a big, red
tasty bottle made entirely of Syrah grapes. The others may be
less spectacular, but they are clean and very drinkable. Up to 95
per cent of production is destined for the export market. 'We
have only just started selling to the French,' she says. 'But we
have been astounded by the demand.'

Charles and Ruth Simpson, both in their 30s, were also
attracted to the Languedoc region due to its potential. They
were living in Azerbaijan when they decided they wanted to get
into the wine business. 'Basically we had a lot of time to talk,'
explains Charles. 'We didn't really know anyone and there
wasn't much to do. So during those long dark winter evenings
we chatted about what it was we both wanted out of life.' At
the time, Charles was general manager of Glaxo-Wellcome in
Azerbaijan and Ruth was working as a consultant for various
charities. 'The way things were going with my job, we realised
we would be forever moving and not really together much at

---

*Terms*

*Bouchonné.* Corked. An 'off' characteristic in wines due to imperfect corks. Often caused by the chemical compound trichloroanisole or TCA. Cork taint is believed to come from fungi that are not detectable on dry corks, or by cork processed with chlorine. TCA diminishes the fruit character of the wine, producing a stale, woody, mouldy smell and taste, possibly accompanied by oxidation of the wine.

*Négociant.* The English translation is 'merchant'. Alternative definition: A wine merchant who buys grapes, must, or wine, blends different lots of wine within an *appellation*, and bottles the result under their own label.

---

all. Which is not the reason we got married.' Charles and Ruth considered several options, including estate management in Scotland and commercial forestry. They wanted something in which they were both interested and to which they could both add value. 'The idea of being involved in wine seemed very romantic,' says Charles. 'Although I'm not sure I would describe it as that now that we've actually done it. In addition, we both have experience in business management, strategy and marketing, so we felt we could work on that side of things, although we knew nothing about actually making wine. We were both fascinated by the fact that a bottle of wine can cost between £2 and £2,000. And the difference in the price is purely to do with marketing and reputation.'

Charles and Ruth bought Domaine Sainte Rose, a stunning estate outside Béziers, in June 2002. The domain itself is 16th century but the *château* was rebuilt after a fire around 100 years ago. They paid around £1.2 million for the property, which includes 46 hectares of vineyards and another five or so hectares of parkland, a winery and of course the *château*. 'Anyone wanting to set up here wouldn't need to spend as much as we did,' says Charles. 'You can buy planted land for between £10,000 and £15,000 per hectare.' If you do need to raise substantial funds, one option is to copy Charles and Ruth's model. They raised a third of the money themselves, 80% from personal funds and the balance from investors, each paying about £5,000 to become members of a group of 12 people who are entitled to free wine as well as an annual dinner at the *château*. A third came from a bank loan and the final tranche in the form of so-called vendor finance. 'We told the previous owner we couldn't afford the whole lot at once, and because he wanted out he agreed to let us pay him a third over time,' explains Charles.

The philosophy of the business has been to define the target audience and then make wine to cater for that audience. 'Our typical customer is a person who is interested in wine, is looking for something different and wants to be close to the product,' says Ruth. 'It's the kind of person you would get buying their meat from a butchers' shop instead of the supermarket.'

'It was always our dream to own the relationship with the customer,' adds Charles. 'As a UK customer you can click onto our website, order some wine and it'll be there within 48 hours. The downside with our method is that it all depends on personal contact. It's hand-selling, so the business takes time to build up.'

Perhaps any non-professional winemaking person should follow the lead of our friend Peter Glynn-Smith. Having sold his Islington-based design business, he bought one of the finest houses in the Languedoc, together with a small two-hectare vineyard. His Cabernet Sauvignon grapes are tended by a local man and sold to the local cooperative. The grape harvest is just enough to pay for his hobby, while he has the satisfaction of owning a vineyard. 'There is nothing better than sitting on my terrace in the evening, watching the swallows drink from my pool, and see the grapes ripening on the vine in the distance,' he says.

# Lesson 8

# Living on Water

Watermills are a popular choice with Brits settling in France, the threat of floods notwithstanding. There are an estimated 5,000 watermills in southern France, many of them derelict, waiting for an owner with money and taste to restore them. The Romans introduced them into France as a key source of power. Many were used to grind flour and olives, as well as irrigating the land. Later they were used to make paper and in the 18th century to power looms for weaving cloth. With the introduction of steam-powered engines they were largely abandoned.

There are two key issues for anyone contemplating buying a watermill. First, check that you get the sun. Second, find out if there is running water in the summer. In the Languedoc, for example, a lot of the rivers dry up in the hottest months. The only way you can verify whether or not the river will run dry is to check with local records at the *mairie*—the mayor's office—or, if you are lucky, you will find a local historian who may be able to provide some data.

The best place to look for watermills is near the rivers that come down from the Massif Central. The *départements* of the Lot and the Tarn are two areas where there are a good number of mills, and to date these areas have not become as popular or developed as some of the regions bordering the Mediterranean. Prices vary sharply depending on location and condition.

There is a watermill in the Minervois region of the south of France whose location is a closely guarded secret of the London family who have spent the last 20 years restoring it. To reach it you have to drive four kilometres down a stone path, which is often cut off in the winter. There is only solar heating, no telephones or television. 'It is our bandit's lair', says the owner.

When the family bought the mill, it was derelict. Working mainly with the family and co-opted boyfriends of the daughters, along with a retired hippy who got lost on the Croisette in Cannes many years ago, it is now an exquisite home that can sleep 16 family members in comfort. On a summer's evening in June it is an idyllic place to linger over a bottle of local wine, listening to the birds and the water.

But this serenity can be seriously disturbed. Rain in the mountains can send a wall of water hurtling towards you at high speed, sweeping all in its path, and often with very little or no warning. 'Three years ago in November there was a sudden huge flood,' says the owner. 'The river rose more than 18 feet. The house was six feet full of water. Trees were uprooted and turned into giant battering rams. The damage was colossal.'

One of the most stunning houses I know is the mill house owned by the writer Stephanie Keating and her husband Norman Berke, a retired American businessman. The first time Peter Glynn-Smith took us there for lunch we were still house hunting. It was one of those lunches you never forget, lots of wine, wonderful food, interesting conversations and sunshine all day long. Stephanie is an amazing character and legendary hostess. Norman is fascinating, one of those people who has done everything.

Their guests are always interesting. On any given day you might find an Oscar-winning screenwriter swapping recipes with Boris Berezovsky's chef; Norway's most famous artist dancing with a local matador; or the organiser of the Rhino Charge, East Africa's most gruelling charity event, holding court in the corner with a glass of whisky, surrounded by attractive women.

Their mill, set in rolling countryside with the hills of the High Languedoc to the north, is on the edge of Saint Chinian, one of the best wine-producing appellations of the Languedoc. They bought the house in 1995 from a French philosophy professor and sculptor, who had been a friend of Samuel Beckett. The house dates from the 17th century. The mill is a later addition, probably from the 18th century. The power from the river was used to power looms to make uniforms for Napoleon's army. The house is set off back from the road, down a drive of enormous plane trees that must each be at least 250 years old.

The house is not only surrounded by water, there are channels that run underneath the house. During one flood the water

---

*Top tips for buying a watermill*
- Beware of flooding
- Check for rot
- Find out if the river runs all year
- See if there is sunshine—in fact, this applies to any house, if you're mad about the evening sun, make sure the house you're thinking of buying actually gets it.
- Be prepared for high maintenance costs

---

rose almost up to the dining room windows. But Stephanie has taken heart from a comment from the French philosophy teacher who sold them the house. 'She told me that if we loved the house it would look after us,' she says. 'The first year we were here, the rain came pouring in. I found myself at 1.30 in the morning sandbagging the place and mopping up with towels. In frustration I went outside and looked at the water rising in the river. But remembering what she had told us, I went to bed. In the morning, the water had receded. And ever since I have slept soundly here, confident that we will be all right.'

If you are looking for a mill you should contact one of the agents dedicated to locating them. I have never really thought about it, but agree that the sound of water would be lovely (not much chance round our way). Others love the proximity to the river, watching the birds and fishing from their bedroom windows. In the south of France there is the bonus that you have access to water all the year round to irrigate your garden for free. Whatever the merits of owning a watermill, it is the housing equivalent of owning a classic car or a Fife schooner. You are likely to end up spending as much time working on the place as you will enjoying its benefits.

Doug and Bethanne Hazelton live on the water at Sète, on the Mediterranean coast close to Montpellier. They have converted a 90-foot former cargo vessel called Sinbad into their home. Doug has been mad about boats since he was 12 and lived on them since 1967. He met Bethanne in the Caribbean, where she was working at the time.

Although he was in the process of building a house for a girlfriend at the time, he and Bethanne ended up at the top of a mast of a boat. 'I guess that's where we fell in love,' says Doug. 'That was the end of my girlfriend's house and we moved on to a trawler.'

Shortly afterwards, they were married on the island of Saba, a volcanic island in the middle of nowhere in the Caribbean 'I wanted some place our relatives would have a hard time getting to,' says Doug. After their children, Antaris and Azura, were born, they spent several years travelling around the world to Thailand, Venezuela, Indonesia, Fiji to name a few places. They settled for a while in New Caledonia where the children went to school, but apart from that Bethanne taught them on the boat through a French correspondence course. 'We got into a routine,' she says. 'We would get up early and do a couple of hours before breakfast, then some more afterwards. We were normally finished by lunchtime,' she says. 'The children got on very well and loved having all that free time. It meant I had to get my French up to speed which was great.'

The most surprising thing they have found about living here is how cold it is, even though they are in the south of France. 'We had no idea the winter would be so tough,' says Doug. 'We were wearing every piece of clothing we had. I don't think we owned a jumper between us.'

Once the summer is over they will go back to the Caribbean, although Doug is full of praise for France. 'If I were a land person I would live in France,' he says. 'It's a great place, in the summer. The people have been really helpful and I like the French system. In some places in Europe we've been treated like waterrats but not here.'

Bethanne agrees. 'It's been great to have a year in France,' she says. 'I have thoroughly enjoyed being here, but then I thoroughly enjoy being anywhere. The only downside about Europe is that you can't anchor at sea, so here we are next to the road the whole time. We're used to getting up in the morning and going for a swim.'

They make a living on the boat from the odd charter and salvage work. 'It's what I call my golden egg theory,' says Doug. 'If you're in a plodding job you won't see the golden egg. Times can get a little tough, but that golden egg always comes by in the end.'

# Lesson 9

# Earth, Wind and Fire

The ancients believed there were four elements. In the thorny *garrigue* where we live, between the Mediterranean Sea and the Black Mountains, it is easy to see why. We have regular storms of a ferocity that occurs perhaps once a generation in Britain. The ditches become raging torrents, rivers flood, and every year a number of unwary people are carried away and drowned.

In the summer there is baking heat, the screeching of cicadas and no rain. These *canicules*—literally dog days—can only be endured by sleeping through most of the day and working at night. These heatwaves end in September, with an enormous clap of thunder and brilliant electrical storms, leaving most of the electrical appliances in the house wrecked.

There is the earth, which the French call *terroir*. And then there is the most quixotic element of all: water. Water for drinking. Water for bathing. Water that does not necessarily gush from the tap. It is easy to understand why the old French peasants always have their eye on the sky. I certainly feel we live much closer to the elements here than we did in England. Here, the relationship with water is more intimate, interactive and at times, threatening.

For example, we are dependent on a spring for all our water. So if there is the slightest problem in any part of the complicated system that brings water from the source via a series of underground pipes and storage tanks to the house, nothing comes out of the tap. This has now happened countless times.

The first time, Rupert had just started a new contract helping to arrange a series of educational programmes for journalists on the importance of water. The irony was not lost on me. As he was away somewhere gallivanting about trying to make water flow to the world, here in our French paradise there was no water at all.

The film *Jean de Florette* by Claude Berri, set in Provence in the 1920s, portrays a crippled ingénue played by Gerard Depardieu, dying in agony trying to provide water to his family as malevolent local peasants, played by Yves Montand and Daniel Auteuil, plot to steal his land. It is odd that this film with its dark portrayal of the French rural character became one of the most successful French films of its time. There were not only evil peasants to consider when our water stopped for the first (but not the last) time.

Normally I am stuck in the house alone when this sort of thing happens. Rupert always contrives to be away when there are domestic disasters and phones me from some luxury hotel, pretending to be sympathetic while working his way through the mini-bar.

The best person to call in a crisis is always my cleaning lady, Geneviève, who has many years of experience in the various disasters that the elements can throw at you here. She thrives on crises, and is brilliant at volunteering her husband Jean-Pierre to sort them out. He has come to my rescue many times as when Sam, our dog, was on heat and seemed to be stuck to some random stray (I had no idea that was how they mated and thought they had crashed into a tube of super-glue or something).

There was the time when the washing machine started smoking and looked as if it was about to blow up. I was convinced we would have to buy another one, but Jean-Pierre fished out a five centimes piece that was causing all the trouble (callously left in a pocket by Rupert). Jean-Pierre also comes to my rescue even when I'm not there. On a trip to England I had a call from Monika, our new Slovakian au pair, who was alone in the house. She has spent a couple of years in Italy where she perfected the art of hysterical behaviour. The lights had gone out. There was an axe murderer outside just waiting to come in and chop her into tiny pieces, after he had tortured her almost to death and stolen all her possessions. I called Geneviève, who told me Jean-Pierre would be there immediately. He got the lights back on and Monika agreed not to leave.

In case of a lack of water Jean-Pierre is phenomenal. He can normally fix the pump, or fiddle with the wiring so the whole thing jerks into action once more. He only failed me once.

'Don't you worry *Madame*,' Geneviève assured me on one particularly difficult occasion, as Jean-Pierre stood looking bemusedly at the empty tank in the garden. 'This is up to the fire brigade now. They can't just leave a pregnant woman alone with children and no water.' She ordered them to deliver a tanker filled with water. Unfortunately the trailer overturned on its way up the small country road. Luckily it was warm enough to have a bath in the swimming-pool.

Even Jean-Pierre was at a loss. The system seemed to be working well, but nothing was happening. The tank was just not filling up. Geneviève said we had probably used up all the water in the source. I was horrified.

How would we survive?

'You need a *sourcier*,' said Jean-Pierre.

'A *quoi?*'

'An expert on natural water sources, he'll tell you if you have any water left.' Jean-Pierre gave me a telephone number. 'Apparently he can tell if you have got any water just by talking to you on the phone,' I told Rupert that evening when I called him in his faraway hotel. 'I would have thought that he could tell that we didn't have water by the fact you were phoning him up,' was his response.

Tony, as the *sourcier* was called, arrived the next day. He was Spanish. I was slightly concerned to discover that he spoke a French as unintelligible as my own. But he also spoke good English. He walked over to the source and produced a two-foot long strip of plastic. Wearing a rather thoughtful look, he moved it around. Suddenly it started twitching in his hands.

'You 'ave water,' he said. 'We know that,' I replied. 'The trouble is that we don't have it in the house.' I explained to him the Byzantine workings of our water supply. It flows from the source into a small tank; this is transferred into a neighbouring tank, which is then pumped 40 metres across the garden into a four cubic metre holding tank, from where it is pumped into the house. Tony wandered around, then came up with the solution. 'This tank 'ere is leaking. Buy some special cement, slap it everywhere, and all will be right as rain,' he said.

He explained to me about springs. I had thought that behind the rock was a large underground reservoir, that once tapped, would spring into life like an oil well. Apparently not. Springs are more like underground gutters, which channel water down through the rocks. Springs can dry up. The water can just go somewhere else. 'Don't be alarmed,' he said. 'I think you will be fine.'

I asked him whether he thought we were using too much water. 'You cannot use too much water,' he said. 'If it is coming out and you don't use it, it will just go to waste.'

It was nice to have one of Geneviève's doomsday theories trashed. Tony relieved me of €30 and disappeared in his white van. Then Jean-Pierre showed up. I told him what we had to do. He did not think there was a leak from the tank. He went down to the large holding tank and got inside. 'There is no water coming in,' he said.

So now we had water coming in from the source and disappearing magically somewhere in the garden. I went down to look at him squeezed in the tank.

'What is that floating on the bottom?' I asked.

The floating ball had fallen from the ceiling of the tank. It was not what was preventing the water from flowing in, but we could see there was another opening that had jammed shut. He opened it and we heard water flow, a dim sound, but as pleasurable as that of a waiter bringing you an iced vodka and tonic.

'We must wait and see,' he said.

All that day I checked the tank to see if it was filling up. There seemed to be the sound of running water, but I wondered if I was imagining it. That evening I went and sat by the spring, watching the small holding tank fill up with water, three litres a minute. After half an hour the moon came out. Then there was the unmistakable sound of a pump. I ran from the tank to the reservoir by the house. There was the sound of running water. From somewhere indoors came the sound of a washing machine starting up and a dishwasher coming to life.

On other occasions, we have problems with too much water. Before we invested in a huge four-wheel drive, we really were often completely cut off during the winter. There are rivers to either side of the house and during the storms we often had to leave the children with the childminder until the water subsided. Rupert and I would drive as close as we could to the water and assess the situation. Was it really worth risking the car, and the children, just to get them home for the night? They would only have to make the same perilous journey the next day to get back to the childminder. And what if rained even more and we were stranded at home with the children? Possibly even more terrifying than being stranded without them.

It is the elemental quality of France that for me, having spent years living in the cramped, temperate UK, is so surprising. This is a place where the forces of nature are genuinely overwhelming. Your everyday life is affected by the elements in a way it is so rarely in England. When did you last not go shopping because it was too hot?

Or when did you last not get on a plane because the airport was closed due to flooding or snow? The French have learned to cope with these natural disasters. They have efficient forces of firemen and rescue workers. The regular floods that burst from the Rhône cause devastation but this is quickly cleaned up by the emergency services. Angela Thomas was very impressed after her house was flooded. 'There was no shortage of organisations coming round to see what I needed,' she says. 'They provided me with a new fridge and all sorts of things I had lost.'

When the *garrigue* catches fire in the summer, spectacular water bombers arrive. I remember seeing a fire over the hills one night, I wasn't sure what to do but thought I ought to call someone. In France the emergency numbers are split up. You call 15 for an ambulance, 17 for the police and 18 for the fire brigade. I dialled 18 and was politely told that they were already aware of the blaze. Ten minutes later the planes arrived and the fire was under control. Around us they cut fire breaks. When I first saw the great machines in action I thought they were razing the ground to build a housing estate. Not so, I was told by the friendly forest ranger, who then offered to cut a circular walk for us on the hill opposite and called it '*La Promenade des Anglais*'.

When the storms come we have to unplug all the computers and the phones. In fact, it was Geneviève who first told me we needed to do this. I of course ignored her, for she is extremely dramatic at times and I thought she was exaggerating. When I went to switch on my computer the hard drive had failed. The phone line was working but crackling terribly. The insurance covered the cost of replacing the computer and France Telecom sorted out the phone. In terms of insurance though, you need to be careful. A lot of policies do not cover natural disasters.

All this is slightly humiliating. Whereas in Britain the transport system can collapse because of rain or the wrong kind of snow or leaves on the track, disasters seem to be on a kinder, more gentle scale than those here. The winds here are usually that much stronger, sometimes just walking into the wind can feel like a workout. The bolts of lighting—the *sturm und drang* from the heavens—is just on a different scale. In places like India, Africa, and the western parts of the United States, there is a similar respect for the rage that nature has in reserve.

It is hard to describe just how hot it gets here in summer. I remember one of the first mornings after we moved in. It was the beginning of September and we set off at 7am to buy our morning bread from the village bakery. Buying my morning bread is one of the things I had been fantasising about us doing since we signed the contract to buy the house. I was heavily pregnant (for a change) and wore a sarong and a T-shirt. All went well until we started for home. By now it was almost 8am. Suddenly the sun tripled in strength and at one stage I thought I was going to have to lie down in the road. I took my T-shirt off in an effort to cool down. Luckily there was no one about.

Seeking the shade is a concept so alien to anyone who lives in England. But during July and August when I go shopping I will cross the road if there is shade the other side. Carrying out any chores is a nightmare, you come back home feeling like you've been bashed over the head with a cricket bat. The heat is so intense around the house you can actually hear it—a sort of buzzing noise combining cicadas with relentless hot air. By the end of August the garden looks as if it's been burnt, everything is dry and yellow.

We have had plenty of problems with electricity since coming to France. When we first moved here it kept cutting out for no apparent reason. We would know it had cut out, not only because there were no lights, but the house alarm would start a high-pitched squeal, usually when we just got the children to sleep. There seemed to be no reason for the constant cuts.

In the summer, I wondered whether it could be the heat. I thought it might have melted the cables. I also used to blame the power cuts on the wind. We don't have the infamous mistral here, but we have what seems to be its younger brother. Once I went for a siesta and woke up to find the three metre square pool umbrella snapped to bits in the water. The wind had lifted it from its stand.

Our most memorable power cut was during our first year in the house on Christmas Eve. We had invited 12 people for a Swedish dinner. Just as we raised our first glass of schnapps, the lights went out. Luckily we had bought a lot of candles from the Toulouse IKEA, along with the schnapps. We lit about 20 of them and waited for the electrician to show up. It was rather romantic, the whole atmosphere suddenly changed and became more intimate. There was a feeling of siege around the table as we fumbled around for the herring. The electrician showed up about 20 minutes later. He is a local man, but married to an Englishwoman. He speaks good English but with an extremely pronounced French accent making it rather like having Inspector Clouseau checking your wiring.

'Theez is most strrrange,' he told the candle-lit company, as he wandered from fuse box to trip switch prodding things. He couldn't understand why some circuits worked and not others, there seemed to be no rational explanation for it. Eventually all the lights came back on, but we decided we liked it better before, so once he had gone, we turned them all back off again.

The electricity still goes off periodically, but we have dismantled the alarm, so I don't really mind too much.

# Lesson 10
# Père du Village
## Local Politics, Planning & Builders

Short of bad news about the children, it was one of the most worrying answer-machine messages one could receive. 'This is Gregory Guida from Château St Martin de la Garrigue,' said a French voice in good English. 'I need to talk to you about a large construction project that will seriously impact the value of your property.'

He left a phone number, but it was already after office hours. We spent much of the evening discussing the problem. What could it be? A new road? A housing estate? A nuclear power plant?

Whatever it was, the mysterious Frenchman certainly had a sharp idea of what it takes to penetrate to the core of Anglo-Saxon anxiety. The British, living on their overcrowded island, are obsessive about property; the French tend to have a more relaxed, continental attitude. If an official in Paris draws a line across a map and decrees it to be the route of a high-speed rail line, it will not be too long before the bulldozers appear and not long after that when the first TGV whistles past at 300 kmh. France is such a big country—three times larger in area than the UK—that policies on the use of land tend to be pretty relaxed. The result is that large parts of France are becoming quite similar to suburban Kansas City.

Virtually every French town and city is now surrounded by hideous strip shopping malls and new housing estates. This carefree attitude to land use—in essence, use it up because there is always more—is one of the reasons why the British have found it so easy to settle in France. As the French have abandoned their old houses in the villages and towns, and moved to the new estates, the British have simply moved in behind them, taking over the old properties and often caring for them with a punctiliousness that is pretty alien to the natives.

'You can tell in any village where the foreigners live. They are the only ones who have painted their houses,' says one of my friends, only half joking. Gregory Guida says the mentality here is very different. 'In Britain you are much more densely populated,' he says. 'So the quality is much more important. In France it doesn't have to be pretty. In Britain if you go to any random village everything will be perfect. In France, three houses will be perfect and they will be owned by Brits. The French have only just discovered the countryside, a little too late I think because the English have made it unaffordable.'

Shortly after we moved in we bumped into a local man pacing up and down the field opposite us. He wanted to build a weekend home there, he told us. I went white and almost fainted. But the mayor wouldn't let him, he went on, the land does not have building permission. We tried to look sympathetic and skipped off home, vowing to vote for said mayor in the next election. Since that day though, we have been on tenterhooks, waiting for something to ruin our view, our peace, in short our pretty perfect location. We were even conned into buying a worthless plot of land adjoining the property for a couple of thousand pounds. The owner of it only had to mention the word steel dump and our cheque book was open.

The evening of the phone message from Gregory we went for a walk and tried to imagine the various hillsides covered with houses, or a road going through the valley. It was a horrible thought. Our rural idyll was over. We would have to go and live in Wales.

When we finally spoke to him the next day, we learned that it was not our view that would be spoilt, but the view around Pézenas. The mayors of two small neighbouring villages had approved a plan to erect 11 giant windfarms, nearly 400-feet in height on one of the most visible plateaus in the Hérault. We were happy that this wasn't happening on our hill, but appalled that this could even be contemplated without lengthy consultation with the locals.

'I only found out by chance a week ago,' said Gregory. 'We have about a month to try to stop it.' His English neighbours, Jonathan James and his wife Anne were equally surprised. They bought Domaine St Hilaire 18 months ago, to escape from the bustle of suburban Dulwich. The 200-acre vineyard contains fruit trees, olives and wild flowers. Now there is the prospect that they will have giant towers overshadowing the wildlife. Each rotor will be the length of a Boeing 747. The towers will be four times the height of a water tower or electricity pylon—they will become the tallest buildings in the Hérault.

'It is unbelievable,' says Jonathan James. 'We would have thought twice before buying the domaine if we had thought such a thing could happen. We found out by chance a few days ago. Now we have less than a month to act.'

Many of the local French seemed either unconcerned or resigned to the fact that the windfarms would happen. But the British community of Pézenas, some 200 strong, leapt into action. Peter Glynn-Smith, says the very idea is an outrage. He renovated his house, rebuilding Roman walls, and creating an enormous garden with a dining area where guests can look out south to the sea. Now that view is about to be ruined forever.

'It seems astonishing that such a unique area of outstanding natural beauty as the Hérault should even consider introducing windfarm pollution to its landscape,' he says. 'We have always believed that this part of France had learnt from the mistakes of other Mediterranean tourist communities. Greed or ignorance today by a few will have a long-term financial impact on thousands.'

This would sound reasonable except for the attitude of

many French. Not only do many locals think the wind farms are actually attractive, but they are queuing up to sell their land to the wind farm developers. It was becoming a curious situation where the conservationists seeking to preserve the beauty of the landscape were mostly foreigners, and those seeking to despoil it were the natives. As Guy de Saint Victor, a French friend of mine who has lived in England says: 'I really have nothing against the Brits arriving in such huge quantities. At least they are environmentally friendly.'

Gregory found it extremely difficult to motivate the local landowners into any kind of action. 'They just don't believe me when I say that the value of their property will be halved if there is a windfarm next door to it,' he says. 'They think the increase in value they have seen over the last five years is set in stone.'

The International Press Club of Pézenas (members: my husband, Jonathan Miller, Frank Johnson, another neighbour and journalist, and of course Peter Glynn-Smith, our official photographer, and me) organised a wind and wine evening. It was held at Jean-Claude and Alex's castle, Château de Conas. The mayor of Pézenas was invited, along with several local British winemakers and members of the expat community. The mayor had expressed an interest in meeting them and the expats wanted to tell him what they thought about the windfarm. The evening went well, the wines were good but not much was achieved. The mayor was predictably non-committal and said of course no decision would be taken that was detrimental to

---

*The mayor's website*

If you want to find out more about the place you're moving to, a lot of the local mayor's offices have websites. I googled our village before we moved here and found out that the local schoolchildren ran a vineyard. Not particularly useful, but I spent many happy hours dreaming about Olivia tending grapes in the sunshine.

---

the region. In other words, he would watch the way the wind was blowing and vote accordingly.

The British activists, more potbelly than Swampy, decided their best bet was to target some of the 22 estate agents in Pézenas. Foreigners won't buy and you'll lose your fat commissions, they warned. The estate agents looked horrified and started frantically taking notes.

One British homeowner who has already had his property ruined by a windfarm is Nick Rogers who lives in Surrey. He decided to buy a holiday home in Brittany, along with a friend. 'We always went on holiday together, so it made sense to buy a place together and split the costs and the work,' says Nick. The two men went house hunting and found the ideal property close to Guerlesquin, a house split into two cottages. 'It was great, a lovely place tucked away in the middle of nowhere, the nearest building was a farmhouse about 50 yards away,' says Nick. Because it was so perfect for them, they decided to buy it without their wives seeing it. 'We took lots of video footage home to show them and they were delighted.'

The sale went through smoothly and a couple of months later the families went out to spend Easter in their new holiday home. As they were coming off the motorway exit they saw nine windfarms shimmering in the distance.

'Oh, I wonder where they are?' Nick said to his friend. As they got closer to the property, they realised the turbines were not far away. When they turned onto the lane towards their house that they realised they were right next behind their place.

Nick is fairly sanguine about it. 'At first we contacted the agent, Vivre en France, and went crazy with them. They said they had no idea. I don't believe that. The guy who sold us the property was a Brit and I think they must all have known about it. The fact is they are at the back of the house so they don't spoil our view. Of course they have affected the resale value of the property but the children like them.'

If Nick had gone to his local mayor's office (*mairie*) before signing, he would have seen the plans for the windfarm. When we bought our house, we had no idea how important the mayor is, but if you do one thing before you sign, go and check out your property and the land surrounding it. The mayor's office will tell you whether there is any public access to the property, whether the land around it is building land or not, whether there are any major projects in the pipeline and so on. You just have to show up with the details of the property or the parcel number of the land it is on. The mayor has the *Plan d'Urbanisme* (habitation plan) for the village and its surrounding areas. This will show you exactly where you can and cannot build. Do not be tricked into buying land and told it has planning permission without checking. However, you should bear in mind that the mayor is under no obligation to tell you of any developments. In the case of windfarms, for example, the village or region will gain from them financially. In addition he is unlikely to give you an honest answer if it means the loss of a sale to a local resident.

The role of the mayor in France cannot be exaggerated. Every village has one, even if it doesn't have a baker, and he or she is involved in everything. A friend of mine who wishes to remain anonymous says: 'I have always believed and advised anyone that if you fall out with your local *maire*, it's time to move home.'

Jacques Kuhnlé, a retired English teacher living near Nancy, confirms the importance of keeping in with the mayor. 'When I built my house in the Alps, I was careful to invite the mayor to see the house and drink a glass of pastis,' he says. 'At first he didn't like the place but after the wood panelling was stuck over the concrete he said it was all right. Thank Goodness! My neighbours have a piece of sloping land which keeps collapsing on to the road. They managed to have the commune buy the part of the property that crumbles to avoid costly maintenance. They couldn't have done that if the mayor hadn't been a friend.'

I remember when I first visited our mayor to talk about some land that was for sale near to the house. I wanted to see whether or not it was designated building land. He showed me a map of the village and surrounding areas. It was rather like those old-fashioned maps of the world you used to get in schools, where all the pink bits were British. Here all the pink bits were protected. The plots that were allocated building land were blue. Luckily the land close to us was pink. I noticed that just outside the village was a whole swathe of pink bits with one little blue bit stuck in the middle of it. I asked him what the blue bit was.

'Oh that's the house the previous mayor is building for himself,' he told me.

Jean Martinez, the mayor of my neighbouring village, Caux, describes the role of mayor as being 'like the father of the village. You are involved in everything, from the psychology of the people, to their quarrels, to the water supply, the school, rubbish collection. In short, anything related to the life of the people.' Jean is a Professor of medicinal and organic chemistry at the University of Montpellier. He has worked and lectured all over the world and speaks flawless English. He is the head of one of the major experimental laboratories at the University, but on Tuesdays, Thursdays, Saturdays and 'Sundays if necessary' he is mayor of Caux, a village with a population of just over 2,000.

'I have always looked after people,' he says. 'And I love this village. This is something foreigners will never understand, this love we have for our homes. It's a kind of atavism. If it hadn't been for the village, I would have stayed abroad, the career opportunities are much better. But the village is the only thing that you never leave, you even end up buried in it.'

If you are planning to do anything at all with your home in France, or even if you're not, it is well worth cultivating your local mayor. He or she will be able to make most decisions that affect you and your home. In terms of planning permission, the decision rests with the mayor unless the land is protected, in which case the mayor would have to refer it to the DDE (*Direction Départementale de l'Equipement*). But don't forget, whatever the mayor recommends will be taken into account. If you live within 500 meters of a listed building, any change you want to make will have to be passed by the equivalent of the English Heritage, *Bâtiments de France*.

Mayors are elected for a period of six years. In the country they are elected on the basis of personality rather than politics.

---

### French workmen

When dealing with French workmen, there are some useful phrases whose real meaning you should be aware of:

*Je ferai le maximum* (I will do my best) = I'm late for lunch

*Ce n'est pas normal* (This is most unusual) = Too complicated for me

*Je vais vous envoyer un devis* (I will send you a quote) = You'll never see me again

*Je vais passer en début d'apres-midi* (I'll be there early afternoon) = I'll be there this week

*Je vais passer dans la semaine* (I'll be there this week) = I'll be there this month

*Je vais réfléchir* (I'll think about it) = I'll think about it for the next 10 years, by which time I shall be retired.

---

'Here people have known me since I was knee-high,' says Martinez. 'It is only really in the bigger cities you have to belong to a political party.'

Our mayor is a retired colonel who drives a vast motorbike. He seems like a perfectly nice chap to me, but Geneviève tells me that he sided with the far right in the last election. There is now a plan to remove him. When I last saw him, he looked stressed. His plans to create a village square had been rejected, he told me. He wanted to knock down the post office, which also houses the doctor and the hairdressers and make that area a place to sit. The post office, doctor and hairdresser would be moved to a new building down the road.

'It's impossible,' he sighed. 'People here want to die as they were born.'

I think they have a point. I rather like the crumbling old post office. And it's not as if the villagers miss having a square. They find plenty of places to sit and watch the traffic go by, even if they have to bring their own chairs.

So the power of the mayor is not limitless, but it is a force to be reckoned with, as Sophie Randall found when she moved to the Mayenne in northwest France with her husband David and their three children.

They ended up buying into a nightmare situation. First, the farm was owned by two families, with five people still involved in the property, including a M. Poulletier, who had a vegetable patch there and grew cider apples. Although the agent who sold it to them had told them it was not occupied, another member of the family still rented out one of the small buildings on the farm. They moved to France with their dogs and had specifically asked the agent if the property was suitable for dogs. He had said yes, although he must have been aware of the law that if you have more than three dogs you have to be further than 30 metres away from your nearest neighbour.

After about a year in the house, they had both failed to get jobs in France. Sophie is a teacher and David is an accountant but their qualifications were not accepted here. They decided to set up a dog breeding business. 'We had bought a legal book on rules and regulations governing breeding livestock which was recommended by *Nos Chiens* (a French glossy dog magazine) but it was desperately out of date,' says Sophie. 'This is yet another lesson that we have learnt, that systems are so complicated in France that no one anywhere seems to know the definitive answer.'

The Randalls sent off their application, put several bitches into pup and sat back and waited. 'It was very nerve-racking,' says Sophie. 'But I felt we might just muddle through until we could start selling puppies.'

The minute Poulletier and the other family member, M. Edard, realised what they were doing, they started a campaign to evict them. 'They knew that if we got authorisation they would be never make any money from the property because no-one can build or live on land within a 100 metres of a breeding kennel, which meant that they couldn't develop the site,' says Sophie. 'We didn't of course know but Poulletier is an ex-councillor, a friend of the mayor.'

Poulletier went around to all the neighbours and told them to complain about the Randalls' dogs. 'Everyone is the village is frightened of him,' says Sophie. 'The next thing we knew the DSV (*Département de Services Vétérinaires*) came round to close us down. The guy in charge was only slightly apologetic and said we should just go back to England. We couldn't really believe it was happening to us as, as far as we knew, we had done everything right. But we are English so as usual fair game.'

The Randalls refused to move. Then things turned nasty. 'Poulletier started coming around drunk and frightening the kids and leaving poison about for the dogs,' says Sophie. 'The mayor stepped in and told us we had to move the dogs or he would get the SPA (The French equivalent of the RSPCA) out to put them down. He also told us that we should go back to England. I told them all at this point that I was going to take them all to the European Courts as technically they didn't have a leg to stand on.'

The Mayor then brought in the region's head vet to strengthen his case. 'Fortunately for us, she is a woman. Not only that, a very tough one who has presumably had to fight men all the way to get to the top and she certainly didn't appreciate the mayor telling her what to do! I don't think she could give a damn about fairness or justice but she certainly wanted to teach him a lesson and so told him that it was nothing to do with him at all, but that it was her decision. After all the anxiety it was at least quite good to see him storming off in the rain with his deputy holding the umbrella for him so his cashmere coat wouldn't get wet!'

Finally her decision was that they would have to move the dogs, but she put no time limit on it. The Randalls found somewhere else to house the dogs. 'Poulletier had the last laugh though,' says Sophie. 'We couldn't go home as we could no longer afford to buy a house anywhere in the UK so we decided to sell the building and put the money into building up the dogs so we could make a proper living out of them. We put it on the market, but every time the agent took someone to look at it, Poulletier was there and he would charge up to them and tell them that if they bought it, he would make sure they were sorry. Eventually we had to drop the price and sell it for probably half of what it was worth to one of his mates.'

Sophie and David have now bought the house near the piggery that houses their dogs. They now have 40 dogs and are selling them all over France and winning prizes for them. 'Fingers crossed, we are a little bit wiser and are not going to get cheated a second time,' says Sophie. 'I would certainly advise people to avoid friends of the village mayor.'

While you are making friends with *M. le Maire*, you should also try to make friends with local artisans. Down in the south, reliable builders, plumbers, electricians and so on are notoriously difficult to find. I must have made almost 100 appointments to see various people, and only half have even shown up.

---

*Planning permission*

In your purchase contract, ideally, you should have a condition inserted to state that if planning permission for a particular project is not obtained, then the purchaser may withdraw. However, this type of clause is not very attractive to a vendor who may have to re-market his property at the end of a lengthy period whilst planning is sought for the appeal period to be passed.

The other trick is to come and give you a quote and then disappear. Or, as in our case, come and take away your TV satellite box to fix it and then vanish. Four years on we have heard nothing from the rather handsome man who showed up in a white van and said he'd be back in a week.

There wasn't much building work to be done, but when we bought our house it had a huge atrium; a sort of death trap for children and also a waste of space. Although it had been very useful for shouting at Rupert to come upstairs when he was watching the cricket, after a year we decided that Olivia and Bea's survival thus far had only been a matter of luck and that it was time to fill in the hole. According to Peter Glynn-Smith you should always live in a place for at least a year before undertaking major construction work, you need to see what it's like through all the seasons and get a proper feel for the property. We asked a local English builder to come along and take a look. It was such a relief to speak to someone who answered back in English and seemed to understand everything I said that I didn't worry when he said he would have to fit in the job with tending his vineyard. In fact, tending his vineyard was the least of our problems. The family only had one car, so when his wife needed it, he couldn't come. He was a keen tennis player and obviously couldn't miss any games on account of our atrium. After six months we were still living in semi-chaos. But eventually the job was finished and we had another room upstairs. When we decided to put a fireplace in, we went for a local builder. He showed up at 8am every morning and worked solidly until 6pm. The whole thing was finished in ten days.

Even if you find it tough dealing with local builders, using foreign help is not to be recommended. A couple who wish to remain nameless managed to alienate the locals by importing workmen from England. They bought a barn in the Aude valley for conversion last Spring. Nine months after they moved in, they still had no electricity or running water. Finally they hired a local architect to take over the project, but by then they had so alienated the local community that even he got nowhere. 'Every time I submitted absolutely water-tight planning permission on their behalf, it would be turned down for some spurious reason. It clearly just wasn't going to happen for them here,' says the local architect, who wishes to remain nameless. 'They came into the community, didn't introduce themselves to the neighbours or the local mayor and then proceeded to use a builder from England to do all the work.' He goes on. 'But these were not nasty people, they were just naïve. And they didn't speak French.' Eventually they sold at a loss and went home.

It is inevitable, especially in regions like the Languedoc where house prices have risen by 30 per cent in the last four years, that there will be some resentment towards the foreign invasion. I went to buy some meat in a local butcher's a year or so ago and was told by the man hacking up my beef with a 10-inch cleaver that it was my fault his children couldn't afford to buy a house. Others are more pragmatic and say that the Brits and most other foreigners too only go for the old houses the French don't want. But still it is true that even a house on a *lotissement* (housing estate) now will cost around €100,000. When we first started looking here you could get a huge old village house for that price.

However, as always the French state is on hand to help. In the village where my girls are at school they are about to build 60 low cost houses for low income families. The villagers are up in arms, saying they will have to build a new school as well to accommodate all the children. No doubt the Brits who live there will get involved. I heard a story recently of a fight in a village nearby to keep a restaurant open. The snooty Parisian lady who had a holiday home next door to it wanted it closed because of the fumes it produced. Colin, a friend of mine who lives there, said the local Brits were at the forefront of the fight to keep it open. They have won the battle and also made a lot of friends in the village. Parisians down here are less popular than the foreigners, so it was an extremely unwise move on her part.

Last time I saw Gregory, he told me the latest news on the

windfarms. He and his father Umberto, a charismatic, handsome gentleman, have managed to use their connections to get a commission to look into the project. This commission then advised the Montpellier authorities that the project shouldn't go ahead. 'After that, we were told the building permit would be refused,' says Gregory. 'But the head of the council has not made a decision either way. I think there is tremendous pressure from politicians in Paris, as well as pressure from big business.'

Another worrying development is that there is a plan to change the law so that

### Easy driving

Short of building a mechanised arm to collect the *péage* tickets on way through France to my house near Cannes, what can you do to make life easier in your right-hand drive car? The answer is a small plastic *télépéage* box. You might have seen the lucky owners. They avoid all the queues and are waved through a barrier with a 't' above it that seems to open magically. I always thought one could only get these boxes if one were a serious commuter or professional driver. Not so. They are available from the small offices at most big motorway exits to anyone with a bank account in France and £15 a year for the administration costs. The cost of your *péage* travel is then deducted automatically from your bank account, and you can avoid further injury from your gear stick whilst trying to lean through car to pay the bill.

mayors can accept a windfarm project without having to go to the regional council. 'This is truly scandalous,' says Umberto. 'In effect the mayor of a village of a few hundred people could give the go-ahead for something that could affect thousands.'

The Guidas question the feasibility of the windfarms. 'Our analysis of the whole problem is that it could become one of the great scandals of the 21st century,' says Gregory. 'Thousands of windfarms will spring up across the country only to placate the eco-Nazis, who don't even live in the countryside. But when the power companies tire of overpaying for this extremely undependable source of power, the windfarms will be left to rot, their thousand ton concrete bases as shameful a remembrance as WWII bunkers. The greens argue that we should put them where man has already ruined the landscape. The landscape around Pézenas has not been ruined, but it soon could be.'

As Umberto sums up: 'The sword is still hanging over our heads.'

---

*The French government and your property*

Bear in mind that if the local council decides to exercise its *pre-emption* right on the sale of your house, it does not have to come up with the money for six months. In the meantime, you keep the right to occupy the property. The council can purchase the property at a lower price than the market value, in which case you may:
— withdraw from the sale and keep the property;
— stick to your price and let a judge fix the amount the council has to buy it for.

Remember, pre-emption rights can also be exercised by the tenant of a property and in rural areas, the agricultural commission SAFER (*Société d'Aménagement Foncier et l'Etablissement Rural*) may do so.

Property is considered untouchable in France and a *compulsory purchase order* can only deprive someone of their property in case of public necessity (road construction, extension of an airport etc). Compensation will have to be paid.

# Lesson 11
# Healthcare

I was doing some late-night admin in my office when I heard my daughter Olivia run downstairs. The two girls, Olivia who was then aged four and Bea three, insist on sleeping in bunk beds in the same room. I use the term sleeping lightly, they rarely stop chatting and playing before 10pm. So to hear her come down at 9.30 was not unusual.

'Daddy,' I heard her say to Rupert, who was watching the news. 'There's a big, big problem.'

So far I was still only half listening. It was the next sentence that had me jumping from my chair, screaming as I ran upstairs.

'The torch fell out of bed and Bea has got blood on her head.'

I found Bea in the bathroom with Monika, the au pair, who was trying to stem the relentless flow of blood. The wound was on her forehead and looked deep.

My husband and the au pair were a lot calmer than me. In fact, Bea was a lot calmer than me. I started phoning every doctor in the region to find out what we should do. I spoke to one who said she might need stitches. So off we went to the local hospital, with Bea wrapped in a blanket. Visions of similar situations at hospitals in London came to me.

'We'll be there for at least four hours,' I said to Rupert.

'Why didn't I bring a book?'

We parked right outside the door of the *Polyclinique Pasteur* and rang the emergency bell. A nurse opened the door and asked what had happened. She asked how old Bea was and then led us to an operating theatre. There seemed to be no one else in the hospital. About five minutes later a young doctor straight from ER arrived looking very cool in his surgeon's kit and black scarf. He greeted us all and looked at the wound.

'She'll have a small scar,' he said. 'But with stitches it will be minimal.'

---

### The French equivalent of Calpol

A word of warning from Ruth Simpson who gave birth to their first child in Narbonne. 'I had been in my hospital for about an hour when the contractions started to get just a little bit too painful. The nurse offered to get me a painkiller. I said yes please. She came back minutes later with a bullet-type pill. I suddenly realised what I was supposed to do with it. Charles and I looked at this thing and then at each other. 'I love you very much Ruth,' he said. 'But there's no way I am putting that up your bottom.'

The French are mad about suppositories. You will find as soon as you have children here you get very used to administering them as they see them as a cure-all, the French equivalent of Calpol.

---

Bea looked horrified.

'Don't worry,' said her father as they placed a gas mask on her face. 'You'll still be a supermodel.'

The nurse asked Bea to blow into the balloon. After a few seconds Bea started giggling, then she fell asleep. About half an hour later we were home. The whole episode, including getting there and back, took less than an hour. Admittedly we live near a small town, so maybe we were shielded from the crowds of drunks and drug addicts one would find in any major metropolis, but, in England, there wouldn't have been a hospital there.

The French pride themselves on their health system. And it is true that after giving birth here (twice) and living with three small children who spend a lot of the time being ill, I have been very impressed with it. It seems to mix the private and public in a way that the English haven't been able to.

But getting onto the system is a total nightmare. Because it is so comprehensive (for example, I paid nothing for Bea's treatment) they are not keen on letting foreigners onto it. They kept turning me away and telling me I was covered in England, until I finally got a letter from the social security there saying they had nothing more to do with us and that we were resident in France.

The brilliant healthcare system does not come cheap. For every employed person around 45 per cent is contributed to the state for social security benefits and healthcare compared with 22 per cent in the UK. 'This percentage is split between the employer and the employee approximately 30 per cent to 15 per cent,' says Sarah Vedrenne, an accountant with CAC Languedoc. 'In France when we talk about what we get paid, we talk in net terms. If I look at my salary slip it's heartbreaking, but that's the price we pay for the benefits system.'

As most people with a business to run in France will tell you, the system is not sustainable. It is just too expensive to employ people. Ruth and Charles Simpson who run a vineyard told me that the people that owned the business before them used to employ eight people. 'We now employ one,' says Charles. 'And for this one person we pay another 100% on top of his salary in tax and contributions. It's a huge problem in France. The system is so punitive it forces people to go underground. If we didn't have to pay such huge charges we would almost certainly employ more people. As it is, we just can't afford to.'

If you live here and want to be covered you need to join the *Régime Obligatoire* (RO) and contribute to the *Sécurité Sociale*. This entitles you and your dependants to medical treatment. Once you are registered, you will be given a magical thing called a *Carte Vitale*, which you hand over to doctors (for automatic reimbursement) and chemists instead of money.

The contribution you make to the social security system will depend on what you earn but is usually around 22 per cent of taxable income. If you are employed, your employer will pay this automatically. If you are self-employed you need to register at your local *Caisse Primaire d'Assurance Maladie* (CPAM). The *Sécurité Sociale* will cover between 75 per cent and 90 per cent of treatment and 40 per cent to 70 per cent of medicines. The patient is liable for the remainder unless the illness is critical. We have a private insurance company (called a *mutuelle* or *complémentaire*) which covers this portion and costs us around £60 per month for the whole family. The *mutuelle* pays the difference between the state's contribution and 100 per cent. There are several companies that offer the service in France and the premium will depend on what level of cover you chose. For example, you may want to have cover for eyes and teeth. You can also opt for cover from a *mutuelle* at over 100 per cent which will then help to offset the cost of a private room or hospital.

If you're retired, you will need to get an E121 form from the NHS. This will entitle you to the same healthcare as a French pensioner.

If you're moving to France contact the Centre for Non-Residents in Newcastle (on 0191 225 4811). Get as many forms as possible. I found having lots of bits of paper helped during my year-long struggle to get us registered. And there was a brilliant form that covered me for childbirth (fairly essential as I was eight months pregnant when we left England). It is called an E112. An E104 is also useful. It is a record of UK National Insurance contributions and could help you to register here. If you're planning to claim unemployment benefit you will need an E301. If you are self-employed you should get an E101. For those of you with holiday homes, the most practical thing is

---

*Postnatal care*

You will have a check-up two months after giving birth and your doctor can then prescribe a course of pelvic re-education. This is normally carried out by a *Kinésithérapeute,* who is a cross between an osteopath and a masseur. Currently this is still reimbursed by the state, but according to my *Kiné,* it soon won't be. It is a most singular experience and you should go wearing your best underwear, which you will have to take off. He measures how fit your pelvic floor is by asking to squeeze his fingers (this is not something for the chronically shy). 'That's not bad after three children,' I was told. 'With some patients, I ask them to squeeze and I feel nothing.'

The aim is to get your nether regions back into shape after childbirth, whether this is to keep you or your husband happy, I'm not too sure. Or maybe it's for the amusement of France's *Kinés.*

---

still the E111, which is a simple form you fill in at the post office. This way you have to pay for healthcare up front, but you get refunded from the NHS once you get home. The list of E-forms is practically endless and you should call the above number to see which ones you need.

The way to get registered is to go to your local CPAM with the form that is relevant to you, which you have already organised from the centre for non-residents in Newcastle. At my

CPAM there is an international department called the *Conventions Internationales*. You should also take along your birth certificate (with both parents on—no I'm not joking), as well the birth certificates of any children, your marriage certificate if you're married and proof of income and tax paid if possible. If you're employed, salary slips will do. If you're self-employed you will need your accounts or at least some written proof of what you earn.

Finding a doctor is easy in France. The French are as interested in their health as they are in their stomachs. There seem to be doctors for everything, and when you see them they prescribe huge amounts of pills and potions. When all three children are ill at the same time our kitchen looks like a pharmacy. If you don't like one doctor you see, you can go to another, you just pay €20 each visit. There are several doctors in the neighbourhood. Our favourite is German. This is partly because he speaks English, but also because he doesn't just hand out antibiotics every time you visit him. He tells me that all is not well in the French system. I asked him if it is, as the French declare, the best system in the world. 'There are worse,' was his reply. However, he points out that in Germany there is a choice of 60,000 different types of medicines. In France there are fewer than 5,000, with brands being discontinued every day as the government tries to save money. I can confirm this. Two medicines I tried to get to treat my six-month old son's bronchitis were no longer available.

But despite drawbacks, the system is magnificent. Where else can you give birth for free and be looked after in a private room with air conditioning and television? Where else can you walk into a hospital at 10 o'clock at night and be given the service we were with Bea?

Posy and Mike Fallowfield had a terrible health scare almost as soon as they moved to France. Mike was suddenly taken seriously ill with a critical heart condition. 'We knew he had a problem before we left England,' says Posy. 'But we didn't realise how serious it was.' The local doctor told them to go and see a specialist in Auch. He ran some tests. He said the results were serious and suggested they go to the Clinique Pasteur in Toulouse for an angiogram. 'We showed up at the hospital on the Thursday before Good Friday like innocents abroad,' says Posy. 'We didn't realise this meant he would have to stay there. He didn't even have his toothbrush.' The test was carried out and they were told that Mike had four blocked arteries. He would either have to have open heart surgery or have four stents (a small cylindrical piece of mesh which opens the artery) inserted, one for each blockage. 'Luckily they opted for the stents option,' says Posy. 'Otherwise it would have meant six months of convalescing in the caravan which probably would

| **Useful medical terms** | |
| --- | --- |
| allergies | *les réactions allergiques/ allergies* |
| anaesthesiologist | *un/e anesthésiste* |
| anaesthetic | *une anesthésie locale/générale* |
| ache | *le mal* |
| blood | *le sang* |
| blood vessels/arteries/ veins | *les artères, les veines* |
| blood test | *le prise du sang* |
| cancer | *le cancer* |
| chills | *sensation de froid* |
| a cold | *refroidissement* |
| to cure | *guérir* |
| diabetes | *le diabète* |
| fever | *la fièvre* |
| 'flu' ('feeling unwell') | *le rhume* |
| inflammation | *l'inflammation* |
| influenza | *la grippe* |
| itching | *démangeaison* |
| medication | *les médicaments* |
| migraine | *la migraine* |

| | |
|---|---|
| muscular tear | *un claquage musculaire/une élongation* |
| on an empty stomach | *à jeun* |
| pain | *la douleur* |
| pins & needles | *des fourmillements/des fourmis/des picotements* |
| Repetitive Strain Injury(RSI) | *les microtraumatismes permanents* |
| shooting pain | *une douleur lancinante* |
| insomnia | *l'insomnie* |
| a splint | *une attelle* |
| surgeon | *un chirurgien* |
| surgery | *la chirurgie* |
| swelling | *c'est gonflé/enflé* |
| to treat | *soigner* |
| vertigo | *le vertige* |
| whiplash | *le coup du lapin* |
| X-ray | *une radio(graphie)* |

have killed us both off.' Mike stayed in hospital for four days. 'Even then, he was desperate to get out,' says Posy. 'He told me he felt like jumping around.'

The whole process, from the first visit to the GP to the convalescence took exactly three weeks. 'I'm not saying that we wouldn't have got good treatment back home,' says Posy. 'But I am sure it wouldn't have happened so quickly.' Mike is certain it made a huge difference. 'I think being here saved my bacon,' he says.

Because his condition is chronic, the medicine Mike has to take every month is 100 per cent reimbursed. His treatment cost £8,000 in total, 90 per cent of which he got back from the state. At the time, he and Posy were covered with an E106. They are now fully paid-up members of the French system. If they had had a *mutuelle* at the time of Mike's operation, they would have got everything back.

Sadly this all-encompassing health service is under threat. The government has been trying to introduce healthcare reforms and according to a recent survey, failure to do so could see healthcare expenditure of £85 billion a year by 2020. Health spending accounts for nearly 9 per cent of GDP compared with 7.1 per cent in the UK. There is an unpopular plan called 'Hospital 2007' which proposes management reforms and a new emphasis on cost management. The core suggestion is that citizens must pay more and doctors must change their behaviour. The French consume almost three times as many antibiotics as the Germans, for example. I have tried to go down the homeopathic route, until my GP retired. His replacement was not *conventionné* (ratified by social security) so the visits became too expensive at £30 per child. One of the ways the state is looking to save money is to reduce the number of alternative, and so-deemed non-essential, treatments available.

We kept Bea at home the day following the torch incident, just to make sure she was all right. At one stage I went to check on her. She was playing with Monika and her Barbie dolls. She was holding a particularly stunning example of a Barbie doll with fluorescent pink hair and a princess dress. Monika was holding Ken.

'If you don't love me any more,' Bea's Barbie was telling Ken, 'then I'm going to tell my mummy.'

I think she is going to be all right.

# Lesson 12

## *Allons Enfants de la Patrie* — Education

About three years after we moved to France, I was hauled up in front of the headmistress at my daughter's school. I had done nothing wrong, although it's amazing how a headmistress's office can make you feel guilty whatever your age. The problem was my five-year old daughter, Olivia. She had apparently bitten a classmate's bottom. 'Was he cute?' was my first question.

'No,' said the inappropriately named Madame Jolly. 'It was a girl and she has teeth marks on her bottom. This behaviour is inexcusable. What are you going to do about it?'

To make matters worse, the girl's mother then phoned me. She was furious. I thought briefly about cheering her up with my husband's helpful comment that he had often wanted to bite her bottom (she is a very attractive single mother) but decided instead to opt for total surrender and promise to take Olivia to see a child psychiatrist.

I asked Olivia why she had bitten the girl's bottom. 'She kept following me around,' was her rather surly response. I told her bottom biting was wrong, but my husband and mother both took a more lenient view and said that kids behave like that.

They might in England, but not over here. At least not without the whole village establishment taking notice.

Education is a pressing concern for many people buying homes in France. Some see it as a way of getting out of school fees in England. For us, the thought of the expense of sending all our five children to boarding school was enough to make us leave the country.

In France there is little social cachet about sending your children to a boarding school. In fact, it is traditionally those who are bad who get sent away. We have become good friends with my gynaecologist and his wife, Kati. He is a rather good-looking man, known in the family as the Dashing Dr Denjean. She is incredibly glamorous, your average French nightmare, a size 8 (if that), impeccably turned out, with beautifully mani-cured nails. Their daughter is ten and whenever she misbe-haves, Kati threatens to send her to boarding school. Our friends Peter and Dominique Glynn-Smith epitomise the cul-ture divide. He was very keen to send their son to Bedales where his children from his previous marriage were educated. She wouldn't hear of it.

'Private' schools, however, are still popular. In total around 15 per cent of the French send their children to private schools compared with 5 per cent in Britain. The private schools were all traditionally religious schools, but there are now some international and bilingual schools. The main difference, it would seem, is that the private school teachers don't strike as much as the state ones. In fact, every time Olivia and Bea have a day off due to a strike, I call my friend Alex to see if her daughter Elisa is around to play. She never is. Alex pays €84 (around £50) per term to send Elisa to a private school and this sum will remain constant as she grows up. French private schools are fully regulated and partially subsidised by the state. The international schools are much more expensive, some are on a par with English public schools.

Several parents of English children I have spoken to have found there is more support for their children within the French private system than the state one. Private schools are more likely to allow more time for French as a foreign language tutoring and there seems to be a consensus that they look after the individual needs of the child. The most important thing is to check with the individual schools and teachers in the region you live in or are moving to as there are of course variations.

My two girls go to school in the village where my child-minder lives. When I tried to enrol Olivia in the local village school here, it was full. To enrol a child you will need immunisation certificates and a piece of paper from your insurance company which provides cover for them at school. Sometimes the insurance company covers the child inside the school but not during outside activities, like trips, so it's worth checking. You will also need to provide proof of residence.

Chantal, my childminder, was already looking after Bea when Olivia first started school, so it was also more practical to have them both in the same place. In addition, she was only going in the morning as she was just over two. So far, I have been extremely happy with the way things have gone. The school itself is a lovely village school, the teachers seem great and she is doing very well. Last term she came home with top marks in every subject, except pronunciation, which she got the second top mark in. I was totally overjoyed, but the somewhat overprotective headmistress has insisted I take her to see a speech therapist. This seemed to me a little ridiculous, but I am going along with it—he may be able to do something about my pronunciation at the same time.

Olivia speaks just about perfect French, so imagine what the teachers would say about an English child moving over aged, say ten. An estimated 50,000 Brits a year are moving to France, and there must be a lot of school age children among them. It is difficult to say what the ideal age is to move to a different culture, although the earlier the better if you want to speak French like a local. When we moved, Olivia was just over one, so barely speaking. My other two children were born here. Bea, now three, speaks English with a charming French accent and is always being corrected by her older sister who seems to have

English somewhere deep down in her memory. In his book *Buying a House in France*, André de Vries, suggests that children under seven settle in most easily. 'Any older and the language deficit, combined with the rigorous nature of the French education, could make their lives unbearable'.

*Liberté, égalité, fraternité,*

I wasn't worried about sending my children to school in France when we first moved here. They were so little I knew they would adapt easily. But the more I learn about the system, the more concerned I become. The first thing you need to remember is that it was set up by Napoleon who decided that all French children should study the same subject at the same level in every region so that the local differences (and objections to his dictatorship) would disappear over time. This gives the whole school system a uniformity, which I suppose is useful if you move within France.

Some 200 years later, however, this fundamental concept remains largely unchanged. According to a French friend, 'We were being attacked from all sides, mainly by the British as usual and so we set up a lot of military schools. Sadly nothing has changed since then.' To illustrate the difference between the two systems, he tells the story of one of his sons who is at Cambridge and decided to go travelling in Peru. He went off happily with a rucksack and came back after two months having had a wonderful time. 'My other son who is studying in France went to Marseille for two weeks and was terrified the whole time. Children in France are just not taught to cope in the world and to think for themselves. The system allows no self-reliance. You learn and shut up, that is it.' Another French friend argues that Marseille is terrifying and far more dangerous than Peru, but that's a different argument.

The other thing you have to remember is that teachers are civil servants, employed by the state to make children perfect little French citizens. 'They are like soldiers in an army,' says a friend. 'Individuality is frowned upon because it can cause dissension in the troops.'

Though the job of the teachers is to produce little republicans, the '*égalité*' breaks down quickly. They are all supposedly teaching the same subjects at the same times, but not all schools are created equal. There are some inspiring professors but many others who just go through the motions. The Bac (equivalent to A-levels) has supposedly been reformed and it now comes in several flavours and just like in Britain, the pass rate constantly goes up. 'But if your plan is that your gifted child should rise to be admitted to one of the *grandes écoles* like the famous ENA, more selective even than Oxbridge, you had better move to Paris and send your child to one of a very strictly limited number of the grandes *lycées*,' says Guy Veillot, a French friend. 'Admissions to these tends to come via connections and is not coincidental with residence in the better post codes. And so the elite renews itself.'

This is not a view shared by all. Rory Clarke, chief editor of the OECD *Observer* magazine, says France is ahead of England in terms of equality in education. 'I wouldn't like to be guilty of dewy-eyed romanticism,' he says. 'But I think the system favours ordinary people with brains in France, whereas well-off people with money and not much in grey matter are guaranteed very little indeed. If you like, it is one of the better vestiges of the revolution. If you compare the two countries' exam results, in Britain, broadly speaking, those who do well come from good backgrounds and those who do badly from poor ones. In France the background is more mixed.'

But still there are elements of French education that are paradoxical. By attempting to reconcile the often contradictory tenets of French Republicanism, it has produced a system where quirky children can be overlooked or ignored. At the same time, the French system somehow produces writers, thinkers, musicians and artists of towering genius. It is like so much about France—hard to figure out.

The marvellous film *Etre et Avoir* offers a glimpse into the survival of traditional schooling, especially at the primary level, which looks rather inspiring. Olivia, aged five, is already doing the beautiful joined-up writing they learn and I am very proud of her, but she will end up with the same handwriting as millions of other children in France, except those who are left-handed and can't cope with writing right-handed. It is peculiar that they all learn to write in exactly the same way. Children will learn how to spell and surf the internet. But it is an open secret (and a comfort to British immigrants) that many French people never really master their own language and are condemned to menial jobs on the minimum wage, or worse, because if you don't pass the French language section of the Bac you get nowhere.

Reform of the education system has been continuous and the results decidedly mixed, or at any rate minimal. Often obstructing change, the teachers tend to be left-wing and also deeply conservative. As soon as the government wants to change something, they strike.

Despite the changes some basic inequalities between schools remain. If you are the sort of parent who cares about this (and not everyone does to the same degree), it is, in fact, exactly like education in Britain and everywhere else—it is absolutely crucial where your child goes to school.

According to Nick Rowsell, who was an English teacher in France, a lot of expat children have problems with the French system simply because they are different. 'One of my American work colleagues was told time and again that her kids were failures,' he says. 'On the advice of teachers, they spent their formative years being shunted around educational psychologists. In later years, in *lycée* and *collège*, their major crime was that they 'didn't fit in.' My colleague's kids have now finished with the system. However, for us the nightmare is just beginning—my daughter has been assigned a special needs teacher because she is 'different'. The French way of education can cause a lot of emotional trauma to non-French parents and their offspring. Even if their children have never set foot in a British school, the simple fact of one parent exerting a British or English linguistic and cultural influence on the child, will set him or her apart from the system.'

Nicole Kuhnlé, a primary school teacher I interviewed, tells me that foreign children are often different from other kids, but usually for positive reasons. 'They are usually better pupils than the rest of the class,' she says. 'I have had countless children from Arab countries, some not speaking French at all, an American, a South Korean, Yugoslavs, Turks, Albanians. And they usually coped quite well or even were top of the class after a few months.'

Stephanie Godwin lives in the Mayenne and her three children are going to school in the region. She has encountered terrible problems, and puts it down to them being English. 'They seem to equate someone who is English with someone with learning difficulties,' she says. 'Joseph's (her five-year old son) teacher told me he would have to stay back a year after teaching him for four mornings. She says she hasn't got the time to teach an English child to read. There are only 12 kids in his class!' Stephanie advises anyone looking to move here to check out the attitude of the local mayor towards the British before they buy. 'I have just discovered that it is the mayor who controls all the primary schools and that is why we have had such a bad time here, as he doesn't want any English kids in the school.'

She also says that bullying is a huge problem in France and that it starts with the teachers. 'They just don't want any extra work so they try to get rid of English children as soon as possible by sending them to another institution like SEGPA (special educational institutions for children with learning difficulties or behavioural problems). This they achieve by being foul, running the kids down as much as possible and refusing to help them in any way.'

As in all schools there are stories of bullying by other children from France. I have had lots of letters from readers on the subject. One from a couple who recently moved to Perpignan with their boys aged seven and nine. They were picked on for being the only English children in the school, the younger boy was hit on the head so hard (by a girl) that he had to be taken to hospital in an ambulance. They also found that the teachers were far more violent than in England. 'To start with our eldest son was in a class where his teacher would suddenly shriek at one child or another and then strike them,' says his mother, who wishes to remain anonymous. 'Our child was never hit, but he was always on edge, not knowing what the others had been hit for.'

---

The French Educational system is divided as follows:

🏛 Nursery School
  Lower Section (*petite*)          2-4 years
  Middle Section (*moyenne*)        4-5 years
  Upper Section (*grande*)          5-6 years
🏛 Primary School (*école primaire*)   6-11 years
🏛 Secondary School (*collège*)        11-15 years
🏛 Sixth Form College *(lycée)*        15-18 years

After the *Baccalauréat* which you take at the end of your time at the *lycée* you have the choice of a technical qualification (a BTS) leading to a job, further diplomas, university or *prépa* for the *grandes écoles* if you have done well enough.

---

My primary school teacher friend Nicole Kuhnlé says that she has given a few smacks in her career, when it was still not illegal to do so and when the child was really uncontrollable. 'Today whenever a child gets hit, a rare occurrence, it usually ends up in court,' she says.

According to Nick Rowsell 'anyone moving to France for the sole purpose of the better quality education their offspring might receive should themselves go back to the classroom. It is a loopy idea'. Nick trained as a teacher here and says that what he saw of the education system was enough to make him leave it. 'French schools might look good on paper,' he says. 'But they don't half screw up your kids. French education is all about following instructions to the letter, and that starts in the first year of infant school.'

Jacques Kuhnlé, Nicole's husband and a retired English teacher himself, says that may be true, but he defends the French educational establishment. 'Seeing bad manners and the way children are (not) educated at home by their parents, I don't find it shameful that someone should set limits to what children can do or not do in the company of others, even in the first year of school,' he says.

To illustrate his point on limits set, Nick tells the story of his daughter, Lena, when she was five, being asked to draw a picture of a Father Christmas (she goes to a nursery school in Bourges in the Cher). 'Just before Christmas, my daughter's class was told to draw a Father Christmas on a sheet of A3 paper. My daughter duly drew a nice Santa, but she added a Christmas tree and presents. With the approach of Christmas, Santas appeared all around the classroom on the wall from all the children, apart from our daughter. When my daughter's work did appear, it was a minuscule Santa since the teacher had cut the offending items out the picture, so it would match the others. I told the teacher that it showed imagination and initiative and was met with a stony silence, followed by: '*votre fille n'a pas suivi la consigne*—she didn't complete the assignment.'

One of the most common criticisms of the French system and the thing that most worried me is the lack of opportunity for self-expression. Pupils are force-fed information like a goose being fattened to make *foie gras* and just expected to regurgitate it when asked. 'This is reflected in the fact Cambridge alone has won 80 Nobel prizes against 50 for the whole of France,' says Alaric Wyatt, a private tutor now based between Oxford and France. 'True and deplorable,' says my friend Jacques. 'But the reason is not so much the lack of freedom given to an individual as the amount of money scientists have in their labs.'

Children are also likely to find there is much more homework than in the UK. Ruth de Latude who brought her three children up in France remembers them having an hour's homework every night from as early as seven years old. She found the system a harsh one. Ruth's eldest son Thomas suffers from epilepsy and has had to take drugs all his life to fight the condition. 'These make your thought process much slower so Thomas found it very hard to keep up at times,' she says 'Here they seem to have either schools for severely handicapped children or nothing at all. And in the normal school you either keep up or you're out. Thomas was terribly unhappy and in the end I took him out aged 16.'

Indeed, the French system is not famous for dealing with any special needs well. Leslie Sorbie from Newcastle-upon-Tyne is considering a move to France with their daughter and two grandchildren. Her grandson Sean is 11 and has Down's Syndrome. In France, says a source at the British Down's Syndrome Association, they are way behind England in terms of education. 'They do not, as we do, offer children with Down's Syndrome access to mainstream schools as a matter of course, although I think things are better in the rural areas.' Jean-Charles Wiart from FAIT 21, the French Down's Syndrome Association, agrees that in France there are vast regional differences. 'In theory parents have the choice of whether or not to integrate their children, but in practice it totally depends on the region and what is available there.' In France a child with Down's Syndrome will be 'shadowed' by a carer in normal school, and some regions do not have this facility. In Nancy, for example, there is the choice of integration in an ordinary school or a special class in a local school.

Some friends who live near Montpellier have a daughter

who is dyslexic—which is not a condition the French look upon as seriously as the English do. 'It has been really tough for Georgie,' says her mother. 'And as far as I can make out, they don't really get much of an education anyway. The teachers are always off sick and the girls are sent home early. When they do get taught it's very old fashioned and they seem obsessed with results.' They moved to France when their triplets were 11 years old. Mike, her husband, is in the army and was posted here. 'There was no question of leaving them behind,' he says. 'That's not what we had them for.' The girls were taken out of the English public school system and put into a school in a village close to Montpellier. It wasn't just Georgie who had problems. 'They absolutely hated it at first,' says Mike. 'I remember one time Jessica calling me to tell me that she was outside the school and all three girls had locked themselves in the car. There was a time when I think they would rather have done anything than go to school.'

Other people, like Melissa Miller, have moved their children back to England to get away from the system. They moved to France when their children were six and nine. 'There was a lot of shouting, humiliation and smacking. And the children, who had nothing to play with but a ball made from old newspaper, did a lot of physical fighting and bullying.' Her daughter did very well. After 10 months she had mastered the language and was among the top of her class, but her son was placed in a remedial class because he refused to speak French to the adults. 'I also found the method of teaching very parrot fashion and narrow-minded,' says Melissa. 'They leave no room at all for imagination or creativity. In the classes for the younger children homework consisted of learning long poems by heart. Older children were taught by copying long passages from the blackboard and learning them for tests. In the end we decided to come back to England for the sake of the children's education. We did not want them stifled. We were grateful for this short educational experience. It did them no harm and there were some great benefits.'

Paul Beaufils, a former naval officer who moved to Béziers just over two years ago to set up a property business, is very happy with the French system. When they first moved here, he told me the school took the arrival of their two daughters very seriously. They were nine and thirteen and neither of them spoke French. 'They got all the governors and the teachers together,' Paul told me. 'They had a meeting that went on all afternoon. I was panicking thinking they weren't going to let them in or something. Finally the headmaster appeared and said they had made a decision. "I know what we're going to do," he told me. "We're going to speak French to them." I could have told them that!'

His daughter Laura learnt the language easily and is now top of her year. 'She loves school,' he says. 'And is particularly good at history.' One day he asked her why she liked the subject so much. 'It's pretty easy Dad,' she replied. 'All you have to remember is that the French basically lost everything except for Africa.'

One of Tony Tidswell's best memories is his daughter's first day at the village school of

*School holidays*
So as to make sure the whole of France isn't on the beaches or the ski slopes at the same time, the school holidays are staggered. There are three zones and the regions within the zones have the same dates.

Zone A:
Caen, Clermont-Ferrand, Grenoble, Lyon, Montpellier, Nancy-Metz, Nantes, Rennes, Toulouse

Zone B:
Aix en Provence, Marseille, Amiens, Besançon, Dijon, Lille, Limoges, Nice, Orléans, Tours, Poitiers, Reims, Rouen, Strasbourg

Zone C:
Bordeaux, Créteil, Paris, Versailles

Nizas in the Languedoc. Miranda was three at the time and he remembers another three year old girl coming out from the classroom, taking her hand and leading her in. 'It was such a poignant moment,' he says. 'And they are still the best of friends.'

What will be the right school will depend on your region. There are notoriously bad schools in the suburbs where it is unfortunately true that very few learn anything much. Most seem to encounter problems are most likely to be in regions where there aren't so many expats and where the children are the only foreigners at the school. Jacques Kuhnlé says 'generally speaking, *maternelles* (nursery schools) are excellent. Primaries are quite good. *Lycées* are fine. Naturally this is a general assessment. You will find poor or lazy teachers even in the best places. The real problem is in *collèges*. Their location is critical. Try to avoid *collèges* or *lycées classés en ZEP* (*zone d'éducation prioritaire*). This means difficult suburbs, problems of discipline and pupils' motivation. As for private schools, beware. They are not all good. Far from it. Some are excellent but the others (I would say over half depending on the region) can be just awful.'

The most important thing you can do as a parent is to stay positive. If you accept the different life, methods of doing things, so will your children. If you are planning your move several months in advance, get your children a French teacher. If you are already here, get a tutor; someone who can come in every afternoon and help with the homework, the syllabus, and of course the language. The tutor can also help your children get used to the endless tests he or she will encounter.

Your child may have been top of his or her class at home and will probably come bottom for a while. This will be very hard to adjust to and totally demoralising. On the positive side, a huge number of Brits I have met who have children in the system here find they eventually overtake their French counterparts. Some parents have chosen to take advantage of the system here and then send their children to private school in England to complete their education. 'Our daughter was going to be held back for a year here aged 13,' says an Englishman who has lived in Paris for 30 years. 'She avoided that by going to England and also has come out with a more rounded education.'

Educational experts say it takes five terms for a child to fully settle in and learn the language. This period may be shorter if they are very small, and of course it gets more difficult the older they are.

Don't forget that their English will deteriorate and it will be up to you to reinforce it, as the level at school is not going to be high enough. At home, we speak English and Swedish, and videos and TV are only allowed in those two languages. If a book is English (like Harry Potter), it is read in English and never in the French translation. I encourage the girls to speak English together and so far they do. Chantal, their childminder, says she loves listening to them chat away, although she has no idea what they're talking about.

Another common complaint among expats is of bias in the teaching in French schools, so you may need to correct that. A wine-making friend of mine in Bordeaux says he will send his son to school in England: 'I'm terrified he will grow up thinking Napoleon is a good bloke,' he says. ('What does he expect?' asks Jacques. 'Nelson presented as a hero or Waterloo as a great victory?')

The mother of the bullied boys above tells me they were extremely surprised by the history material the boys came home with one day. 'We noted with interest that the French teach them that Franco-American forces landed on D-Day and went on to win the war,' she says 'On the plus side, our son has overcome his aversion to Maths, as it is a subject he now really fully understands.'

You will also have to have a decent level of French to be able to help them with their homework as they get older. All conversations with teachers will be in French and you will also need to communicate with your children's friends. Assuming you're not moving to the Dordogne, they are likely to be French.

Graham Richardson, who moved to Montpellier with his

wife Karen and their children ten years ago, has three daughters who have been through the French system. He advises throwing children in at the deep end. 'When we first got here, Charlotte was eight,' he says. 'There was a French-Canadian girl in her class who spoke good English so we thought it would help her to sit with her and learn from her. Not a bit of it. Whereas Sarah (ten at the time) and Josephine (four at the time) both picked up French in two months, after six months Charlotte still wasn't making progress.' In the end, Graham told her that if he ever heard her speaking English to her friend she would never see her again. 'That was a turning point, after that she was fine.'

Graham's girls are among those that love the system here and have had no problems at all. 'They have responded well to what is really a very structured and organised system,' says Graham. 'They seem to enjoy the constant scoring that goes on.' A small blip came early on when Josephine found she was losing a mark on every test at school, even if she got all the answers to the questions right. She asked her teacher what the problem was and was told that she was spelling her name incorrectly, she needed to put an accent on the first e. 'But I'm English,' Josephine told the teacher. 'That's not how my name is spelt.' 'It *is* in France,' was the response.

## Higher education

The higher end of the French system is even more impenetrable than the English. There are the *grandes écoles*, the top schools, and then everything else. Only a small percentage of *grandes écoles* students come from a working-class background, although there are efforts to change this. The *Sciences Politiques* school in Paris, for example, recently opened admission to suburban schools where the students are traditionally French lower-class of Arab origin.

Graham Richardson's daughters Sarah and Charlotte have both got extremely good Bac grades and are carrying on into higher education. Sarah is doing *prépa* (intensive teaching in smaller classes which the top 10 per cent of the Bac students have the option of doing) at the *lycée*, and may go on to one of the sought after *grandes écoles*. Charlotte has decided to go straight to university to study law. 'We moved here to give the children a better education without having to pay for it,' says Graham who is preparing to move back to England to become a teacher. 'I think we've achieved that.'

The problem is the low standard in the universities has made it even more essential to get into a one of the *grandes écoles*. 'Now that the government has decided everyone needs to pass their Baccalaureate, the standards at universities have gone down so the only people who will get decent jobs are those who make it to the *grandes écoles*. And to make it to them you have to have the right family, not just for support, these students work from 8am to 11pm, but also the contacts,' says Guy Veillot.

Many people don't agree and maintain that as it is all based on your exam results there is no room for elitism. 'The written

---

### Don't mention the War

In small communities across France there is still much bitterness going back to the Second World War. When Francis Cammaerts, a celebrated British secret agent who helped the French resistance during the War from within France, moved into his new house, he made friends with his next door neighbour. About a year later, his neighbour's wife showed up at his house in tears. 'I can't tell you the difference it has made,' she said. During the war, the Germans had said they would release one imprisoned French soldier for three workers. Her husband had, mistakenly, thought that by volunteering they would let his favourite uncle come home. The villagers had shunned him ever since, until the British secret service hero became his neighbour and friend, nearly 60 years after the end of the War.

part of the exam is nameless, precisely to ensure that only the best succeed (the old republican principle of equality),' says Jacques Kuhnlé. 'Only at the orals (when they exist) can the examiners see who the students are. And even then, letting in a bad student because you know him or his parents is dangerous, not only legally: if he fails miserably the other teachers will demand to know who let in that awful student,' he says.

'Most people think that the Bac is equivalent to English A-levels but it's not,' says Graham. 'The real selection for top grade higher education takes place the following year at the universities themselves where a huge percentage of the intake fail to carry on. I think this is an interesting twist because it means that everyone who gets even a mediocre Bac [80 per cent pass rate] can go to university [*égalité*!]. And then they find themselves sifted ruthlessly before being kicked out if they are no good. Which means that just like anywhere else, the French have an elitist system but are clever at pretending otherwise.'

In order to get into a *grande école* you have to be at the right preparatory school. Peter and Dominique Glynn-Smith have been forced to run two households so that their son can go to school in Montpellier. This is the closest city that has a school that is a feeder for the exclusive preparatory schools everyone is aiming for. Once you have got into the *prépa*, you have two years of unimaginably hard slog ahead before the ultimate prize of the *grande école*.

Jérôme did get into the *prépa* in Versailles, in fact, he came top in the whole of France in Geography and History in the Bac for his year and was even telephoned by a government minister who congratulated him. Astoundingly, the very first question he was asked in his interview at the *prépa* was: 'Here in Paris, we have the impression that in the south of France you find it difficult to work hard. What do you think of this?' My friend Jacques would say that the fact the interview took place is proof that there is no prejudice or elitism in the system. Jérôme comes from a family who live down south with no smart Paris address.

As far as the expense of the best education in France is concerned, now that Jérôme has got into his *prépa*, his parents will have to find around €2,000 a year tuition fees and at least €600 a month living costs. 'There are very few boarding facilities,' says his mother Dominique. 'And in France not everyone gets a grant.'

*The Arts*

One of my main concerns about the educational system is that there is really not much beyond academic subjects taught at French schools. In primary schools there is no art, music or sports to speak of. In secondary schools, according to Jacques, they have one or two hours of music a week, the same with arts and sports. Drama is not usually on the syllabus. Originally Wednesdays were free because of an arrangement with the Catholic Church so the children could go to catechism in the morning. Nowadays the idea is that pupils have Wednesdays off to pursue their interests. This of course is difficult for those who have parents who work and can't drive them to which ever club they want to go to.

Sarah and Matthew Cookson have decided, after 12 years in France, to move back to England with their children Rosie and William for secondary school. 'I'm fed up with driving around the county all the time,' says Sarah. 'If we want them to get a balanced education we have to take them to the various clubs or classes ourselves.'

Sarah recommends finding out about something called the *Forum des Associations*. This is an open day, usually a Saturday, where all the associations and clubs display their courses and you can register your children for them.

This lack of sporting and artistic culture means that if your child is incredibly sporty but not keen on course work, he or she may never be seen as anything but a low achiever. 'If your child is not academic, he or she may not be very happy in the French system,' says Laurence Micklethwait, who is French and married to an Englishman. 'They will feel like a failure all the way through.' Laurence has decided to send her two boys to French school for the moment, partly because the English schools around Paris are so expensive and because she feels the academic level in French schools is higher. 'This may change,' she says. 'My husband was at boarding school in England and he may want to send the boys there one day. I'm not against the idea.'

There are special schools geared towards dance or sport, so if you have a child prodigy who is not academic, he or she could go to one of those. But remember they are not in every region. I am worried Bea will not be academic. She seems to have more of a crazy Viking Swede gene in her than her sister, and she is definitely the actress of the family. When Olivia was her age she would come back at the end of term with a folder full of work with little smiley faces the teacher drawn on. This is their system of marking little ones. Smiley faces means good, non-smiley means mediocre and turned down mouth is bad. Bea has more of the latter two, but I guess there's still time.

I am keeping an open mind. So far the girls are happy where they are and they will stay. Our older children, Hugo and Julia, will stay in England. Hugo has an unconditional place at Eton and if we can afford it (no chance) we'll send him there. Julia wants to go to her local comprehensive because she likes the red uniform (there are worse reasons for choosing schools). When the little girls are older I may decide to send them to the international school in Montpellier, or even England for a year or so. I would like to think they will grow up truly bilingual (with enough Swedish to talk to attractive Scandinavian men when they come across them) and I don't think they will do that if they are educated here 100 per cent. Leonardo will never learn to play cricket if he is totally educated here, unless his father teaches him. But I guess he will play rugby and I never really understood the rules of cricket anyway.

Whatever else, it's a lot better than Heathfield Comprehensive or 15 years of trying to find £4,000 a term each for some middle class training ground in the home counties.

# Lesson 13

# Tax

The intransigence of the French might be scary, but the tax and social security regime is positively terrifying. France is well known for being impossibly bureaucratic and punishing. For French friends who run successful businesses here it has got to the point where they are considering moving them to the UK. Bill Blevins, of the financial advisers Blevins Franks, tells me one of his most successful French clients in Paris is moving his whole operation to London. 'Despite the prices there, he will save around 40% in costs due to the punishing social security regime in France,' he says.

A lot of English people who move to France or have a second home here think that they can simply stay out of the system. As a warning to them I quote a terrifying statistic from a book written by a former tax inspector. He states that if you are a French farmer, you are likely to be inspected by the tax authorities once every 135 years. If you are a foreign entrepreneur you are likely to be investigated once every six years. Is this institutionalised racism?

'I don't think that tax offices target foreigners specifically, but in areas where there are a lot of foreigners there are often various forms of abuse going on, some of which they catch up with eventually,' says Dawn Alderson, lawyer at Russell

Cooke. 'Some people think they can go and live in France and pay tax neither in England nor France. It's just not realistic.'

Despite doing everything legally, Tony and Carole Tidswell have been through the hellish experience of a tax investigation. Bill Blevins describes the process similar to 'having a concrete mill wheel around your neck'. Those who have been through it agree.

Tony and Carole were wrongly advised when they first moved to the south of France over ten years ago. 'As a self-employed person, I was told I had to register my profession with the relevant association or *Chambre*,' says Tony. In France there are several *Chambres des Métiers*, one for commercial professions, another for artisans and another for writers and artists. As they were in the process of setting up an internet business, Tony registered as a photographer—which had been his previous profession. Belonging to a *Chambre* means that you pay a monthly contribution to your social security and pension payments. Tony ended up paying €500 per month over six years, even though they had no income at all. They were living on capital whilst doing up their home and starting the internet business. 'What we did was totally wasteful and unnecessary,' he says. 'Although I had several meetings with tax people and accountants here not one of them gave me the right advice. If you ask five people the same question, expect five different responses and often conflicting replies.'

Finally they went to a UK accountant for advice. He told them they only needed to register with the *Chambre des Métiers* if they wanted to operate any business or trade in France where they were going to invoice people locally. They then resigned from the *Chambre des Métiers*. 'Immediately we were jumped on for tax on all income that had gone through our bank,' says Carole. 'This included the sale of our personal effects, private loans and expenses we were paid whilst trying to set up our business.'

The tax authorities are not allowing any expenses they have incurred during the years they are investigating to be offset, so Tony and Carole now face a tax bill of around €17,000 on 'nonexistent income.'

'For people coming into the French system', says Tony, 'just appointing an accountant or talking to the tax people is not enough. It is really necessary to dig deeply into the implications of trying to work in a system where you will be assumed to be guilty of trickery and are guilty until proven innocent.'

Brent and Susan Calvert moved to the Dordogne in 1995. Brent had owned a number of estate agent offices in Blackheath, but when he was offered a substantial profit by one of the large mortgage players, he decided to take his money and flee abroad. He moved first to Andorra, but after seven years of skiing and hill-walking he bought a large farmhouse with land in the Dordogne area of France. Immediately they ran into trouble with the French taxman. 'Looking back on it, maybe we were a bit naïve,' says Brent. 'We declared everything we had and once we had done that, we didn't stop paying. Even though we love France, it couldn't continue. I was paying more tax than I was earning. I said this to the taxman and he just laughed and said 'sometimes it is like that'.

The easiest way to avoid trouble with the French taxman is to work for a French company. This way your employer gets to pay for your social security contributions (around 40% on top of your salary) and deal with the authorities. However, the average wage is only €800 per month net, hardly enough to pay most mortgages. Nick Rowswell, head of studies at the French Air force language school in Avord, south of Paris, has been in France for 13 years. 'Since the introduction of the Euro,' he says, 'living and working as the French is getting harder. I have an annual salary increase of 0.5 per cent, inflation stands at 2 per cent and prices have risen by 17 per cent.'

You should also take into account that you may have to pay wealth tax (*Impôt de Solidarité sur la Fortune* or ISF) if you have net assets which are valued at over £500,000. This applies to anyone who is resident in France or has assets in France on January 1st of more than £500,000. When calculating the value of your assets you have to take into account things like your car, furniture, yachts etc. You may also be asked to produce receipts to justify your valuations. You will pay a percentage of the value of your assets calculated on a sliding scale at 0.55 per cent on assets of between £500,000 to £770,000 up to 1.80 per cent on assets of £10 million and above.

The capital gains tax law changed recently. This tax is paid when you make a profit on a property that is not your principal home. A French resident selling a property that is the principal residence will not be taxed on any capital gains. Residents and non-residents from the European union selling a property, where it is a second home, within five years of purchase will be taxed in full at 16 per cent on any profit. Residents from outside the European Union will be taxed at 36 per cent. Between six and fifteen years after purchase any gain on the sale benefits from a discount of 10 per cent for each year of possession, thus after 15 years of ownership no tax is payable. The cost of property extensions, major improvements and renovations, supported by receipted accounts, may be deducted from the gain. Bear in mind that social taxes, in some cases as high as 10 per cent, are also payable on any gain from property sales, although not by non-residents.

There are several property taxes you need to be aware of. First and foremost there are two types of local tax: *taxe d'habitation* (residential tax) and *taxe foncière* (property tax, similar to council tax in the UK). Residential tax is payable by anyone living in a property in France, property tax is paid only by the owner of the property. Both taxes are payable on main or second homes and whether you are a French resident or not. If your property is habitable (ie furnished) on January 1st of any given year, you are liable for tax for that year. The amount of tax you pay will usually be based on the rental value of the property for the previous year, as well as the living area and factors like whether or not you have central heating, a swimming-pool, location and so on.

You must also pay tax on any rental income received in

France. It does not matter where you live, where you collect the rental money for your home in France or where your personal tax is paid. If the house you are renting is in France, all income from it is considered as being earned in France and tax must be declared on that income in France. Tax must be paid in France, even if you declare and pay tax in another country.

If you are already making a tax declaration in France you can add the property income to your declaration, deduct all relevant expenses and you are liable to tax at 25 per cent on the balance. If relevant expenses are greater than your income no tax is due. If you do not already send in a tax declaration, the simplest system for your property is a *régime micro*. Under this scheme, you are only liable for tax on 30 per cent of the income; they allow you the balance as expenses. You pay tax at 25 per cent on the 30 per cent of the gross rental income.

In addition there may be local tourism and occupancy taxes. Your local *mairie* or *préfecture* can help with this information. These taxes are usually payable per bed, and are usually around one Euro a night.

You are not likely to face double taxation if you have paid your taxes in France and then take the balance back to the UK. You can ask in person what forms are needed at your local tax office. They are usually helpful. More information can be found at the government site (www.service-public.fr).

The one piece of advice everyone gave us when we moved here was that we should keep all our accounts in England.

As it turned out, it just wasn't a realistic option. You have to pay tax in the country in which you live and with children at school here, there is no way we could avoid that. In fact, ultimately the children were the answer. The French are extremely keen on population growth and there are all sorts of benefits for *'familles nombreuses'*. This is classified as a family with more than three children. You get to go on the train for half price, for example. In terms of tax, the level you pay is reduced drastically with every child after the third one. With five children between us, the tax man is very nice to us.

# Lesson 14

# Mad Dogs and Englishmen

In Conan Doyle's story *Silver Blaze*, Sherlock Holmes is able to deduce who nobbled the horse from the fact that the dog did not bark. If Holmes had been in France, he would never have solved the mystery, because there has never been a French dog that did not bark.

One of the few drawbacks of living in this fine country is that, wherever you are, somewhere in the distance you will always hear a dog barking. In villages some owners seem to encourage their dogs to bark to dissuade intruders.

The first house we wanted to buy in France was a relatively isolated property, about half a kilometre between two villages. We liked everything about it until my husband went for a walk in the fields and came across the footings of a building. When he asked what they were for, he was told 'kennels'. Although the owner assured us that if we were bothered by the noise the mayor would have the dogs removed, we preferred not to take the chance. Passing the property by chance recently, we stopped to have a look. As our car pulled to a halt in front of the kennels, 50 dogs jumped up and started howling.

These dogs were kept purely for hunting, a practice that is common all over France. Even though we live in the middle of nowhere, we can often hear two dogs kept in a cage barking from across the valley. 'These animals are not normally regarded as pets and once they stop being useful are usually shot,' says Stephanie Godwin, the English breeder based in the Mayenne. I often feel like wandering over the hills to let them out, but as the hunters traipse around my house with rifles for much of the year it's probably not a good idea.

My friend Carla, who is mad about dogs, says she could never live here because of the way the French treat their animals. She once went to stay with a friend in Provence. Close to the house were two dogs, locked up in a shed, which the owners used for hunting now and again. 'It was appalling,' she said. 'They would throw them bits of stale bread once a day, the poor creatures were starving and frantic.' One evening she could stand it no longer and let them out, having fed them a dinner bought especially from the local butcher. The next day the owner of the shed arrived at her friend's house, furious. 'He knew that only the English would let his dogs out. We had to own up and my friend apologised for my behaviour. I just wanted to kick him.'

Julie Fletcher says that when they first moved here they used to see a hunting dog tied up all day long across the river from their house. 'He was never let off except to hunt,' she says. 'They would throw him some scraps and give him water every day. We got so distressed that we approached the people one day and talked to them about it. 'Oh don't worry about him,' they said. 'He's used to it.' 'Eventually he died, and still attached to his chain they carried him off to bury him.'

How does one explain this fundamental difference in attitude? The dogs I describe above are purely for hunting purposes. But it is not only hunting dogs that are cooped up all day long. Guard dogs in France have a pretty bad time as well. These animals are seen as purely functional and are not part of the family or kept for pleasure. At Château de Conas, they have an Alsatian called Bush (named after the elder American president) who is a guard dog. He is tied up most of the day and barks whenever anyone arrives. Alex, my friend who lives there, would as soon take him for a walk as invite him to dinner, although her father-in-law does take him round the vines occasionally.

One of Simon and Julie's neighbours, François, has a dog called Bruno. Bruno spends 22 hours out of 24 locked in a pitch-dark basement. At 8am every day, François brings him out and ties him to the railings in the road. Bruno then stands there barking for an hour while François gets ready to take him for a walk. 'If we've had a late night we always sleep in the spare room at the back,' says Julie. 'Otherwise we get woken up by poor Bruno who comes out literally blinking at the light.'

But does every French person behave the same? Curiously it was a Frenchman, Blaise Pascal, a 17th-century philosopher, who said 'The more I see of men, the more I admire dogs'. But maybe this says more about French men than French dogs. Pierre Desproges, the French stand-up comedian (an extraordinary thought in itself) came up with the following:

*Plus je connais les hommes, plus j'aime mon chien.*
*Plus je connais les femmes, moins j'aime ma chienne.*
(The more I know of men, the more I love my dog.
The more I know of women, the less I love my bitch.)

Pascal seems to be in a minority. I have never seen so many stray dogs and dogs left tied up as I have in France. Why would a dog never be tied up and left to bark in an English village? Because someone would report it to the RSPCA. Here it is such common practice that the French equivalent, the SPA (*Société Protectrice des Animaux*) would be snowed under.

Although I have never seen dogs cooped up in England and let out only to defend a property or hunt, Laurent Garosi, a French qualified vet who has been practising in Suffolk for seven years, says the Brits are as bad as their French counterparts. 'The main difference, at least in the south of France, is that dogs are sometimes kept outside,' he says. 'Obviously then they are less a part of family life but I wouldn't say there is any difference in their treatment.'

Not all vets agree with him. I spoke to one based in the Loire. He preferred to remain anonymous. 'I hate the way the French treat animals as something to make money out of,' he says. 'They have no feelings. They only see animals as objects. I can't wait to get the USA, Canada or Britain where I will no longer feel like I'm battling against the rest of the population.' He thinks vets in France are undervalued and underpaid.

There is a huge difference in mentality and it goes all the way up to government level. In the UK so-called puppy farms have been wiped out because of new Kennel Club rules that took effect in the year 2000. These rules state that any breeder of pedigree dogs is only allowed to register one litter of puppies a year. In France, no such rules exist and consequently unscrupulous farmers are breeding two litters a year from young bitches until they are aged three and four. Then they sell them on to even worse puppy farms where they breed them to death and take their offspring to the markets where unsuspecting people buy them. Clearly these will not be very social or healthy dogs.

I heard about Thérèse Pelon, a Frenchwoman who has dedicated her life to dogs. She was a vet but decided against having a surgery and began studying dog behaviour. She also started to breed Leonbergers, a fine old breed measuring over one metre at the withers. The French canine society found that selling the dogs was easier if they were smaller and more aggressive, so they encouraged breeding with the runts of the litter. Thérèse gave her breeding card back and decided to go it alone. She has thus saved this race from extinction. However, the canine society has refused to allow her to call them Leonbergers, so she has given them the name *Lion d'Occitanie*, from the region in which she lives.

When we first moved here people would ask me if there was anything I didn't like. There are two things, the drivers and the dog poo. My local town is a beautiful medieval town with a wonderfully illustrious history and stunning buildings. When my mother first came to visit she said she felt like writing a letter to the mayor that read: 'Dear Sir, I have enjoyed my trip to your glorious town enormously. I would have liked to look up at the historical buildings, but was too busy scanning the streets for dog poo.'

Montpellier, another elegant place, has become a meeting place for Europe's down and outs. If you were homeless, where would you rather sleep rough: in the sunny south of France or in Glasgow? Many vagrants have dogs because the French system is such that arresting someone with a dog involves so much paperwork the police can't be bothered. These dogs live, eat and defecate all over the city. There are specially equipped little vans that go around cleaning up, but wherever you step in the exquisite pedestrian centre you have to watch out. I once asked an official at the mayor's office what they were doing about the problem. He conceded that it was a difficult issue but said that it was really up to the police.

If you complain to your local mayor about a dog wandering around loose or barking, he or she will write a letter to the owner or visit them. 'Dogs are a big problem in villages,' concedes Jean Martinez, the mayor of Caux. According to Martinez, it is the foreigners (and by that he means not only the Dutch, English, Swedish, German and so on, but also the people from northern France) who have a problem with dogs. 'If you are born in the village, dogs wandering around is part of daily life. You don't see it as a problem. It is only those who don't come from here who complain about them.'

I have always thought of myself as a cat person, probably because I was bought up with a mother who surrounded herself with cats and found dogs 'smelly'. But since I came here, my life has become linked with dogs in several ways. The first thing that happened was that the house came with a dog. I remember the first time we came to see it. As we drove up the drive, a wolf-like creature came bounding towards the car, frothing at the mouth. We sat in the car while it circled, looking menacing. Eventually the owners came out and released us. Jazzy, as he

*Dog laws in France*

🐕 The land belongs to private owners. You are only allowed to walk on designated tracks and footpaths across it. (Look for yellow and blue signs.) Your dog could be shot if found running free in a hunting reserve or on farmland.

🐕 Most walks around parks or leisure environments demand that you keep your dog on the lead. You are also supposed to have a rabies certificate with you at all times to show the authorities if required.

🐕 You can face a prison sentence of up to six months if you abandon your dog. Your dog must be identifiable at all times; breeders like Stephanie sell puppies with a microchip and a medallion to wear so that people can take your dog, if found, to the vet to be identified. Make sure they wear this on their collar at all times!

🐕 Have good strong fencing to prevent your dog escaping and think of getting third party liability insurance for him/her. Remember that healthcare is private in France, and if your dog causes a car accident, someone—in all likelihood the owner—has to pay for the ambulance, hospital, and the fire brigade.

🐕 Put a notice on your gate warning people that they enter at their own risk. (Do not, however put one of those '*chien méchant*' signs up as you may be admitting liability.) If your dog bites anyone who enters uninvited, you are covered. If your dog attacks under other circumstances, you could face hefty fines and even prison.

🐕 Watch out for ticks, they are much more dangerous than in the UK. You need to get a potion which you put on your dog when the tick season starts in the Spring. We have a plastic contraption with which you get them out, and it doesn't risk leaving anything embedded. Dogs die of so-called tick disease in France and you need to take precautions.

🐕 Issues about noise with neighbours are always difficult. In France, the basic rules are that you can have up to nine dogs in kennels without having permission, and any number of them in the house! You are definitely allowed one guard dog, which can bark when visitors arrive. Beyond that, if someone wants to complain to the mayor they can, and it will be investigated. The best thing is to be at least 100 metres away from your neighbours. At a distance of one kilometre, you are generally safe. As a rule of thumb, allowable noise is determined by the type of neighbourhood. If you live by a busy main road you can make quite a lot of noise; if you live in a secluded hamlet virtually any noise will be frowned upon.

🐕 No one can stop you from having dogs in rented accommodation. If your dog damages anything, you obviously have to pay for it, and it will be grounds for terminating your lease.

🐕 You can take your dog on holiday with you to campsites and hotels, as long as it is well behaved and covered for rabies. Dogs are also allowed in most shops and restaurants.

was called, turned out to be friendlier than we first thought. In fact, when we sat down in the drawing room on our second visit, once the sale had been agreed, he sat next to Rupert and put his nose in his hand.

'I see you like dogs,' said Mme Millière, the previous owner of the house.

'Oh yes,' nodded Rupert and smiled, anxious not to offend her or jeopardise the sale.

'Good,' she smiled back. 'Because it's his house. He belongs here. We can't possibly take him with us to a flat in Nîmes.

Anyway, you'll need a guard dog here.'

It seemed like a fine idea. In fact, we were both so overjoyed at the thought of moving there she could have said she was leaving her ten grandchildren and we probably wouldn't have objected.

We took a picture home with him to show Hugo and Julia. They were delighted. In fact, they seemed more interested in him than the house itself.

When Rupert arrived to take possession of the place, a few days before me, Jazzy was there to greet him. At that stage our furniture hadn't arrived and Rupert slept in the garden while Jazzy guarded the entrance of the house.

He was an extremely effective guard dog. He would bark if there was a car within a few hundred metres of the house. He was a brilliant alarm when you were swimming naked in the pool. Jazzy was also very good at keeping guests under control. That first summer a rather hungry friend of ours was staying. When she got up for a midnight snack she found Jazzy blocking her path to the kitchen, snarling menacingly.

The problem with Jazzy was that he was slightly unstable. He would chase cars and bark at them as if they were trying to murder us. He once chased a lone jogger into a water-filled ditch, and only a few very fast cyclists made it past the house without being overturned. The previous owners had got him from a rescue home and, although no one knew anything about his background, he gave the impression that he'd been badly treated. The other disadvantage was that he had cataracts in one eye so would often knock over the babies because he couldn't see them.

But the climax of Jazzy's menace came one night during a dinner. We had started with homemade saffron risotto, and were finishing off a leg of lamb when disaster struck. Our friend Norman is extremely fond of dogs and had spent the evening telling us how lucky we were to have Jazzy. 'He's a great *dawg*,' he said, in his New York accent. A former chief executive of a car manufacturer and big player on the stock market, he was talking about the world of high finance when Jazzy slunk in from the terrace and sat next to him. I briefly heard Norman talk about some director or other whom he had known, before I went into the kitchen to check on pudding.

A minute later I heard an awful howling noise. At first I wondered whether it was Norman getting dramatic while telling a story, or whether he had been given some bad stock market news. I was on my way to see what had happened when Georgia, Peter Glynn-Smith's daughter, came into the kitchen looking pale.

'Can I have some ice and some tea-towels,' she said. 'Jazzy has bitten Norman and it looks bad.'

I gave her the ice and towels and ran after her to see what was going on. Norman was leaning back in his chair, with blood pouring from his nose.

'Stand aside,' said one of the guests in a rare display of energy. 'My father was a doctor.' (A psychoanalyst, it later turned out.)

He put the ice and tea towels on Norman's nose and declared he would have to go to hospital. Peter's wife, Dominique, being French, was volunteered to go with him.

'It's only a scratch,' said Norman, as we all tried to stop him looking in the mirror as he left the house. 'Don't remonstrate with Jazzy,' were his last words as he was led off to hospital. Jazzy was outside on the terrace looking sheepish.

I went to sit down when I spotted something on the floor. It could have been a piece of lamb but looked a little under-cooked. I went white and pointed.

'It's not Norman's nose,' said Rupert, grabbing a piece of kitchen paper. 'But I'm going to make an executive decision and remove it anyway. We don't need it here.'

The next day we visited Norman in hospital. He had had a serious operation, whereby they grafted some skin from his thigh onto his nose. He was absolutely wonderful about it all.

'Don't do anything to that *dawg*,' he told us. 'It was my fault.'

Rupert told me that Norman had hugged Jazzy after feeding him a piece of lamb. Jazzy had got frightened and lashed out. There was much discussion as to whether the dog was to blame or not, but I think we all knew there was only one thing we could do.

The dog had to go. But where? France is not like England. There are not mad people on every street corner willing to take on a nose-eating, cyclist-chasing Alsatian. There are over 10 million dogs in France according to the *Société Centrale Canine*, (compared with 6.8 million in Britain) and not much of a support system.

This became evident not only when we were looking to re-house Jazzy, but when Cordelia and Tim, friends of mine who eventually bought a house down here, rescued a dog.

They were driving to meet us for dinner in a café on a particularly nasty road called the D13 when they saw a small dog thrown through the air. The car that hit him simply carried on and as they drove past they saw the dog lying in the middle of the road bleeding. Tim turned the car around and pulled over. Cordelia and the children, Katie aged 17 and Orlando aged 12, stayed in the car as Tim braved the relentless traffic of the D13 to reach the dog.

'It was awful,' says Tim. 'He was lying there with blood coming out of his mouth. The only part of his little body he could move was his tail, and he wagged that when I spoke to him. My French really isn't good enough to soothe someone, so I spoke half in French, half in English.' By now other cars were stopping to see what the problem was and one lady telephoned the fire brigade.

Up at the café, some other friends arrived who had driven past the scene on the road. They hadn't recognised Tim but when they told me that there was some dog dead on the road 'and some lunatic with it,' it didn't take me long to work out that it had to be him.

The firemen arrived and Tim was convinced they would just scoop the little dog up and that would be the end of it. 'They were amazing,' he says. 'So careful and gentle.'

The following day they went to the fire station to see if the little dog had survived the night. They were told he was at vet's in Clermont l'Hérault and so they went up to see Roujan as he had now been named, because they had been on their way to the village of Roujan when they'd rescued him. They were told he was a wonderful patient and had charmed all the staff at the clinic. He had some terrible injuries including a ruptured stomach and a broken back leg.

'I think by this stage our fates were intertwined,' says Tim. 'We asked what would happen to him if no one claimed him. The vet just shrugged her shoulders. I asked if we could take him and she was visibly delighted.' They were told that if they wanted to take him on they would be liable for some of the costs of his medication, as well as ongoing treatment and vaccinations. But they said they would stand the cost of the operation to insert a clamp in his leg.

'In total we would have to give them about €400 and so we decided to adopt him on the spot. He really was such a lovely dog and I'm convinced he recognised my voice from the day before. The only question then was what to do with him for the six months' quarantine before we could take him back home to Scotland,' says Tim.

But the problem of where to house him for six months was getting urgent. They were leaving in two days' time and Roujan needed a home. It was after the second visit to the vet and about two weeks into Roujan's quarantine that Jean-Pierre and Geneviève showed up at my house looking slightly embarrassed.

'Madame,' said Geneviève, wringing her hands. 'It's about the little dog.'

'Oh God, what's happened?' I asked her. My first instinct was to panic. Cordelia and Tim would be heartbroken if anything happened to him.

Geneviève beamed. 'Nothing has happened to him. But he's adorable.'

'Yes?'

'Madame, Jean-Pierre and I were wondering if we could look after him until he goes back to Scotland.'

Sadly for Jazzy, we couldn't find anyone willing to take him on. We thought about keeping him as an outside dog, but it would have meant we could never ever relax with the children around. They didn't understand that he could be dangerous. Julia had had a scary moment with him some months earlier when she got her head too close to his and he snapped at her.

There was only one thing to do. I called the vet to make an appointment.

Sometimes life in France can seem really complicated. This was one of those times.

'You can't just bring him in for an injection,' said the vet.

---

### Bringing your dog back into the UK

To move a dog from France to England you need proof that it doesn't have rabies and also a good-health statement, which must be signed by a vet between 24 and 48 hours of your trip home. This is a form saying the dog has been treated for fleas, ticks and tapeworms. When Tim took Roujan back to Scotland he had to delay his trip while he found a vet in Calais. Although he had the necessary paperwork, it had been signed three days prior to departure. There is a Pet Travel Scheme within Europe (PET) which requires pets to be fitted with a microchip.

You can call the PETS helpline on 0870 241 1710.

Roujan arrived in Scotland in the early hours of a chilly Spring morning. He immediately chased the cats and ate their food. Tim's other dog, Derry looked on fairly unamused. After two days of trying to mount each other, he and Derry finally realised it wasn't going to work and are now the best of friends.

---

'He has to come in and be psychologically assessed. This takes at least three visits. If, at the end of the third visit, it is deemed the logical solution, then we will put him down.'

This seemed like a ridiculous way to deal with the situation. In the end, Rupert and his brother took Jazzy for a final walk with a gun borrowed from Ray, our neighbour. It seemed a more dignified way of dying than an injection from a vet following psychoanalysis. One minute he was wandering around the mountains, the next he was gone. It was one of the most difficult decisions we ever had to make.

We decided to get a new dog almost immediately. Partly because the house felt empty without Jazzy, but also because Geneviève said we couldn't live here without a dog. It wasn't safe, she told us.

After much discussion we agreed on a Labrador puppy, though quite what we thought it would do if we were ever threatened by burglars I don't know. Anyway, I remembered my grandmother's Labrador with much fondness.

I started scouring the small ads for a suitable candidate. For some reason we decided it had to be female and a purebred, in some moment of madness we must have thought about breeding from her. We found a dog for €280 in an ad. She whimpered on the way home as she snuggled into my shoulder. This little bundle obviously wanted her mummy. Sam, as she was now, grew. And grew and grew. A fatter dog I have never known. We decided what she needed was a friend to run around with. When a neighbour of friends was about to drown 11 puppies we said we would take one, Coco. We had had Coco for about a year when our third dog arrived. A stray Alsatian, he was attracted by her being on heat. Sam had also had her admirers, one a rather mangy-looking longhaired stray, who was nicknamed Shoe. This is because every time I saw them I would say 'shoo', so Olivia thought that was his name. When his even less attractive mongrel friend arrived for a piece of the action he became known as Box. These two quickly went away again once Sam was off heat. But Wolfie, as we'd nicknamed him, showed no signs of leaving. This was probably because I kept feeding him. He was painfully thin, and, although Rupert kept telling me not to feed him, because 'the last thing we need is another dog,' I just couldn't help myself. I later found out that Monika was doing the same thing.

Wolfie was very shy and would keep away from everyone. Sometimes on a walk he would lift his head as he passed me and lick my hand, which I think had something to do with the fact that I fed him. I adored him; he seemed to have such a noble spirit, unlike the two Labradors who were sweet but terminally stupid.

But Rupert was just not happy with him around. 'Remember what happened with Jazzy,' he warned me. And then one night Wolfie started barking at 3am and wouldn't stop. When the French want to get rid of dogs, they just abandon them. I have always found this an abhorrent practice, but now found myself agreeing to do the same.

'Wolfie will be fine,' said Rupert. 'He's a survivor. He'll find another home. We just do NOT need a dog barking all night.' As we drove away, I watched him look at the disappearing car and felt horrible. He was intelligent enough to understand what was happening. I would almost rather have left one of the others behind.

It was around lunchtime the next day when Rupert walked into the kitchen looking amazed.

'You will not believe who is wandering up the road towards the house,' he said.

I rushed out and there was Wolfie, looking a bit thinner and certainly stragglier than the day before, but fine. And he was home.

'Oh well,' said Rupert. 'I guess it was meant to be.'

Wolfie settled in well. He began to nuzzle Rupert's hand as well (once he'd forgiven him for trying to abandon him), and it seemed to me a little as if we had resurrected Jazzy.

# Lesson 15

# Disasters

Someone told me recently that 60 per cent of Brits who move to France give up and go back home within the first two years. At first I thought this couldn't be possible, but the more I meet people who have moved here, the luckier I realise we have been.

We came here with no real idea of what we were doing. I spoke almost no French at all and was heavily pregnant. We arrived in a house we knew nothing about except that we loved it, in a region we had only seen as house hunters. I had no idea who would look after our children when I was working, or even if I would be able to continue to work.

After we had moved, people kept telling me how brave we were. It didn't seem brave to me. All we had done was swap a stressful life for one where the fundamentals, such as our home and the climate, were so much better. Already that made a huge difference to our lives. Then there are all the other factors like good state education, a safe environment, fantastic healthcare, great food and so on. It seemed to me it would have been braver to stay in southeast England. But when I see the sorts of awful things that have happened to people on moving here, I can begin to understand why people thought us brave, or even mad.

Countless things could have gone wrong which would have made our lives extremely difficult. They could still go wrong, but I hope now that we're settled here we will be in a better position to handle them.

*James and Alice—a nightmare sale*

James and Alice are good friends of mine from Sussex. They had always wanted to move to France and finally bought a lovely house in a village near to us two years ago. 'Living in France had always been James' dream,' says Alice. 'He had quite a continental upbringing and works in the wine business. He was so enthusiastic about it that it became my dream too.' When James sold his shares in a wine freight business, they had the money to start looking. They decided to look close to the city of Montpellier and the beaches, with the benefits of the Mediterranean climate.

'We'd been down several times and really hadn't seen anything we liked. Then we saw this place and just fell in love with it. It had everything we needed. We wanted to be in a village, to be able to walk to the bakery and the bar, and to be involved in village life,' says Alice. During the sale there was just one point that worried them. There was a right to buy on the part of the council for a piece of land in their garden. Four metres of their garden could be taken, if necessary, to build an access road from the main road, down the side of the property to a vineyard, which was designated building land. 'We were not unrealistic about living in a village, we know they expand, and four metres we could just about cope with. It still meant we could build a swimming-pool, which was something we had stipulated as a condition to the sale all along' explains Alice. 'We were assured by the vendors that there had been talk about this project for years and that it had never come to anything. They said the project would never happen because the bend in the road was far too dangerous.' They had a London-based *notaire* handle the sale and, satisfied with his findings, the sale went ahead.

Once the sale had gone through, James and Alice discovered that the project was far from dead. In addition, the reserve was not for four metres, but for eight. And there was going to be a

> ### Roads along your property
>
> Sarah and John Palmer bought a house near Aix-en-Provence four years ago. It is in the middle of a village, on the main road. 'It didn't occur to us that this might cause us problems in the future,' says Sarah. Six months ago, they had a letter from the mayor informing them that the road was going to be widened and that three metres would be taken off their garden to carry out the project. 'We have tried to fight it,' says John. 'But apparently there is nothing we can do.' The Palmers will lose a significant amount of their garden, which is small in any case. 'Luckily the swimming-pool is at the other end from where they want to chop up the garden,' says Sarah. The Palmers will not be paid for the land, as the mayor has a legal right to the land in the interests of the community. In some instances the land owners might be paid compensation but not where the alignment is of fairly limited effect. Before you buy, check whether your land is close to a road that could be upgraded, straightened or enlarged. This is called alignment and your lawyer should be able to obtain a something called a certificate of alignment stating your property is exempt. However, be aware that the situation may change in the future.

housing estate in the field next door to them. 'This will totally ruin the property, the whole ambiance will go,' says Alice. 'In addition, we won't be able to build a pool. Our home is going to be decimated. It is a very stressful experience. I always knew they would build something on the land, which I had accepted, but never imagined half our garden flattened to make the access road.'

James and Alice's first mistake was to trust the vendors. Because they were English, they believed them when they told them the project was dead. 'When we signed, the previous owner was busy cracking open bottles of champagne,' says Alice. 'I realise now that they were more for them than for us.' The building work on the estate starts in a few months. There are going to be 55 houses and the only access road will be the one they build by taking part of James and Alice's garden. Alice is being pragmatic. 'We will just let them get on with it and then eventually build a big wall to regain our privacy,' she says. 'Once it's all done and the garden has grown back up again we'll decide whether or not we want to sell it.'

To add to the stress of the housing estate, James and Alice's 17-year-old son Adam was attacked by a dog as he stopped at a nightclub on his brother's birthday to find out what time it opened. 'He was approaching the barrier to the car park when he saw a man with a dog. He just had time to say '*Excusez-moi monsieur*' before the dog jumped on him, bit through the muscle in his forearm and took two chunks out of his leg,' says Alice. 'The man then called him off, but not before he'd done a lot of damage.'

Adam's brother and sister-in-law took him to hospital where they treated him for the bites. The next morning the police were called and took a statement. An identity parade was organised but Adam couldn't positively identify the owner of the dog, so the case was dropped. 'I can't fault the police,' says Alice. 'They came straight away and were very professional. But you wonder what sort of people would set a dog on a boy who was just asking for some information.'

The dog incident was James and Alice's second encounter with the local police. Just a couple of days before they had been broken into while out at lunch with friends. 'We left around 11 and when we came back the place was ransacked. I have no idea who could have done it, but there were a few people in the street as we waved goodbye to our neighbours.' They were told by police that it was quite a common occurrence and that a house just up the road had been burgled three times recently. 'They knew exactly what they were looking for, just cash, credit cards and jewellery. In fact, the most valuable thing in the house were my pearls, which they left. They probably thought they were fake. I'll never leave money or credit cards in the house again.'

James and Alice's whole French experience seems to be jinxed. About six months ago the sewers in the village broke and the sewage poured into their garden. James decided to do something about the mess and started clearing it up. He was already practically blind in one eye due to glaucoma. Whilst he was cleaning the mess up, a small particle got behind the retina of his good eye, causing a serious infection. They rushed back to England but after much treatment the doctors declared they could do nothing to save his eyesight. He is now almost blind, is unable to drive and can't carry on working, which means they have no income. Despite all this, they still love it here and want to move here full time one day. 'In spite of everything, I just relax as soon as I get here,' says Alice.

*Angela Thomas—death and floods*

Angela and Ken Thomas retired to a village in Provence called Vallabrègues in 1996. They had come from Wrexham where Angela was a night theatre sister and Ken was a crane driver. They had always loved France and Angela spoke French. 'We thought about going around the world,' says Angela. 'But then we thought, what's the point? What do we end up with at the end of it. Better to invest in a house in the sun.'

They had been living in Vallebrègues for seven years when Ken had a stroke. 'I came downstairs one day and found him with his head in his hands saying he didn't feel well,' says Angela. 'He looked terribly pale, so I called the doctor.' The doctor was there within ten minutes and immediately called an ambulance. Ken was taken to hospital where he was given all manner of tests within half an hour and Angela was told he would have to stay in for a few days. She moved into hospital with him and only went home to feed their cats and tend to the garden.

Ken was not in a good way, hardly speaking and losing weight. He hadn't spoken to her for three weeks when one day, as she was straightening his arm, he looked at her and asked: 'What are you doing?'

She was totally taken aback. 'I'm straightening your arm,' she replied.

'Oh why don't you piss off you soft sod,' was Ken's response.

'I have never been so happy to be told to piss off in my life. I cried and hugged him and it felt like I had my Ken back.'

Ken seemed to make a remarkable recovery. He started moving, eating a bit more, and talking. The doctors couldn't explain what was going on but agreed he could go home. Angela was given a prescription for all the things she would need like a wheelchair, an electronic bed, an invalid armchair and went off to kit the house out. She didn't have to pay anything for any of this and in addition a nurse came twice a day, as well as a home help three times a week.

Ken was delighted to be home. He spent a lot of time talking to his cat and watching sport on TV. But after a few days he started to develop a terrible rash. Angela called the doctor again who said an emergency blood test was needed. At 6am the following day, a nurse came round and by midday they had the results. They were not good. Ken's kidneys were malfunctioning. He would have to go back into hospital. This time Angela was not able to stay with him so she commuted from their home to spend the days with him.

Then it started to rain, and rain and rain. 'It seemed like it was never going to stop,' she says. One morning she was about to leave when she heard the flood warnings on the radio. They were telling people to cancel all non-essential journeys because the roads were too dangerous. 'I called the hospital and told them what had happened. They said he was fine and that they would send him my love. I told them to tell him I would be in the following day.'

Angela had a visit from the fire brigade, asking if she wanted to be evacuated. No, she didn't. She was told to move as many belongings as she could to the top floor and to turn off the electricity if the water started to come in through the front door.

Some friends offered to move her car to a hill above the village. Her neighbour Marie arrived to stay in her hall, as she didn't have a top floor. Angela had also rescued a cat she found hanging onto a piece of wood floating in her garden. She carried what she could upstairs, including all her bottles of wine, and she and Marie lifted the heavier furniture like the sofa onto tables.

The next day there was no way she could get to the hospital. The water was now all over the first floor of the house and the streets were full of water gushing past. She called again to make sure Ken was OK. He was fine, they told her. That night the stray cat and Ken's cat had a fight and knocked Angela's stack of wine bottles down the stairs. Now the house was not only flooded with water, but wine, and broken glass. Angela was clearing away what she could when Marie came downstairs.

'Aren't you cold?' she asked her.

'It was only then I realised I was picking up the broken glass stark naked,' says Angela.

They were four days into the siege by this stage. On the fifth night she spoke to the nurse on duty at the hospital, a man she and Ken had got to know well.

'He's not good,' he told her. 'He's not talking to me any more. I think you'd better get here.'

Angela managed to get to the hospital by taking a hugely roundabout route. When she finally saw Ken, she was shocked.

'He had lost so much weight, he looked terrible. I went completely mad with the staff and asked if they were trying to starve him to death.' Angela moved back into the hospital to be with him. A day later she went off to get a coffee and on her way back to room was met by a nurse.

'She told me Ken wasn't well. I told her I knew that. 'He's really not well,' she said. I said I knew that too. But when I opened the door I saw what she meant, he was an awful ivory colour. I ran over to him and took him in my arms, I told him we would never be apart and that I loved him very, very much. Then he died.'

'I felt like death was trailing me around like a cloak. I went back to England for Christmas, and on the boat over it got very choppy. We're all going to sink, I thought to myself, and it's my fault.'

Angela's advice to anyone who goes through what she did is to have someone at your side who knows how the system works. For example, as with births, deaths need to be registered within 24 hours. At least in the south, the French are much keener to bury or cremate people quickly, the norm is within 48 hours. The custom here is also to put a table with a book of condolences outside your house. According to a friend who lives near Nancy in the Lorraine region, things are different up north. People either offer their condolences at the cemetery when the bereaved are standing in a line after the burial or people leave their card in a basket at the entrance of the church.

'I was amazed at how many people signed the book,' said Angela. 'Even though Ken didn't speak any French, he was universally liked in the village because he was such a happy person.'

Ken was cremated and Angela has kept his ashes. 'The agreement was that whoever died first would keep the ashes of the other one. When I die our ashes will be mixed together and put in the garden of our house.'

There is no question of going back to Wrexham though. 'My life is here now,' she says. 'I like the people and the way of life.'

*Colin and Tuk Hudson—a swimming pool saga*

Building a swimming pool is a top priority for many Brits coming to live in France. Our pool was already here, but I had a swimming pool drama about a year after we moved here. Having handed over £1,800, 30 per cent over the original estimate, to change my pool from a chlorine to a salt system, I watched it turn from crystal blue to murky green.

The crunch came when a guest asked if it was safe to go swimming, or 'are there alligators in the pool'? I called my pool man to ask him to sort the problem out. The system he'd installed obviously wasn't working. His response, 'read the instruction manual. If you want me to come out it's €95 a visit.' I was furious. Rupert threatened to throw the man in the pool if he showed up and tried to charge us €95.

Finally I telephoned the manufacturer of the salt system, they promised to sort out the problem. A technician arrived at 9.30pm the next evening and checked out the whole operation. 'Your pool man didn't put enough salt in,' said Nicolas Tedesco, Export Manager of Pool Technologie. 'Add a bit of hydrogen peroxide to get rid of the green and salt and then it should all be fine.' A week later I had my blue pool back again. I thought maybe I had been foolish to go for a small operator and that maybe a big name with a reputation to protect would be safer.

Not so. Some friends of mine, Colin and Tuk Hudson, ordered a pool from Diffazur in Montpellier for their house in France. Diffazur is one of the biggest names in swimming pool design and manufacture. Just after Colin and Tuk paid their final installment of €4,500 the Diffazur office they were dealing with went bust. They were left with a concrete bunker having paid almost the whole cost of the pool. 'We made several calls to the head office,' says Tuk. 'They have been incredibly bad at responding. The work was supposed to be guaranteed but they refused to confirm that at first.' Meanwhile the Hudsons, who paid for three quarters of the pool up front in order to get it finished before the summer, were left in the sweltering heat looking at a hole in the ground where mosquitoes breed. Finally Diffazur took responsibility for its franchise and finished the pool.

*Anonymous—divorce in France*

Divorce laws in France are quite different from those in England. When I first moved here a lady got in touch with me who had been the victim of what can only be described as a confidence trickster. They were married in England when the lady, let's call her Susan, was around 30. Her husband, we'll call him Tim, didn't work but was instead going to do up the house, which Susan had bought and they had moved into. Susan worked full time as a psychiatrist. 'He did nothing,' says Susan. 'He told me he was depressed and that he wanted to start a new life. By this stage we had a daughter and she was having a terrible time at school in England, so I agreed to sell up and buy a place in France.'

When they bought the house in France, although it was all with Susan's money, it was easier for inheritance tax purposes to put it in their joint names.

'As soon as the deal was done, he changed. He became violent, cruel, even lazier than he had been at home, simply horrible,' says Susan. 'I put up with it for three years and then eventually told him to get out. He turned to me and grinned. 'I think you'll find my dear, that the law in France is very different to the law in England. Here this house is half mine and there's nothing you can do about it'. We sold the house and he took half. I was forced to move into a small flat with our daughter. Looking back on it, I think the whole move to France was just a way to get some money for nothing.'

In a recent case, a family had been living here three years totally outside the French system. The husband worked for cash as a plumber and the wife looked after their five children. He then ran off with someone else, leaving her alone with the kids and no income. As they had not been paying any social security contributions, she is not on the system and therefore not eligible for help. It is worth remembering that you do need to register with the social security otherwise you could find yourself seriously strapped if you become ill or, as in the case above, your source of income runs off with a local doxy.

A friend of mine is just going though a divorce. She and her husband have three children together. When they bought the house, they bought it in his name. 'It never occurred to me that we would ever fight about ownership,' says my friend. Because the house is in his name, she has no right whatsoever to any of the proceeds from it. In fact, her husband doesn't even have to sell it. In addition, as her husband has been working for cash and declaring his income as nil to the tax authorities, any judge will assess him as unable to pay any alimony at all. 'Quite how I'm going to survive with three children, I don't know,' says my friend, who is now struggling to find a job having been a house-wife and a mother for the past ten years.

*James and Barbara Sands—cash come-back*

A lot of people who buy properties or land here pay a portion in cash. This means that both parties avoid tax and is often seen as a goodwill gesture. The problem with doing this is that you have no recourse should things go wrong, as James and Barbara Sands found when they bought a fishing lake in the Mayenne. They took a career break from their jobs in a police force in the north of England to move to France and set up a Carp fishing holiday business.

'We were fed up with the massive stress we were under at work, the rising crime rate and the rat race that is life in England,' says James. 'It sounds cheesy, but we wanted to give it a go and live the dream while we were still young.' James and Barbara, both in their early thirties, sold their respective houses in order to buy a lake with four hectares of land. 'I'm a keen angler and Barbara is a keen gardener,' says James. 'We both love the outdoors so this was an ideal thing for us.'

They paid for the land and the lake above board, but paid £8,000 for the stock of fish in cash. When they got to France, they paid a company £1,000 to net the lake so they could see exactly where they stood in terms of fish stock. There were only four Carp left in the lake. There should have been around 150. When they asked their neighbours what had happened they were told that the previous owner had had a party there a couple of nights before they got there, had the lake netted, killed all the fish and sold them.

'We have absolutely no comeback,' says James. 'But we were in the wrong for agreeing to buy them for cash in the first place, but that's just how it works over here, everyone seems to do it.'

James and Barbara's problems continued. They had been told

when they bought the land that they could have a mobile home on it and that getting mains electricity and water to the land wouldn't be a problem either. When they applied for permission to put a mobile home there, they were told that this was not possible. They could have a static caravan but not a mobile home. They bought a second-hand caravan from some people in Nantes. It was only when they got it home and told their neighbours about the transaction that they realised they had been tricked into paying VAT on it. 'You don't pay VAT on second hand goods in the UK, but here I didn't know what the form was so I just paid up,' says Barbara. 'It seems to me the locals here see the Brits as having more money than them and something to fleece at every opportunity. Every single time we have bought materials we have been quoted a price and then told to pay way over that price at the end.

On top of this, James and Barbara had their applications for mains water and electricity turned down. They are going to have to dig a well and pump out water from that. 'Our wonderful neighbours, who are from Paris, have agreed to install a second meter and we will run an underground cable from that for the electricity,' says James. 'But we're going back to the UK in the winter, we have to go back to work. I'm told 50,000 Brits are leaving the UK every year to come to France. They need to know it's not all as rosy as it is on the TV. If you come out here with your life savings, they soon disappear. And people might say we were naïve, but isn't everyone when they move to a foreign country?'

James and Barbara will carry on with their plans to run fishing holidays but only as a sideline. 'All this has totally put us off moving here full time,' says Barbara.

*David and Jan Denholm—insurance, what insurance?*

David and Jan Denholm bought a holiday home in the Languedoc and insured it with Groupama, the French insurance company. During severe winds one winter, part of their roof was blown off. As a result, their bedroom was totally flooded and everything in it ruined. 'The walls and ceilings were stained,' says David. 'The bed and mattress ruined. We came to France immediately and repaired the roof with the help of a local builder.' They went along to the Groupama office to deal with the insurance claim and were told that under the section dealing with floods none of the roof repairs were covered, as they were caused by natural events.

'We were totally amazed,' says David. 'And we also felt we didn't get satisfactory answers to our questions like, what if we had neglected to mend the roof and the rain had eventually caused it all to collapse?' The Denholms were only given 50 per cent back on the cost of replacing all the bedroom furniture and had to pay for the painting, roof and repairs to the walls and ceiling.

According to my friend Jacques, this happens all the time. 'If the village is not declared the victim of a *catastrophe naturelle* by the *Conseil des Ministres* after studying the dossier presented by the commune, the expenses are yours to cover,' he says. 'After the last earthquake in eastern France I noticed a few cracks in the walls. But apparently there were not enough people who had suffered damage and the town has not been declared *catastrophe naturelle*.'

The moral of the Denholms' story is obviously to check your insurance policy very carefully. If you don't speak good enough French have it translated, or if you live in a region that is likely to flood then ask specifically about the cover for this. Don't assume that things are run in the same way as in the UK. Stephanie Godwin (mentioned below) found her premium was too much one year so decided to cancel the policy and buy another cheaper one. You can't do this in France, you have to give at least two months' notice by registered letter. Her old insurance company is now trying to sue her for the premium.

*Stephanie and Jeremy Godwin—not qualified to work*

Stephanie and Jeremy Godwin moved to the northern

Mayenne in search of a better life for them and their three children. Originally from Beaminster in Dorset, their children were being bullied at school for wanting to study and they were generally fed up with England. Jeremy had worked as an accountant for 15 years and Stephanie had worked as a teacher for 15 years. 'I have a PGCE and an MA in education, as well as my 15 years' experience,' she says. 'But when I tried to get a job here, they told me I had no relevant qualifications and no relevant experience. It was the same story for Jeremy. The only place he could get a job was with an international firm in Paris. The French system is impenetrable.'

A lot of people I have spoken to have found that there is no way you can carry on with the career you had at home without getting the equivalent French qualifications. 'Most of the English out here are totally broke,' says Stephanie. 'They just can't get work. We've used up all our equity just keeping going. Now we can't even go back.' Stephanie and Jeremy decided to abandon their job search and have instead started breeding dogs, something they started while still in England. 'Thank God we brought some of the dogs with us,' says Stephanie. 'At least we can start trying to make a living from them.'

Jacques says Stephanie was unlucky. 'It sounds as if she didn't knock on the right doors,' he says. 'In my 32 years at the university I have used the services of countless English people as teachers. They set themselves up as *professions libérales*, which is a little tricky at first (tax, URSSAF tax etc) but quite feasible. And there are also private schools which don't have the same requirements as public ones.'

In my experience, those who have best succeeded here are expats who work for companies in the UK. They get paid well and they don't have the hassle of trying to make it within the French system. If you have a job that is transferable, like teaching, you should talk to your local education board or equivalent and find out exactly where you stand before you move.

*Tony and Carole Tidswell—denounced by Brits*

You may remember reading about Tony and Carole's problems with the French taxman in chapter five. The reason they had problems in the first place was probably due to someone denouncing them. Denouncement is a phenomenon the English normally find hard to cope with, although it is quite common in France.

'It's just not part of our culture in the UK,' says Carole. 'However much I hated someone, I would never denounce them to the taxman. It's just not something that would ever cross my mind.' The French are constantly wary of denouncers. They advise you not to get a new car, in case your neighbour denounces you. All the local artisans I know are always extremely wary of working for cash anywhere they might be spotted by the village denouncer. This is obviously a habit that goes back to the war when the French were busy denouncing each other to the Germans.

If you denounce someone, the taxman has to look into it. So the person is faced with the enormous hassle and expense of a fiscal investigation. If the taxman gets any money out of this, the denouncer gets a percentage. It reminds me of the secret police in communist Russia, the whole system is too nasty for words. And what is even more shocking in Tony and Carole's case is that they were denounced by Brits.

The person who denounced them had contacted Tony with a view to offering him his services in terms of advice on tax and insurance matters. He visited him and talked to him about their situation. 'After some meetings and general discussions it become clear that the advice was not relevant,' says Tony. 'And told him I didn't want his services.' The man then said Tony owed him £250 for the time he had already spent with him. Tony told him not to be so ridiculous, paid him £100 and told him to go away. A few days later Tony and Carole received a very threatening letter from the man saying that if Tony didn't pay the balance he felt he owed him, he would report him. 'You might consider it unwise to build up a collection of disgruntled ex-advisors and helpers who know—or can guess at— the foolhardiness and danger of your background,' he wrote.

Tony ignored him and a few weeks later he found out he had been denounced and the investigation began.

Over the next six months the tax authorities demanded a series of interviews and examinations where every penny which was paid into any bank account anywhere in the world for a two-year period was scrutinised and, unless they were able to prove with certified documentation that the money was not income, tax was demanded.

Under French law a person accused of anything has to prove their innocence. The proof required is dictated by the tax inspectors and this invariably means only officially stamped and certified documents will be accepted. All receipts are treated as income, no expenses of costs are allowed or offset so Tony and Carole are now having to pay tax on personal items they have sold as well as loans from friends they have had and repaid. 'Apparently what we should have done was get a contract drawn up and signed in front of a lawyer stating that this money was a loan,' says Tony. 'But when a friend helps you out, you don't think about doing that.'

Having gone through their bank statements, the tax authorities decided they owed them €17,000. They appealed against the decision and I went with them to the tribunal just outside Montpellier. It was a terribly impersonal building and there was no indication of where we had to be. Even the receptionist, when we showed her the letter stating room C1 in some annexe was confused. Eventually we found our way to the right place, but the tribunal was running late. There were two other cases to be heard before Carole and Tony's. We were shown into a waiting room and after a few minutes a rather pinched looking woman showed up and started rustling papers. Carole and Tony both nodded towards her. 'That's the woman who's ruining our life,' said Carole.

Carole, who speaks flawless French, spoke to the woman and

explained that they had new evidence to show the tribunal. They had managed to get their bank to find the originals of cheques the tax authorities had labelled as non-declared income and this was proof that they were, in fact, not revenue. The tax inspector took them and added them to her dossier.

After about an hour's wait, we were shown into the hearing room. Inside there was the judge, two men from the tax authorities and two others whose role it was to ensure that there was a fair hearing. The judge started off proceedings by going into the background of the case. Then it was up to Carole and Tony to defend themselves. Carole explained that during their 14 years in France, they had tried to do everything in the right way and that they had not tried to hide anything. She was incensed that they were being told to pay tax on the sale of highly personal possessions like a painting she had sold that her father left her and Tony's camera. The judge nodded and said that was all very well but in France you have to declare everything. He then asked the tax inspector if she had any additional information to bring to the hearing. She told him about the photocopies of the cheques Carole supplied. After that we were allowed to leave.

The judge upheld the decision of the tax authorities and Tony and Carole are paying the €17,000 off, in instalments. 'It is so galling,' says Tony. 'Because we don't owe one penny of it and we're now really up against it.' To add to their problems, Tony recently had a letter from the fraud squad who have demanded an interview with him. 'At first I thought I had been denounced again,' he says. 'People don't really realise, but the expat community is very bitchy. But apparently the fraud squad thing is an automatic process after a tax inspection.'

*Mrs X—compulsory purchase*

When Mrs X (who wishes to remain anonymous to avoid further proceedings from her local authority) moved to a lock keepers' cottage on an island in southwest France, she imagined a stress free life listening to the sound of the river flowing by. She had been there for two years when she received a registered letter from the county council.

The letter informed her that the council wanted to purchase half her island, restore the locks and put interlocking steel gates across the island to stop water from seeping into the ground. This would effectively cut her island in two. 'It's amazing how really bad post always arrives at the weekend when there is nothing you can do about it,' she says.

Mrs X, unlike most foreigners that buy in France, had had the foresight to meet the mayor before buying the property. 'We discussed the possibility of making the river navigable again and opening the locks before I bought the cottage,' she says. 'The mayor seemed perfectly reasonable and I even confirmed in writing that, if it would come to it, I would gladly grant the necessary rights of way to enable the river to be navigable again. I therefore thought this registered letter was a mistake.'

As with all compulsory land purchases, there would have to be a public enquiry. During this enquiry, Mrs X reiterated that she would not stand in the way of the project. 'Because I did this, the council could not proceed with a compulsory purchase order,' she says. 'They had to come up with something else. I was completely floored by what it was.'

The council told Mrs X that although she had bought the property, including the lock, from a private individual, she was in fact not the owner. The council had made a mistake, they told her, when they said they wanted to buy the lock, because it wasn't hers to start with. It was already theirs. While the public enquiry had been going on, they had bought a water mill further up the river which they maintained gave them a right to the lock right in front of her lockkeepers' cottage. 'At some stage in the 1960s the properties had all been owned by the same proprietor,' says Mrs X. 'According to them, they had simply become the owner of the lock when they became the owner of that water mill. You have to hand it to them, it's highly creative.'

Mrs X decided to get a lawyer involved. What followed was six years of legal wrangling and stress. At one stage 17 people showed up to start work on the island, including two policemen and two lawyers. Mrs X and her lawyer saw them off.

'The thing you must remember if you're going to take on the authorities is never to be intimidated,' says Mrs X. 'I was determined not to give in. Their attitude made me apoplectic with rage and fired me to continue the fight, despite a lot of people around me saying I should just give in.'

Mrs X thinks that she would still be fighting the case today if there had not been a change in personnel at the county council. 'Some new employees at the council were given the case, possibly because the others were worn out or bored with it,' says Mrs X. 'Anyway, it suddenly became possible to discuss matters. Someone realised I had not been hindering the project and what should have happened six years earlier happened in 2000: we started discussions. We agreed that the council could take 300 square metres of my island, namely the two sides of the lock and the water in between, instead of the proposed 3000 square metres. They paid me a symbolic Franc.'

Compulsory purchase rights (the right of the local authority to buy the property) are often overlooked by Brits buying property in France. 'The laws have come about because in France land is often divided up into small parcels. This makes it very difficult for the community to carry out any major projects so it has to earmark land for development and collate it as and when it comes up for sale,' says Dawn Alderson, solicitor with Russell Cooke Associates

According to Dominique Semenou, the mayor of a village called Souilhe in south west France, cases like Mrs X's are extremely rare. 'We don't compulsorily purchase land on a whim,' he says. 'We would try to come to an amicable agreement. I have only had to expropriate land once, when we needed to build a purifying plant and the owner of the land wanted to sell it at several times the market value.'

# Happily Ever After?

Almost everyone from England I meet asks me the same question. Will we ever go back?

There are plenty of reasons for staying here. Climate, healthcare, value for money in housing market, quality of life. The list goes on and on. Where in England there are frustrations getting from A to B, here the roads and trains are superb. The doctors here wait for you, not the other way around. The schools are good. The quality of life is hard to beat. The bread is fresh daily. But there are also some reasons for returning to England. Language, culture, sense of humour, friends, Waitrose.

There was an astonishing opinion poll reported recently in Britain in which three-quarters of people asked said they would leave the UK if they could. Certainly for those coming to France the formula is superficially simple. You leave England with some money in the bank, having sold your house at the top of the market. You buy somewhere in rural France, which is five times the size of your terraced house in England, and you still have some change left over. 'Twice as nice for half the price,' as one estate agent neatly puts it. The rest will see you through until you can get your career started again, from your new headquarters in the middle of nowhere. The children will go to the village school, where they will be fine, even though they don't speak French. You will have lovely family dinners together made up entirely of fresh produce purchased from your local market and a bottle of wine from your new wine-making neighbour and soon to be best friend.

It used to be that the people who moved to France were retired. They didn't need to make a living. They had their pensions and their savings and muddled along quite happily. The kind of people who are moving out here now are totally different. Of the estimated 50,000 Brits who relocate to France a year at least half, if not more, are young families who need to earn money. In France, earning money is not as easy as it is in England, which could be why there are 250,000 young French people living in the UK, because they cannot get jobs at home. The options open to a Brit moving here are even more limited than those open to the locals. First, the language barrier is a problem. Unless your French is fluent, you're going to have to get a job that only requires English. Even if your French is fluent, a professional qualification from the UK doesn't necessarily translate in the French job market. You can set up your own business, but the administrative nightmare associated with this is horrendous. You could also end up like Tony Tidswell, the subject of a tax inspection. The French taxman doesn't on the whole like entrepreneurs.

The people who seem to do well here in my experience are those who can still work for people in the UK. Of course you have to pay tax here, but the whole thing is less complicated. You also don't have to struggle to find work here and the money is often better.

I have never heard of anyone giving up and going back because of the bureaucratic nightmare that life can be here. But there were times when I felt like it. Getting onto the healthcare system was almost impossible. Getting our *Carte de Séjour* (a residents' permit, now no longer a requirement) was tougher than A Levels. When the time came to get my *Carte Grise* for our new car I was terrified that I would have to spend more than half the day fighting with bureaucrats.

As it turned out, the official couldn't have been more helpful and the whole thing was over in ten minutes. I think what had happened is that by then I had learnt not to fight the system. The bureaucracy is unbearable, but it works. And if you have the right piece of paper then it all goes well. The problem with coming here as a foreigner is that you often don't have the right piece of paper. For example, as a foreign family we will never have a *Livret de Famille*, an official record of your family. This means that to get a family railcard (50 per cent off rail travel if you have three or more children and lots of other perks) we have to produce all sorts of other documentation that I still haven't had the time to do. I spoke to the regional council about this problem and asked if there was any way at all I could get one. 'Oh yes,' came the helpful reply. 'Marry a Frenchman.' Seems a little excessive just to get cheap train tickets. If you're not already married and intend to get married, you can beat the system by getting married in France. That way they have to give you a *Livret de Famille*.

Many older people I have met have gone back because they miss family, especially their grandchildren. I came across one couple who had lived in Provence for 12 years and were moving back because the wife wanted to see their grandchildren grow up. Not having family and friends around is undoubtedly one of the big downsides to living in France. We have been quite lucky as most of our friends and family seem to have bought houses here as well. But it's true that some of my good girlfriends are still in England and I do miss seeing them a lot. Some argue that it's nice, because when they come out and stay you get to spend much more time with them, but in my view nothing quite compares to seeing someone every couple of weeks.

When you start a new life in a different country, you have a lot of expectations. You expect things to be better than they were at home. You have an image of your new life and the way you will settle in happily. This image can be very easily damaged if the reality is that your children, for example, are totally miserable.

Renting before you buy is a good idea for some people, though we didn't do it because once we saw our house we knew we didn't want to live anywhere else. It means you can get to know the area you are thinking about moving to and really see if it's for you.

One of the problems a lot of Brits find is that rural France, however idyllic, can be quite limiting. If you come from London and are used to how things work there and having everything around the corner, ending up in a big farmhouse in the Auvergne might sound like a blissful idea. But you should think about the practicalities of living somewhere where the nearest supermarket might be 40 minute drive away. You should also be aware that the people in rural France can be quite conservative and may not be as friendly as you'd hoped. I have found everyone here extremely nice, but I think they're quite used to foreigners by now. In places like the Mayenne and Lorraine there are those who have found they are not. But wherever you are, if you learn the language and join in, you will be accepted. That is easier said than done.

Moving house within the same country is a stressful experience. Add to that a change in culture, language and bureaucracy and you can begin to imagine how tough moving here can be. The language thing is something that gets a lot of Brits down. Moving abroad is not a new concept for the British. They have been moving abroad and taking over vast parts of the world for centuries. But nowhere in those former colonies did they have to learn another language. They simply imposed their own system. In France you can't. You will find that a lot of people only speak French. I was amazed when I first came here at how few of the locals spoke or understood any English. In retrospect this was typically British of me. Why should they speak English in the south of France? How many Devon farmers speak French? The English are notoriously bad at languages. And French is a notoriously difficult language. Something somewhere has to give. And I don't see the *Acadamie Française* budging.

In answer to the question will we ever go back—ever is a long time. But at the moment I really can't see it happening. We have sold our house in England now, so even if we wanted to it would be difficult. I thought I would get very emotional when it came to selling up, that it was the final link and so on. Of course it's not. We will always go back to England to visit people and maybe the children will be educated there in part. England will always be there. And even if we live here for the next 50 years we will always be seen as '*les Anglais à Sainte Cécile*'. We will never be French, however much we integrate and however long we live here. I don't think our children will be either. But does that matter?

It is a difficult place to live in some ways, for many of the reasons I have written about in this book. But the upside is huge. A German proverb speaks of 'living like God in France.' It's the German equivalent of living the life of Riley. Most days, that is exactly how I feel.

# A More Successful Move

1. *Adequate Research*:
Carry out a full analysis of what you are looking to achieve
from moving abroad and then spend as long as possible
reviewing all the possibilities regarding areas and then precise
locations in those areas. Check out the selected location at
ALL times of the year. Some places are very hot in the
summer but suffer from unexpected cold and wet in winter, as
well as horrendous winds. Some places are a dream in the
winter and a mass of tourists and the related activity in the
summer (fun fairs, noise, clubs which are open all night in
summer but are virtually invisible in the winter). You should
also check that the house you are planning to buy gets the sun
when you most want it, be it morning or evening.

2. *Obtain a precise costing for renovation in advance of buying*:
Too many people assume that because the price of property is
cheaper in many locations than in the UK, renovation of an
old property will also be less costly. This is almost always
NOT the case and material and labour costs can be significant-
ly higher than expected, and this can break the budget you
have set for the property and the work.

3. *House size and income*:
Remember that if you are buying for long term retirement
the big house at the top of the hill may look everything you

ever dreamed of now, but in ten years' time you may regret that it is not more suited to more limited mobility. Too many people buy the most expensive home they think afford- able and believe that the cost of living will remain constant— it does not. Being over-housed and under-capitalised is a common mistake a few years down the line. Jane Austen said 'Nothing in life is as comforting as an adequate income.' Make sure your income is adequate in the long term. Make sure that whatever it is that brings you an income at home, can do so abroad. Many UK qualifications won't be valid in France, for example.

4. *Tax matters*:
Do not think that what works in tax planning in the UK will also work in the country you are moving to: most frequently the opposite is the case. You must take advice from an inde- pendent qualified adviser who understands and has experience in both UK tax matters and those of the country you are moving to, or you could end up paying more tax than is necessary.

5. *Pension matters*:
Get advice from a pensions adviser who knows the rules in the place you are moving to, as in most non UK locations the rules are very different. For example, the UK concession that allows you to take part of your pension fund as tax free cash is almost always taxable income in the new country. You can avoid this risk if you act early to establish your fund in a manner designed to avoid it.

6. *Language barrier*:
Learn the language of the new country as this will prove to be possibly the best investment you make in settling into your new home. Too many Brits expect foreigners to speak English and in many cases they do, but it is to your advantage to be able to converse at a reasonable level if you are to integrate

into your new community. Many people give up and go home as a result of isolation caused by the language barrier. You can start learning as soon as you decide to move. The internet is a great resource, try www.french.about.com for daily French lessons. For more information on French correspondence courses please go to www.cned.fr. This stands for *Centre National d'Enseignement à Distance*.

*7. Medical facilities*:
Check out the precise facilities regarding local medical facilities from the local doctor to the nearest hospital, and the likely costs. It is too late to find out the facilities are inadequate or expensive once you have a problem. This is especially true if you have a pre-existing medical condition. Arrange suitable medical insurance and also make sure it includes repatriation cover so that in the worst event you can be relocated back to the UK for specialist treatment should you choose to do that.

*8. Integrate*:
Don't just join the local community of expats. Get involved in local community activities. By taking part in all the local events and assisting wherever possible, you will find a new level of acceptance in the community. Too many expats miss out on the best of their community by limiting their contacts to other expats living locally.

*9. Investment arrangements*:
What you needed from your investments before you relocated abroad may not be suitable once you have arrived. There are many investments that are tax favoured (PEP's, ISA's, TESSA's etc) in the UK but which are fully taxable in the new country. You will need to rethink what you want from your investments both in the short and longer term, and to receive advice from an independent adviser who knows what the investment tax breaks are in your new country.

10. *Legal advice*:
Never purchase without independent legal advice. It is common in Europe, for example, to use the same lawyer as the vendor. This is not sensible. If you have a problem with the purchase in which you need your lawyer's advice, you have to be sure that he is on your side in any dispute and not trying to serve two masters.

Always have legal documents translated into English and ideally use a lawyer who understands both UK and local property laws, so that he can relate all the various aspects in your own language and culture.

# Make Your Move Go Faster

*Utilities*

There are lots of things you can organise in advance of your move to make life easier when you get to France. For example, most agents will help you have a phone line connected and also sort out electricity and gas with the local EDF (Electricité de France) and GDF (Gaz de France) branches. If your agent can't help you, you can contact your local utility direct via website www.edf.fr.

*Phone*

The easiest thing if you want to get a phone number sorted out before you move is to go onto www.francetelecom.com/en/worldwide/europe/focus and contact a France Telecom representative there. Cordelia, a friend of mine who recently bought a house close by, was extremely impressed with the service. 'They found someone in the nearest France Telecom office to us who spoke English. She took our details and then gave us our new phone number. The whole thing took about 15 minutes. We immediately phoned the number and imagined the phone ringing in the lovely house we had just bought.' The lady even arranged for them to have the French equivalent of call waiting (called '*Top Message*').

*Bank account*

Before you do all these things, though, you need a French bank account. You should probably think about opening one as soon as you start looking for a house. Go to the bank of your choice with your passport, marriage certificate if you want a joint account, and proof of your UK address like a phone or electricity bill. You can also open an account from the UK. Several of the large French banks have branches in London. Crédit Lyonnais, for example has a branch in the City (www.creditlyonnais.fr). You can call them on 020 7588 4000. You can also go to a website specifically designed for British clients and run by Crédit Agricole, www.britline.com. This tells you how to open an account and gives you all sorts of useful information.

The word for current account in French is a *compte chèque*. One of the most notable differences between the banking systems in the UK and France is that it is illegal to write a cheque in France if you don't have the funds to cover it. If you do so, you are given 30 days to rectify the situation, after which a block will be put on your account for one year. During this time you are banned from writing cheques. In addition, your details are kept on a central list with the Banque de France, and if you try to open another account the police are informed. We have just discovered a brilliant overdraft facility which gives you up to an additional €2000 automatically as and when you need it. It's called *Compte Open* and is available with Crédit Agricole du Midi.

*RIB*

You'll find that in France it's impossible to do a lot of things without a *Relevé d'Identité Bancaire* known as a RIB. Even when you register at the social security office you need one, so they can take your contributions out and pay any refunds for treatment in. It's a small piece of paper you'll find in your cheque book, with your bank details on. You also use RIBs to set up standing orders.

### Birth Certificates

France is a country full of bits of paper. I sometimes wonder how it doesn't sink with the weight of them all clogging up bureaucrats' offices all over the country. When you move here, you will need not only your birth certificate but your birth certificate with BOTH parents' names. You will also need your marriage certificate if you are married, along with countless copies of your passport and any other official document you ever owned. These will all have to be translated by an officially recognised translator. They are very easy to find through the British consulate in Paris (+33 (1) 44 51 31 00, www.amb-grandebretagne.co.uk) or the French embassy in London, if you want to get them done before you move. You should take at least 20 photocopies of everything, so you have them to hand.

# How to Buy a House
# — The Law

Unlike English law, French law does not recognise the concept of subject to contract. An offer on a property should not be made unless you are absolutely certain you want to buy it. Before the offer is made you should consider all the conditions that you wish to include in the contract. We included a clause saying the purchase was contingent on us being able to raise the financing to buy the house as well as the findings of the land search being satisfactory (in other words that there were no plans for windfarms, motorways and so forth, close to the house).

✦

The next step is to sign either a *Promesse de Vente* or a *Compromis de Vente*. This may be prepared either by the *notaire* (a French lawyer who deals with property transactions) or the agent.

✦

In many cases, only the vendor's *notaire* is inserted in the contract. A buyer should not automatically agree to this, and should consider instructing his own *notaire*. Nonetheless, we were told it would make things easier if we used the same *notaire*. It is the purchaser who pays the *notaire's* fees. If there are two *notaires* involved, there is no extra cost to the purchaser as the notaire's fees are fixed by law and the fee will be shared.

✦

Contracts are signed early on in France and contain '*Conditions Suspensives*'. These are the conditions mentioned above and must be satisfied before completion can take place. Until the conditions have been fulfilled, completion of the contract is not possible. If any of the *Conditions Suspensives* are not satisfied, the contract is deemed to be null and void and the purchaser is entitled to the return of his deposit.

✦

These conditions are important and need to be checked carefully. In particular, the contract may need to be amended to take into account the fact that a mortgage is needed to finance the purchase. This clause cannot be added at a later date. The drafting of the contract is very important and a pre-printed form can *never* replace professional advice.

✦

French contracts are also usually conditional upon rights of pre-emption, in other words, that nobody with a right to buy the property does so. A strange quirk in French law is that it gives certain parties—such as the local mayor—the right to buy in place of the purchaser. If the right is exercised, the deposit will be returned to the purchaser. I have watched countless friends go through the nail-biting experience of waiting to see if the commune wants to exercise its right to buy their house. So far, it has never happened.

✦

The purchaser of a residential property is given a seven days' cooling-off period after signing the *Promesse de Vente*, during which he can withdraw from the contract without penalties.

✦

Following signature of the contract, searches are made. The *notaire* will obtain the equivalent of a Land Registry search from the *Conservation des Hypothèques*. This search will disclose any restrictions on the vendor's right to convey title and the existence of charges.

✦

In addition, either a *Note d'Urbanisme* or a *Certificat d'Urbanisme* is obtained. This is a document from the local authority which declares the existing use of the land and administrative restrictions or requirements which apply. The

*Certificat* may also give information on whether building is allowed, the density and other details of development. If the *Certificat d'Urbanisme* is positive, planning permission—*Permis de Construire*, will normally be granted.

✦

Once all these issues have been satisfied, the final completion deed, called the *Acte de Vente*, is drafted by the *notaire*.

✦

The signing of the *Acte de Vente*, the final deed of sale, has to take place before a *notaire*. The expenses, the *Droits d'Enregistrement* and the legal fees are also paid at the signature of the *Acte de Vente* by the purchaser.

✦

These fees include the *notaire's* fees, stamp duty and registration fees. Where the property is more than five years old, these will amount to approximately 6.5 per cent of the purchase price. These are payable in addition to the purchase price.

✦

For newly built properties, French VAT (TVA). at the rate of 19.6 per cent is usually included in the price as well as *notaire's* fees and taxes of approximately 2 to 3 per cent of the purchase price.

✦

If you do not wish to or are unable to attend completion in person you can appoint an attorney to execute the *Acte de Vente* on your behalf using a Power of Attorney or *Procuration*. This document must be drawn in French, signed before a Notary Public and forwarded to the Foreign & Commonwealth Office where a Certificate—*l'Apostille*—is annexed to give legal effect in France.

✦

You may find the *Acte de Vente*, a document many pages long in French legal jargon, bewildering. An independent advisor can review this document and explain the procedure to you in your own language and in terms you can understand.

✦

For exact and up-to-date information and help on legal issues always contact a legal professional first.

*An example of the right of pre-emption*

Before you buy a house you should check the classified zone of the particular piece of land or house you are buying. If it is an area designated for development you may find yourself pre-empted by the local mayor. Tim and Cordelia Simmonds recently bought a small village house with some adjoining land close to Perpignan. Before they signed the *Compromis de Vente* (the initial contract to buy) they were told by their lawyer that the mayor had a pre-emption right on the land just outside their house, where they were planning to build a swimming pool. He advised them to insert a clause in the contract stating that the property could only be sold as a whole entity. 'This meant the mayor would have to fork out for the house as well if he wanted to pre-empt us,' says Cordelia. 'It also means we are protected when we sell it.'

In France 90 per cent of all property is subject to pre-emption rights. This means the mayor of the local council has to provide a certificate of pre-emption before you can sign the final *Acte de Vente* (act of sale). Just 18 days before they were due to move into their dream chalet in a small French ski resort close to Geneva with their two young children, keen skiers Ian and Gill Edwards were told there was a problem. 'The house was sold, the removal was booked, the children registered at the local school and nursery,' says Ian. 'Then we had a call from the *notaire* to say that the council was buying the chalet.'

They went to France immediately to meet the mayor, and to see if the situation could be resolved. 'We found we had no rights,' says Ian. 'The chalet was needed for the local lift company.'

Gill admits that their first reaction was total shock.

'We felt very frustrated and extremely disappointed. We had understood that the chance of pre-emption was extremely remote, and would normally happen within the two months following the exchange. Pre-emption took place seven months later, by which time clients had reserved rooms, contracts had been signed and workmen engaged for the realisation of our long-held dream. We understand and see the reasoning behind the decision, it was the incredibly late timing of it which caused the major frustration. We were extremely unlucky.'

Ian and Gill are now waiting for a new-build in the village to be completed. 'We have had wonderful support, not only from the removal company Britannia Beckwith of Brighton, but also from both French and English friends in the village, whose advice and help in putting us up has been absolutely invaluable.'

(*Check also for alignment, see p. 204.*)

# Renting Out Your Home

There are some fundamental questions you need to ask yourself before you rent out your property.

*First*, why do you want to rent it out? Is it to make money or is it to cover your costs?

*Second*, how often do you want to be there yourself? Do you want to go there on certain dates, ie peak times when the rates are highest?

*Third*, what sort of person do you want to stay in your home? Will you accept children and/or pets?

The answers to these questions will determine how you should furnish and equip your property. You should probably in all cases go for good quality, robust furniture that can be easily cleaned and is low maintenance. Bear in mind that items like dishwashers and washing machines are essential. White tiles in the kitchen are not a good idea. You should sleep in all beds of your home to make sure the bedrooms are comfortable. Wooden or tiled floors with washable rugs and throws for soft furnishings are a good idea. *Do not put carpets in the bathrooms.* You should allocate a storage area or cupboard for your personal items, but try to leave a few things like vases out so the place doesn't look too impersonal.

Before your first guests arrive, you should prepare an inventory and a guest manual. This should contain relevant information about the property and the area such as information on the local town, leisure activities, house rules and how things work, who to contact in emergencies, as well as a contact number for someone who can sort out plumbing and electricity problems, and so on.

Also, before they arrive, make sure everything is as perfect as it can be. First impressions are vital. Make sure essential supplies, such as loo rolls, soap and kitchen paper, are available. Kitchen cupboards should have the basics like tea, coffee, sugar and UHT milk. If the property has been let out for more than a week, it is normal to provide a cleaner and a change of linen at the end of the first week. If at all possible have someone take the key from the guests and say goodbye at the end of their stay.

Keep a track of anything you spend on the house so you can offset the costs against tax. You must also let your insurance company know when you decide to rent out your property; your premium will probably increase, but if something happens and you haven't informed them, they won't pay up.

The cheapest option for renting out is to go for a website like www.frenchconnections.co.uk, www.frenchcountry.co.uk, www.holidayfrance.com, or www.holiday-rentals.com. You will pay an annual fee of between £100 and £190 for an advertisement with pictures, depending on how much space you want. The potential tenants contact the owner direct and the rest is up to you. This option is really only viable if the owner is on-site.

Holiday letting companies like Bowhills or www.somethingspecial.co.uk can also be useful. But owners should make sure there is an agent nearby. As far as using an estate agent goes, the fees vary. An owner can expect to pay at least 20 per cent. However, it can be well worth it if the clients turn out to be tricky. On the Riviera, www.francenetvillas.com offers a personalised service.

If you are buying to rent, bear in mind that house prices vary enormously across France. The south is more expensive than the rest of the country, and the Riviera the most exclusive. In the Languedoc, you can buy a tiny village house for around £35,000. On the Côte d'Azur, that will get you a garage. For a five-bedroom family house with pool, depending on location and views, you will pay between £200,000 and £400,000 in the Languedoc. Along the Riviera a similar property with a sea view would be around £1 million. In terms of living costs, the Languedoc is a lot cheaper than the Riviera. Cleaning staff cost around £6 an hour as opposed to £8 an hour. You can get a cook for £15 an hour, on the Riviera you will pay up to £40 an hour. Pool maintenance is around £240 per month, on the Riviera it is £300. The property tax (*taxe foncière*) depends on the size of your house, but for a five-bedroom house in the Languedoc expect to pay around £800 a year. On the Riviera a similar sized house with a sea view will cost about £3,000 a year. Insurance for a five-bedroom property will cost you up to £350 a year in the Languedoc. On the Riviera it is around £400–£500.

---

*Renting out your second home—a case study*
Tom, a friend of mine in our nearest village, owns a three-bedroom house, which he bought for £100,000 three years ago. He rents it out for July and August, as well as some weekends off-season, and sometimes for half term. His average rental income a year is about £10,000. During the peak season he gets £1000 a week. Out of this come his local taxes, both the *taxe foncière* (property tax) and *taxe d'habitation* (residential tax). The total combined is £1500 a year. The amount you pay is calculated according to how much land and property you own but also differs between local authorities. On top of this, Tom has to pay income tax on the rent. The standard rate for non-residents on their rental income is 25 per cent on the profits, which the revenue calculates as 28 per cent of gross income. In

other words, they give you 72 per cent relief for expenses such as maintenance and repairs. The gross income should also be declared in the UK and you will get a credit for the tax paid in France. After taxes Tom's profit is around £6500.

'That sounds great,' says Pat Bellis, of Riviera Search International. 'But he hasn't even started to pay for all the maintenance costs. These include a gardener, a cleaner, a pool man, the cost of water, fuel, electricity and so forth.'

The cost of employing people in France is astronomical. As an employer, you can end up paying 45 per cent on top of their salary for social charges. And employing people for cash is not an option, according to Dawn Alderson of Russell-Cooke Solicitors. 'It is totally illegal,' she says. 'And the authorities take a very dim view. It's a complete no-no, which could see you end up in court.'

Most of us don't have big enough houses to employ full-time staff, so what are the options for casual labour, if cash is out of the question?

*First*, and easiest, use a company or a sole trader registered in France, who will invoice you as a business complete with a *Siret* number, which proves the company or entity is properly registered.

*Second*, talk to your bank about setting up a *chèque-emploi-service* through which you can legally pay a casual worker via your bank account. This is a scheme within the French system to allow people to employ cleaners and gardeners cheaply and easily.

*Third*, draw up an employment contract whereby you, the employer, would have to issue pay-slips and also be responsible for the employees' social security contributions. This would also mean you need an accountant to with the pay-slips and so forth.

Tom uses self-employed gardeners and cleaning staff. The gardeners get £10 an hour and the cleaners get £6. In 2003 he spent £1,600 on both. His total profit is now £4,900. And he has still to pay for fuel (around £400 a year), electricity (another £600 a year), pool maintenance (on average £500 a year) and water, which is £700 a year. All these costs obviously vary according to the region you are in and how big your property is. Another thing to factor in is the changing rentals market. 'Gone are the days when people just went away in the summer for three weeks,' says Marcelle Spelling, Director and Co-Founder of holidayfrance.com 'Now they come for the weekend, for short breaks and so forth. But as a landlord you have to remember that the changeover costs the same whether they have been there for two weeks or two days.'

In addition to the costs of maintaining the property, Tom also pays to advertise it on the Internet with www.rentalsfrance.com. The amount varies, if he doesn't get any bookings, he pays nothing. If he does, he pays 10 per cent of the rental income up to a ceiling of £195. Another 15 per cent of his rental income goes to a local lady who sees the guests in and out and is on hand to deal with any problems. His profit is now down to £1,020. And that's before he's paid the mortgage.

# Working in France
# — Taxation

If you are living and working in France, you will be liable to pay tax in France on your earnings. In addition, you will also have to pay social charges and healthcare charges on your French earnings.

If you are employed in France, your employer will deduct all social security contributions at source. These include contributions to the healthcare system, unemployment insurance and old-age pension, and are usually around 18 per cent of your gross income. Employers do not deduct tax at source, so you will need to keep aside a portion of your income to pay your tax bill at the end of the year.

If you live in France but work for a UK company and your duties are carried out wholly in the UK, you are liable to pay tax in the UK on your earnings. France will not tax this income directly, but will take it into account when calculating the tax rates to apply to any other income arising in France (*taux effectif*). This method of double taxation relief is likely to change when the new 2004 UK/France Tax Treaty will come into force after ratification by both countries.

If you live in France but work partly in France and partly in the UK for a UK company, you need to split your earnings between the UK and France on a time apportioned basis. The portion of your earnings relating to your UK duties will be taxed in the UK, and taken into account in France for the *taux effectif*, as described above. The portion relating to French earnings will be directly taxed in France.

⇝

If you are self-employed in France, different taxation regimes apply, and the correct regime will depend on the nature of the activity carried out, and whether your profits are classed as 'commercial' or 'non commercial'.

*Commercial profits (Bénéfices industriels et commerciaux—BIC)*
Income from trading activities is taxable under this heading. Where your gross annual income is below €27,000, your profits will be taxed under the *Micro-BIC* regime. This allows you to deduct a flat 52 per cent for expenses, so only 48 per cent of your income is taxable.

*Non commercial profits (Bénéfices non commerciaux)*
This regime would apply to income earned from 'intellectual activities' and would apply to teachers, doctors, lawyers, accountants, architects etc. There is a *Micro* regime which applies where your gross annual income is below €27,000. The *Micro* regime allows you to deduct a flat 37 per cent for expenses, i.e. only 63 per cent is taxable.

The disadvantage of the *Micro* regimes is that they will always show a fixed profit. So, if your expenses are higher than the 52 per cent or 37 per cent flat deductions, you may choose to opt into a 'real' regime, which allows you to deduct actual expenses incurred, although you are required to prepare accounts which must be approved by the French tax authorities. The cost of preparing formal accounts under the latter regime should be taken into account when deciding which regime you elect to be taxed under.

⇝

In addition to tax, France levies social charges and healthcare

245

charges on all earnings, whether from employment or self-employment.

## Social Charges

These charges go towards funding the social security system in France. You will usually pay at a rate of 8 per cent on your earnings. In general, it is the gross amount of income received that is subject to the social charges, although for earned income you get a 5 per cent deduction for expenses, so the social charges are applied to 95 per cent of earned income. If your income relates to duties performed in the UK, you may be exempt from paying these charges on your UK earnings.

## Healthcare Charges

Healthcare charges are payable on your net taxable income at a rate of 8 per cent above a threshold of €6,721. Again, if your earnings arise in the UK, you may be exempt from the health-care charges on your UK earnings.

*This is a brief summary of what are complicated issues. I would recommend you always seek professional advice by a qualified practitioner in relation to your individual circumstances.*

# Learning French

Many of my friends have used the Michel Thomas CD set. This is for total beginners and costs around £60. It is published by Hodder & Stoughton. He maintains that you can learn without writing anything down or trying to remember it. On the CD you listen to him teaching two 'pupils', one of whom is so stupid you wonder how she ever found her way to the recording studio. But I suspect she's there to make us feel better. You can always tell his disciples, as they are very good on the word *confortable*, which he pronounces confortaaaaable.

There are hundreds of websites offering French courses. One of the most user-friendly is the BBC one. The address is

*A free language course*
One of the most maddening things about moving to France is the amount of bureaucracy you will be exposed to. It took me about 20 visits to the social security office in Béziers to get the family registered on the health system. Bureaucracy plays a central role in your life in France in more or less everything, from registering your car to enrolling your children at school. What you should do is to treat these bureaucratic battles as a free French lesson. That way they won't seem like a waste of time.

www.bbc.co.uk/languages/french/index.shtml. It is free, easy
to navigate, and has lots of different areas depending on what
you're after. For example, you can take a train, go for a drink
with a friend or practice your grammar. It seems especially
geared towards the beginner, but there is a fast-track section
for those with some French.

If you have Sky Digital you can tune into the French TV 5
on channel 825 before you get here and become an expert on
French culture, as well as language.

The Laura K Lawless site (www.french.about.com) is great,
lots of resources you can use to learn French from your
armchair. She sends you a French lesson every day, and when
I have the time to look at it, I find it extremely useful.

The *Alliance Française* organises courses all over the world
and can be contacted at www.alliancefr.org.

There are also several websites offering CD-ROMs for sale
either combined with online teaching or alone. The most
popular is probably www.linguaphone.co.uk. The tapes or
CDs are expensive, for example, £250 for a French course that
promises to take you from beginner to expert.

A company called Learn Direct at www.ad.uk.dou-
bleclick.net also offers CD-ROMs and an online French
course. Unfortunately neither are available to buyers outside
the UK, so it's only of use if you're still based there.

For a live teacher you could go to an intensive course in
London at BSL Interlenguas (www.interlenguas.co.uk, 020
7263 7589) but it would set you back £575 per day. I think
this must be more geared to business people. They also offer a
ten-day course for £5,500.

In France you can have a week's intensive language learning
for £275 with www.languagesabroad.co.uk. They have centres
all over the country and provide all manner of courses.

Along similar lines to Michel Thomas, there is the Rosetta
Stone learning method. It calls itself a 'dynamic immersion
method' and claims you will learn naturally without writing
or memorising. They kindly sent me a course to test, suggest-

ing I chose a language I know nothing about in order to assess how effective it is. I chose Russian and can now say lots of useful things like the boy and the dog, the boy on the aeroplane and the girl in the boat. I highly recommend it to people who have a visual memory. It is an active way of learning in that you have to pick the picture you think the person is describing, and quite a challenge to improve your marks every time. The website is www.therosettastone.co.uk. There are two levels for French CD-ROMs, level one is £149.00 and level two is £169.00.

But don't despair if the language issue gets on top of you and progress is slow. According to a recent survey of French adults aged between 18 and 65, 12 per cent of them find writing, reading and understanding simple texts in their native language difficult.

# *Vive la Différence!*
# — Frequently Asked Questions

Some people who think about moving to France are terrified by how different it is. The fact that you can't leave your property to whomever you like is hard to grasp for an Anglo-Saxon. The banks being closed every Monday seems crazy until you get used to it. I have found that a number of the same issues come up all the time so have decided to put them all together in one place.

### Capital Gains Tax

Capital gains tax is paid when you make a profit on a property which is not your principal home. A French resident selling a property which is the principal residence will not be taxed on any capital gain.

Residents and non-residents from the European union selling a property within five years of purchase will be taxed in full at 16 per cent on any gain, where it is a second home.

Residents from outside the European Union will be taxed at 36 per cent.

Between six and fifteen years after purchase any gain on the sale benefits from a discount of 10 per cent for each year of possession, thus after 15 years of ownership no tax is payable. The cost of property extensions, major improvements and renovations, supported by receipted accounts, may be deducted from the gain.

Bear in mind that social taxes, in some cases as high as 10

per cent, are also payable on any gain from property sales, although not by non-residents.

### *Taxe d'habitation* and *taxe foncière*

There are two types of local taxes relating to homes: *taxe d'habitation* (residential tax) and *taxe foncière* (property tax, similar to council tax in the UK). Residential tax is payable by anyone living in a property in France, property tax is paid only by the owner of the property. Both taxes are payable on main or second homes and whether you are a French resident or not. If your property is 'habitable' (i.e. furnished) on January 1st of any given year, you are liable for tax for that year. The amount of tax you pay will usually be based on the rental value of the property for the previous year, as well as the living area and factors like whether or not you have central heating, a swimming pool, location and so on.

### *Wealth Tax*

If you are living in France, wealth tax is usually assessed on your worldwide assets. The tax is payable on assets over €720,000 and rates start at 0.55 per cent and increase on a sliding scale.

The new 2004 UK/France Tax Treaty, which will come into force after ratification by both governments, provides substantial relief from French wealth tax for UK nationals (who are not French nationals). For the five years after becoming a resident of France, your wealth tax will be based on assets in France only; all other assets will be ignored. In the sixth year following French tax residence, wealth tax would then be payable on world-wide assets. Therefore, once the Treaty is ratified, you should try to arrive at the beginning of a tax year, rather than the end of the previous tax year, in order to stretch out the five year exemption time period.

### *Tax on rental income*

It does not matter where you live, or where you collect any rental for your home in France, or where your personal tax is paid. If the house you are renting out is in France, all income from it is considered as being earned in France and tax *must* be declared on this income in France. Tax must be paid here, even if you declare and pay tax in another country.

If you are already making a tax declaration in France you can add the property income to your declaration, deduct all relevant expenses and you are liable to tax at 25 per cent on the balance. If relevant expenses are greater than your income, no tax is due.

If you do not already make a declaration, the simplest system is a *regime micro* for your property. Under this scheme, you are only liable for tax on 30 per cent of the income; they allow you the balance as expenses. You pay tax at 25 per cent on 30 per cent.

In addition there may be local tourism and occupancy taxes. Your local *mairie* or *prefecture* can help with this information. These taxes are usually payable per bed, usually around one euro per night.

You are not likely to face double taxation if you have paid your taxes in France and then take the balance back home.

### Inheritance laws

This is a huge topic as the French inheritance laws are incredibly complicated and very different to the English ones. Even if you die in England, your French property will be subject to the rules of French succession law. In France you cannot disinherit your children. You are not free to dispose of your estate as you wish. Certain members of your family, such as children and parents (but not spouses), have an absolute right to inherit certain parts of your assets. Percentages vary according to the number of children, but where there are children and/or parents, a will that leaves everything to the other spouse will not be upheld. If you have one child half the [French] estate goes to that child. If you have two, two thirds of the estate are shared equally between the two children. If there are three or more children, three-quarters of the estate is shared equally between them.

One of the major problems is protection of the surviving spouse. Under French law he or she is only entitled to one quarter of the estate if children from a previous marriage involved. If there are only children in common involved, the spouse is entitled to a life interest in the whole of the property, which means he or she can live there for the remainder of his or her lifetime. However, the property cannot be sold without the approval of the children.

This is a complicated issue and you should always take legal advice about your personal circumstances, but here are three examples to guide you.

❧ A married couple—one of the partners has children

'I'm married to a man who has three children,' says Linda Lewis. 'I have none. We live in a house with no mortgage, which is in my name only as I alone paid for it. I want to know whether, in France, women can own property independently of their husbands as I don't want to be in the position of finding myself widowed and having to 'hand over' a share of my home to other people's children.'

The answer is that, as the property was purchased solely in Linda's name, it will not fall into her husband's estate and his children will have no rights over the property. If Linda had children, under French law on her death a percentage of the property would be divided between them.

According to Dawn Alderson, solicitor with Russell-Cooke, there are other issues Linda should be aware of. 'If Linda and her husband move to France, it would not only be the house which could be subject to French rules and rights for children,' she says. 'It would also be the couples' investments and other assets worldwide with the exception of any immovable property outside of France. This is because in all likelihood, they will be considered to be domiciled in France very shortly after taking up residence. Linda should bear in mind the question of who is paying for the property. If the funds are in her sole name at the present time, there is no problem if she purchases the property in her sole name. Should the funds belong to both her and her husband, we would need to ensure that the money for the purchase is in actual fact paid from her own assets and is not made from a jointly owned account.'

❧ A married couple—have children together and one has a child from a previous marriage/relationship

To make things easier, I will take the example of a father who has one child from his first wife, and two children from his second and current marriage. (It is worth noting that French law now considers children from non-married couples in the same way as children from married couples in terms of succession rights on their parents' estate.)

On the first death:

Scenario A: Should the father be the first spouse to die, the three children will equally have reserved rights in respect of his share, i.e. in this case, each child receives a quarter outright and the wife may by will receive one quarter outright also. If a valid will has been made and the spouse was given the maximum available portion, she could choose to inherit either a one quarter share and a life interest in the three quarters or a life interest in the whole.

Scenario B: Should the wife be the first spouse to die, then only her two children inherit her share as the third child has no parental connection with her. In this case, the two children would inherit each one third of her share and the spouse the remaining third by will. Again, the surviving spouse could receive a life interest in the whole property if a will had been made and the interest would be owned by the two children or the spouse could receive a quarter outright and three quarters in life interest. (Please note inheritance tax is payable by the beneficiary depending on the amount.)

On the second death:

If a life interest had been selected by the surviving spouse, this will obviously be extinguished and the children (three of them in scenario A, or two of them in scenario B) would become automatically owner of the whole property.

♣ An unmarried couple without children

The parents are also reserved heirs. If the deceased spouse had one parent, this parent is entitled to one quarter of his son's or daughter's estate and the surviving spouse can inherit the remainder by will.

If the deceased has both his parents, each parent is entitled to one quarter, and the surviving spouse to one half of the property. If no parents are alive, the property can be freely given between the spouses by will, subject to the payment of inheritance tax.

### Inheritance Tax

The French take the view that all the worldwide income and assets of a resident are taxable. The system is under review at the moment, but currently this is how things stand.
Inheritance taxes paid in France range from five to 60 per cent depending on the value of your estate and how closely your heirs are related to you. The amount of tax each child has to pay will be based on the sum inherited less an abatement of €46,000 each. The rate of tax for a spouse is based on the net sum less €76,000. The maximum tax rate for close relations is 40 per cent. For more distant relatives like brothers and sisters the rate of tax is 45 per cent and the nil band is only €100.

French law regards unmarried couples as unrelated to each other so the surviving partner has to pay inheritance tax at 60 per cent, except for the allowance of €100. Cordelia and Tim aren't married and have two children together. They decided to buy the house only in Cordelia's name to avoid the inheritance tax. In addition, both her parents are dead so there are no inheritance issues there.

So-called *donations* are an alternative way to pass money or property to children or grandchildren. Under this scheme, each parent can give €46,000 every 10 years and each grandparent can give €30,000 every 10 years. From 1 June 2004 to 31 May 2005 you can give €20,000 in cash or cheque on top of the above sums. To do this you don't need to involve a lawyer or *notaire*, just ask for a form from your local tax office.

You can give part of a house or flat to a child, up to €46,000 for each parent every 10 years and renew the operation for the following 10 years until the whole property is the child's. But this involves an official *acte* with a lawyer, with the corresponding expenses.

### *Legal costs on house purchases*

It was close to the end of the purchase process of our house that we were suddenly presented with a bill for £25,000 that we had no idea we would get. This was for the legal (*notaire's* fees) and taxes. As a rule, this sum is normally between 6.5 per cent and 8 per cent of the purchase price, and it is worth working out what the property will cost you, including all taxes before you decide to buy it. Of this amount, the *notaire* actually only takes between 1.5 and 2 per cent, the rest is taxes.

🍃 Who is responsible for the agent's commission?

This is something you need to know in advance, because the agent's commission in France is huge compared with the UK, it starts at 6 per cent and can go up to about 10 per cent. It is usual practice for the vendor of a French property to settle the agency's commission, although they will normally just factor it into the price. However, in some cases it depends on the negotiations. You should ensure that the price you agree is clearly stated inclusive or exclusive of commission and that the vendor is responsible for this.

❧ Is it possible to obtain a survey of the property?

Yes, although this is not usual practice in France, you can instruct an architect or a UK-trained surveyor to carry out a survey on your behalf. This can be arranged through a law firm, see for example www.frenchpropertylaw.co.uk.

❧ How long does the transaction take to be completed?

It varies from one case to the other and is normally something you agree with the vendor. In our case, we signed the *Compromis de Vente* (agreement to buy) in May and the owners said they wanted one last summer here so we agreed that we would take possession on September 1st. From the moment the *Compromis de Vente* is signed and the cooling-off period has expired, a three month delay is the norm. However, if the local searches or other paperwork have not been received by that time, the process will take longer.

# Swimming-Pool Laws

Pool owners should install one of the following:

1. A fence or a wall. This should stand 1.1 metre high from the ground and have a self-closing gate. It should be a minimum of one metre from the edge of the pool. The maximum is determined by whether the fence is still deemed to be effective, but it is probably not more than 10 metres. According to Tim Hammond, director, at Safer Pools, a network of 30 individual pool companies throughout France, this solution is the safest of all the devices. 'Because of the gate, the child cannot get in if the pool is unsupervised. The other advantages of a fence are that it will be accepted by all the insurance companies as a safety device, and also can take it down in ten minutes when the property isn't let or you're there on your own,' he says. With Safer Pools, a standard-size pool of ten by five metres costs around £1500 to fence plus £250 for the gate and another £250 for installation.

2. A cover. This is more expensive than the fence, but can replace both your existing winter and summer covers. They cost around £2800 plus an installation fee of £200. The disadvantage is that when the cover is off, you are not insured, so if your tenants decide to leave the cover off and someone drowns you could still be liable. Nets have not yet been approved but may gain approval at a later stage.

3. An alarm. The alarm sets off a 150-decibel siren in the house and by the pool, as well as flashing lights. It costs £600 and installation around £70.

4. A telescopic enclosure vaulting over the pool. This costs £8,000 or more. However, it does have the added advantage that you can swim all year round.

Hammond says people have been so confused by the law and its specifications that some have chosen to sell up and move back home rather than deal with it.

'Everyone will have to do something come 2006,' says Hammond. 'But there are questions as to how they will enforce the law.' As it is a law of the senate, it means it can be enforced locally. 'I don't think they will be too active about it initially,' says Hammond. 'But they will make an example of cases when accidents happen.' The punishment is a fine of £30,000, enough to buy several pool enclosures. As the mother of three young children, I am well aware of the risks of a pool, but can there really be a substitute for keeping your eye on the children at all times? Research from some states in America suggest that such legislation adds to the number of deaths by drowning, because parents stop supervising the pool area.

Cynics who remember the furore when France introduced a ban on smoking in 1992 in public places will take heart from the fact that nobody has yet been prosecuted under the tobacco law. I might well decide to cover my pool, but I'd like to be able to decide when and how I do it myself.

Whatever next? A law telling me I have to wear a swimming costume?

---

*For more information*:
www.equipement.gouv.fr
www.saferpools.co.uk, contact@saferpools.co.uk
Hotline     (calls from the UK)     0871 711 3371
                (calls from France)    06 62 28 04 79

---

# Buyer Beware
# French Leaseback Schemes

One of the most popular ways to sell new developments in France is through a leaseback scheme. Potential buyers get a free holiday home, while making a sound investment and getting a return on their investment.

This is how it works. The purchaser buys the freehold of the property and then leases it back to a developer or rental company. The owner is guaranteed a rental income, usually between 3 per cent and 7 per cent of the initial investment. At the end of the lease period the property is returned to the purchaser. The big advantage with leaseback is that the government refunds the VAT (19.6 per cent), providing that the lease runs for 20 years and you don't sell within that time. However, you usually have the option to use the property for three to six weeks a year at no cost.

So far, there seems to be no downside. You get a guaranteed return on your capital, the property is increasing in value, the developer takes care of all the rentals, you get to go there for your holidays and at the end of 20 years you can move in.

'For us it seemed like the ideal solution,' says Grant Hitchin, who was looking to buy a place via the leaseback scheme at the beginning of this year. They were considering an apartment just outside Paris for £35,000. 'My wife and I knew we wanted to retire in France and this way we could buy something now while prices were still affordable. The government VAT refund was our deposit, the monthly return was more than our mortgage would cost, and we could use the place for holidays.' Grant was about to sign up for a development in Paris when he came across a web site called www.frenchpropertydigest.com whilst surfing the web one evening. 'There was a huge amount of information on leaseback and after I'd read it, I decided to forget the whole thing.'

Tony Tidswell, who runs the site, is concerned that potential investors are being led astray by the leaseback scheme. 'It seems like a great idea,' he says. 'But having studied the leases these management companies are asking people to sign, I am seriously worried about what people are letting themselves in for. They may find that there are heavy penalties for opting out of the leaseback agreement and that they never actually have control of their property.'

The law stipulates that the management company has the right to renew the nine-year agreement automatically and that the purchaser is not able to cancel the lease without paying a huge indemnity and refunding the VAT on the purchase price.

'These schemes are moving towards deception in the way they are marketed by some web sites and agents,' says Tidswell. 'They are telling buyers they can get a house for no cash up front, which looks very attractive. But when you go into the small print, it can be a very different story. What people end up with is a steady return on their investment, but not much more. In some cases it can be described as an investment plan and not a property deal.'

According to Dawn Alderson, solicitor with Russell-Cooke Solicitors, leaseback schemes are not suitable for the average purchaser. 'What you have is a commercial-lease situation, which for the right investor is fine. But it is not geared towards the individual looking for a home. In that situation it can be a very dangerous thing to get involved in.' Alderson points out that the VAT refund is contingent upon the man-

agement ensuring that the development remains classified as a
*Résidence de Tourisme* during the 20 year period. 'What
happens if the management company doesn't fulfill these
criteria, or simply goes bust? They lose you the VAT refund
and it's a situation you can't possibly control.'

Web sites selling leaseback schemes describe it as a 'buy-to-
let with a free holiday.' In their frequently asked questions,
they maintain that after nine years the choice is yours as to
what to do with the property. In fact, the lease has to be
renewed legally so you do not have the choice. In other
words, even if the management company has said they will
hand over the property to you, they do not have the legal

---

### Leaseback checklist

- What is written into the lease agreement after the first nine years?

- What are the terms of the renewal or cancellation?

- Is the renewal automatic and will you have to pay a penalty if you do not renew it.

- How much does the management company charge for upkeep of the property?

- Are there any penalties, either in the purchase or the leasing contract if you want to sell?

- Are you free to sell to whomever you chose and free to advertise the sale openly?

- What happens if the management company goes into liquidation?

- Can another company take over the property and if so will you have the same contractual terms?

- As well as contractual issues, you should check whether there are any other factors that could affect the resale value such as proximity to flooding or strong winds.

right to do so. Some management companies get round this by setting up shell management companies that give you a lease that looks like you can opt out but that can in fact be wound up and replaced with another at the time of renewal.

Before signing anything, you need to go through the lease and check the points listed in the box. You would also be well advised to see a solicitor. If you do sign and regret it, there is a seven-day cooling off period, but you should send your letter of cancellation by international courier. There have been cases where the management company have simply ignored the registered letter or maintained it arrived outside the seven-day period. 'Leaseback is getting as bad a name as timeshare,' says an English estate agent based near Paris who does not wish to be named. 'I certainly won't be recommending any of my clients get involved with it.'

# Having a Baby

I moved to France when I was seven months pregnant. I knew
nothing about giving birth here, I didn't even speak the
language. I had already had one baby in England, at a natural
birthing centre, with no drugs and no doctors. It had been a
good experience and I was keen to repeat it. As it turned out,
for my first birth here I was fully drugged and had a
Caesarean. Here are things I wish I had known earlier.

*Covering the costs*

If you haven't yet left the UK the first thing to do is to get
hold of an E112 available from the NHS international services
(number below). This entitles you to medical care abroad for a
pre-existing medical condition, such as pregnancy. It was a
passport to free scans, x-rays, consultations and ultimately
childbirth and postnatal care. The only thing it didn't cover
was the £20 a day I had to pay to be in a private room. If you
are moving permanently, you should also look into getting an
E104 which is a statement of all your contributions in the
UK, and will mean you can transfer onto the French system.
You can get this statement from the Department of Health
(number listed below).

All costs should be reimbursed, you just have to fill in the
*Feuille de Soins* (a piece of paper, normally brown, which
details the care you have had and the cost) and send it off to
your local CPAM (*Caisse Primaire d'Assurance Maladie*).

If you live in France and are already on the French system, your costs should be covered automatically. It may be worth signing up for a private insurance (called a *complémentaire*) company to cover anything the social security doesn't cover for the full 100 per cent. I was able to sign up for one even though I was already pregnant.

*Prenatal care*

If you get pregnant in France and you want to have a baby within the French social security system, the first thing to do is to go to your doctor and fill in a '*Déclaration de Grossesse*'. This will normally take place towards the end of the third month of pregnancy and gets sent around to the various authorities and means your pregnancy is registered. The doctor you go to is up to you, but they must be agreed by the social security (*conventionné*). My local doctor recommended a gynaecologist to me who carried out all my monthly checks. This includes monthly blood tests to check for toxoplasmosis, measles etc. You take the blood tests to a laboratory of your choice, to find one look under *Laboratoires d'analyses de biologie médicale* in the yellow pages. During my first pregnancy in France they sent a nurse to take blood samples at my house to ascertain my blood group.

You will also have several scans during your pregnancy. Very early on they will be able to determine the sex, and if you don't want to know you should tell them. Most people in France find out, if they don't, they call the baby '*un bébé surprise*'. If you are over 35 you will be offered an amniocentesis to determine any genetic disorders. When I had mine they left the results of it (all fine) and the sex of my baby on the answering machine (which I didn't want to know). Towards the latter stages of pregnancy you will also have to meet the anesthetist who will talk to you about the kind of pain relief you are likely to require. Epidurals are freely available and having given birth without one, I thoroughly recommend them. In fact, the French are not big on natural childbirth, when I arrived with my ideas of a drug-free labour they all looked at me as if I was deranged. I know of only one woman here who has given birth at home, with the help of a midwife.

*Midwife*

A midwife is called a *sage-femme* (literally, a wise woman). Once your pregnancy declaration is in the system, you will

| | |
|---|---|
| *Useful baby vocabulary* | |
| Amniocentesis | *l'amniocentèse* |
| Baby | *le nourrisson/le bébé* |
| Birth/delivery | *l'accouchement* |
| Breastfeeding | *allaitement maternel* |
| Breech | *une présentation par le siège* |
| Formula milk | *le lait en poudre* |
| Forceps delivery | *l'accouchement au forceps* |
| Maternity | *la maternité* |
| Maternity benefit | *l'allocation de maternité* |
| Maternity leave | *le congé de maternité* |
| Pregnant | *enceinte* |
| Pregnancy test | *un test de grossesse* |
| Prenatal | *prénatal* |
| Postnatal | *post-natal* |
| Postnatal depression | *la dépression post-natale* |
| She is three months pregnant | *elle est enceinte de trois mois* |
| She's overdue | *elle a dépassé le terme* |
| Shit, it's twins | *merde, c'est des jumeaux* |
| The baby was two weeks overdue | *le bébé avait deux semaines de retard* |
| To get pregnant | *tomber enceinte* |
| Twins | *des jumeaux* |
| When is it due? | *c'est prévu pour quand?* |

have a letter from your local midwife inviting you to attend a course. Although this was my third baby, I went along. Not so much because I wanted to learn how to give birth, but partly to have a contact to call if I had any worries. Also it was a very good French lesson.

### Giving birth

You will give birth in a clinic or a hospital and are liable to pay only for extras, like having a single room, TV and phone. The average stay is five days. I loved my time at the *Clinique Champeau* in Béziers. I remember the first time being totally amazed when a lady in a white coat came in to tell me the day's menu and ask me if there was anything I didn't eat. Don't forget to bring all your social security papers with you to the birth, the whole system thrives on bureaucracy and the first thing they ask you for, as you come panting into the clinic, is your social security status.

Both my births in France were relatively pleasant experiences. The first one was more like surgery than childbirth, but all involved did their jobs admirably. The second one was overseen by the midwives at the clinic, one of whom fought the obstetrician in charge to save me from a second Caesarean. My son arrived just as he was getting the operating theatre ready. I am eternally grateful to the midwife, the whole birth experience and the recovery was the best of all three.

### Admin for the child

The admin for the baby starts as soon as s/he is born. You are legally obliged to register the birth of your child within three days at the local mayor's office, so you'd better have a name ready. When my husband went to register Beatrice (our second daughter) at the Béziers *mairie* he was told that one of the reasons for the registration was to make sure the child w1asn't given a ridiculous name. He asked who decides whether the name is ridiculous. Apparently it is whoever happens to be dealing with your registration. He thought briefly about Kylie Budgerigar or Gianluca Vialli, but decided to stick with Beatrice.

At hospital you will be given a *Carnet de Santé* for your baby. This is a book that contains his or her health records, things like vaccinations, and check-ups. Your baby will have a check-up once a month by the doctor of your choice. Your child has to have certain inoculations (like TB) in order to go to a crèche or school. You will be sent reminders when it is time for your child to have inoculations, once they are pre-school age. For the baby, the hospital should give you a list of timings.

## Nationality

When both parents are foreigners (say British), the baby takes on their nationality. When the child is 13, providing s/he has lived here for at least five years, the parents can ask for French nationality on his or her behalf. When the child is 16 s/he can ask for French nationality him or herself, providing again s/he has lived here at least five years. At 18 the child becomes automatically French, but keeps his or her British nationality.

## Postnatal care

The baby will leave hospital along with a whole medicine cabinet of vitamins, fluoride and creams in case of nappy rash. You will also be given some ghastly red stuff to treat the umbilical cord sore with. It dries it so it falls off more quickly.

## Benefits and maternity/paternity leave

If you have fewer than two children you are entitled to 16 weeks' maternity leave (six before childbirth and 10 after it). If you have more than two children, this goes up to 26 weeks (eight before childbirth and 18 after it). Fathers are entitled to a leave of 11 consecutive days, to be taken within four months of the birth.

In order to be eligible for family allowance you have to provide the CAF (*Caisse d'allocations familiales* www.caf.fr) with the *Déclaration de Grossesse* within the first 14 weeks of pregnancy. Allowances depend on your personal circumstances and you should contact your local CAF for more information. However, the most frequently provided ones are:

✓ *L'Allocation pour jeune enfant* (APE) which is generally given to those on low incomes. It starts from the fifth month of pregnancy and goes on until the child's third birthday.

✓ *Allocations familiales.* If you have two or more children you are entitled to this allowance which does not depend on your income.

---

*Useful associations and addresses*

NHS International Services Team +44 191 225 4811; Department of Health +44 20 7210 4850

*Caisse d'allocations familiales* (www.caf.fr), the government body responsible for paying out. There is one in every city, contact them for more information on your rights.

*Protection maternelle et infantile*, a service provided by the *Conseil Général* where social workers, midwives, doctors and paediatricians answer your questions. Look for your local branch on the Internet.

*Mouvement français pour le planning familial* (www.planning-familial.org), the French family planning organisation with 67 branches throughout the country. Information on contraception, abortion, sexual violence, etc. Information is confidential and free.

*Centre d'information et de documentation femmes et familles* (www.infofemmes.com), +33 1 42171200. Advice on women's rights, legal help and so on. Advice is free and confidential.

---

# Planning Issues

Planning permission is required in France for any new construction (subject to certain exemptions) or any proposal which changes the architecture of an existing property, its dimensions, its drainage or the layout of the surrounding area. It is also required for a change of use e.g. conversion of a barn into a dwelling.

Work on an existing building also requires planning permission where it affects the volume of the building or creates supplementary levels.

Certain categories of construction are exempt from planning permission and are instead subject to a *déclaration préalable* (prior declaration) from the mayor These are works such as terraces, with certain restrictions, and the creation of a balcony or veranda, again within certain restrictions on size. A *déclaration préalable* is also required prior to re-facing work being carried out, for instance.

The *déclaration préalable* is a simplified system whereby the application *dossier* is completed on a standard form and submitted with appropriate plans. The employment of an architect is not obligatory. The form is filed at the *mairie* and, if following the publicity the authorities remain silent for a period of one month, their tacit agreement is deemed to have been given. However, for certain buildings, e.g. historic monuments, the period is increased to two months.

If a full planning permission is required, a formal application *dossier* should be prepared, with comprehensive plans drawn up by an architect. The architect's involvement is obligatory, unless an individual wishes to build or modify a construction for their own use (as long as it is not agricultural) and the habitable surface area does not exceed 170m² (current rules).

After the planning application is filed with the local *mairie*, it will again be publicised. The normal period for consideration of the file is two months, but this can be increased for certain types of building, such as those classified as historic monuments. Once planning permission has been obtained, it can still be appealed by third parties within a period of two months from the date of granting permission.

The situation is complex and professional advice should always be taken prior to proceeding. Once the permission is obtained, building work must commence within a period of two years. Following completion of the works, a letter must be sent to the *mairie* confirming that the works have been completed (*Déclaration d'Achèvement des Travaux*) and the *Certificat de Conformité* (certificate of conformity) is requested which, if granted by the *mairie*, will confirm that the works were carried out in accordance with their permission.

Bear in mind that planning regulations vary from region to region. You should check with you local *Service de l'urban-isme* at the *mairie*, or go to www.vivremamaison.com or www.equipement.gouv.fr.

# Le Troisième Age
## France after Sixty Five

For those contemplating retirement to France it is comforting to know that the French healthcare system is among the best in the world, and that it also covers dental care, which is increasingly difficult to find in the UK under the National Health Service. Furthermore, those of retirement age in receipt of a state pension do not have to make social security contributions to the service. It is essential however, before leaving the UK, to obtain form E121 from the Department of Work and Pensions, Tyneview Park, Newcastle upon Tyne, NE98 1BA. This needs to be filled in and taken to your local *Caisse Primaire d'Assurance Maladie* (CPAM) to get on to the French system.

The most striking difference between the healthcare services of the two countries is that in France payment is made in full, following treatment and then reimbursed. Normally 70 per cent of the cost of treatment, which includes some acupuncture and homeopathy treatment, is reimbursed, and the balance can be funded by additional private medical insurance. While you are not required to register with a particular doctor and can obtain medical assistance from any doctor or specialist in France at any time, it obviously makes sense to find a doctor and dentist near where you live. Also bear in mind that many French doctors do not speak English, so brushing up on your medical vocabulary might be useful.

When choosing a doctor or dentist it is important to verify

that he or she is approved by social security (*conventionné*), otherwise you will not be reimbursed any costs. You can obtain a list of doctors registered with social security from your local social security office.

In order to be reimbursed, you need a *Carte Vitale* which you will get from your social security office once you're on the system. You give this to the doctor following treatment and your bank account will automatically be reimbursed.

Prescribed medicines are also covered by the system, and are reimbursed on a sliding scale up to 100 per cent, depending upon how essential they are. In every case payment has to be made in full following treatment, and the costs are reimbursed.

Emergencies are covered by the *Service d'Aide Médicale d'Urgence* (SAMU). Dial 15 for your nearest unit. It provides ambulance services manned by trained staff with cardiac and resuscitation equipment. Payment is made and reimbursed in the normal way.

There are both private and public hospitals in France. Most private hospitals specialise in some particular type of treatment. The cost of treatment in private hospitals is normally higher than in public hospitals, although some may have an agreement with social security and operate in the same way as public hospitals. Admission to hospital is normally subject to a recommendation by your doctor, except of course in the case of emergency treatment. In the case of life threatening conditions, reimbursement is normally made in full.

It is worth bearing in mind that the French healthcare service is heavily indebted and costs are out of control. At some point in the future one must imagine that this issue will be addressed and means will need to be found for greater contributions to support it.

*French taxation considerations for pensioners*

Anyone contemplating retirement to France and therefore

becoming subject to French taxation and succession law needs to consider carefully in advance three aspects, namely income tax, wealth tax and inheritance tax. These need all to be thought through before becoming domiciled in France as some of the tax advantages available can only be accessed *before* becoming a French tax resident. Professional advice should be sought if the sums concerned are significant.

## 1) Income Tax

There is a sliding scale for Income tax, as in the U.K. and although the top band is 48.09 per cent, most families will pay less in France especially if their prime source of income is a pension. French income tax is calculated on the basis of 'parts', which in fact equates to a family member. A retired couple would therefore consist of two 'parts'. Any income is split equally, taxed at that rate, and multiplied by two. A retired couple would therefore normally pay less income tax than in the U.K.

Most pension income, whether it be from a personal pension plan or UK state pension, is only taxed on a portion of its value, normally 72 per cent due to allowances. Furthermore pensions are exempt from French social charges, normally 8 to 10 per cent. However investment income, bank interest and Premium Bond winnings would be taxed at an additional 10 per cent to your French income tax band. It follows therefore that Premium Bonds are not a tax efficient vehicle for French residents.

There is however another form of investment, life insurance investment bonds (*Assurance Vie*), which are very tax efficient as the growth within the bond is tax free, and if income is taken, a large part of it is considered as return of capital and is tax free. Specialist advice should be taken on these investments.

## 2) Wealth Tax

This is levied annually on a sliding scale on wealth above

€720,000 on all assets whether in France or elsewhere. The value of a French home is discounted by 20 per cent for wealth tax purposes and there are exemptions for fine art, antiques and 'collectors items'. The rates start at 0.55 per cent between €720,000 and €1,160,000.

However the funds in a personal pension plan written in trust are not considered part of your assets for Wealth Tax purposes, although of course the income is taxable as above.

3) Inheritance Tax.
This is a complicated subject, not least because French succession law divides an individual's assets into a disposable portion, and a reserved portion. The reserved portion must go to a protected heir, normally the child or children. A spouse is not considered to be a protected heir and therefore arrangements have to be made to ensure that a surviving spouse is taken care of. A French will is essential. This can be as simple as a hand written note along the following lines:

*Je soussigné[e]* [full names] *révoque tous testaments antérieurs. Je déclare en décès vouloir laisser tous mes biens mobiliers et immobiliers m'appartenant en France et en Angleterre à mon épouse* [full names + maiden name] *et en cas de son décès avant moi à* [full names and relationship] *habitant* [address]
   *Fait ce jour* [date] *à* [place]
   [Signed]
   [Print full name]

You can either pay your lawyer or *notaire* to keep a copy of this or just put it somewhere safe at home. Please note though it must be hand written.

Inheritance tax regulations are completely different from the U.K. While at first they appear draconian, for example inheritance tax is chargeable between spouses above a basic allowance of €76,000, and legacies to stepchildren are charged at 60 per cent above a basic allowance of €1500, there are a number of ways of mitigating these taxes. The life insurance investment bonds (*Assurance Vie*) mentioned above allow you to pass €152,500 to each beneficiary, free from French inheritance tax. There is no limit to the amounts that can be gifted to each beneficiary in this way if the investments are made before becoming tax resident in France. Furthermore this type of investment is not subject to French Succession law so you are at liberty to leave money to whomsoever you wish within certain limits. These investments also offer certain guarantees that protect your capital and as a result are not very exciting, but they make 4 to 5 per cent at present, and pensioners are usually interested in safety rather than the excitement of the market for most of their funds.

It is perfectly possible to reduce your liability to the three main taxes levied in France within the law and maintain a good standard of living provided you plan well ahead and seek advice before moving to France. In that way there will be no surprises, and you will not be subject to unexpected tax demands which can blight a happy retirement.

# The Twenty-Two Regions of France

The last time I was in London, I took a cab from Sloane Street to Wandsworth. 'England's going to the dogs,' said my East End cabbie. 'Too many immigrants. I bet you was the only English person in Sloane Street.'

I was too scared of being thrown out of the cab to tell him I am, in fact, half-Swedish, half-Italian.

'I'm moving to France,' he continued as he swung into the Wandsworth Bridge Road.

'Oh really,' I said. 'Whereabouts will you go?'

'Dunno, probably Limousin.'

My first thought was—thank God, nowhere near me. My second was, how would one decide?

France is so diverse it could almost be a continent. It is the largest country in the EU and with a population density of 49 people per square kilometre compared with 361 in the UK it is far less populated than most EU countries. It is divided into 22 regions and 96 numbered *départements*, which are the equivalent of British counties. The departments are sub-divided into *communes*, which also have their own authorities (run by the mayor) like British town or parish councils.

There are four main climatic zones in France. The *Continental zone*, which is characterised by warm summers but heavy rainfall and cold winters. This zone includes the north-eastern corner of France as well as the Auvergne, Burgundy and the Rhône Valley. The average winter temperature is 9 degrees and 24 in the summer. The *Mediterranean zone* comprises the south and southeast corner, including the Languedoc-Roussillon, the Riviera and Provence. The climate in this zone is hot and dry. The winters are generally fairly warm (although it has snowed twice since we moved here) and rainfall is unpredictable. When it does rain it really pours and we are often stranded as our house is in between two rivers. In the winter, temperatures are on average around 11 degrees. The *Oceanic zone* affects the regions from the Loire to the Basque and is characterised by warm summers and mild winters with heavy rainfall, with average temperatures of 8 degrees in the winter and 24 in the summer. Finally, the *Mountain zone* which affects the Alps, the Pyrenees and the Massif Central. In this zone you can expect cool summers and very cold winters. The average temperature in the winter is 3 degrees and in the summer 25.

## Alsace

*Area*:
8,280 km²
*Population*:
Around 1,700,000
*Climate*:
Continental and wet
*Capital City*:
Strasbourg
*Departments*:
Bas-Rhin, Haut-Rhin
*Miles from V&A Museum in London to Strasbourg*:
460
*Estimated driving time*:
6 hours
*Cost of tolls*:
£26.50

*Where is it?*
On the German border in the northeast of France. Lots of flights from London to Strasbourg where the Council of Europe and the European Parliament sits.

*History*:
Was incorporated into France in 1681 by Louis XIV but re-absorbed into Germany after the Prussian victory of 1870. Then back to France in 1918. The Alsatian or Allemanic language can still be heard in some villages but less and less.

*What do they eat?*
Choucroute was invented here, sauerkraut with smoked ham, sausages and potatoes. The term *à l'alsacienne* means with sauerkraut.

*What do they drink?*
There are seven Alsace wines: six whites and one rosé, all named after the grapes they are made from. Gewurztraminer, Muscat, Pinot Blanc, Pinot Noir, Riesling, Sylvaner, Edelzwicker and Tokay Pinot Gris. The Alsatians are also big on beer, Kronenbourg being the best known.

*What do you do there?*
Go shopping across the border in Germany where everything is cheaper. Ski, walk in the mountains, fish and ride horses. Walk in the lovely countryside.

*Who lives there?*
The Alsatians, a Population that sees itself as neither French nor German. They say '*à l'intérieur*' when they mean the rest of France and will not hesitate to speak of the Boches when speaking of the Germans. They have a very strong identity. Far more reliable than the French (Geneviève, my cleaning lady is Alsatian and shows up for work ten minutes early) and much more Germanic in outlook.

*What does it cost?*
A lot. The classic Alsace house is half-timbered, gabled and expensive. You will pay around £80,000 for a two-bedroom apartment.

*Why is it hot?*
A rich region. Close to Paris, good connections with major German cities. The upper Vosges mountains. Pretty villages. Beautiful countryside.

*Why is it not?*
Bad crime rate in the major cities of Strasbourg and Mulhouse. Not much to do if you don't like sauer-

kraut or wine that comes in funny shaped bottles. Also very hard to adapt at first, according to friends who have tried it.

## Aquitaine
*Area*:
41,308 km²
*Population*:
Around 2,880,000
*Climate*:
Continental
*Capital City*:
Bordeaux
*Departments*:
Dordogne, Gironde, Landes, Lot-et-Garonne, Pyrénées-Atlantiques
*Miles from V&A Museum in London to Bordeaux*:
493
*Estimated driving time*:
10 hours 50 minutes
*Cost of tolls*:
£20.18
*Where is it?*
In the far south-west on the Atlantic coast.
*History*:
Was the capital of the Dukes of Aquitaine in the 11*th* century. The Brits bought so much wine the capital of Bordeaux became very rich.

*What do they eat?*
Truffles, foie gras, duck, pâté, snails and walnuts. The Périgord (the French name for the Dordogne) is known for its truffles, apricots and strawberries.

*What do they drink?*
Wine, wine and yet more wine. This is the world's most famous and prestigious wine-growing region. The vineyards of Bordeaux produce Margaux, Médoc, Sauterne and Saint-Emilion wines among others.

*What do you do there?*
Drink, eat, swim, surf. The region covers a vast area, stretching from the borders of the Massif Central to the Spanish border and the Pyrenees, so there is a lot of potential.

*Who lives there?*
Basque region separatists, although they are now very peaceful, wine makers, wine sellers, wine snobs, in fact, every kind of wine buff you can imagine. Bordeaux itself has a reputation as one of the least friendly places in France. The population is said to be more closed than the rest of France. However, closer to Spain, in the Pyrenees-Atlantiques it is a totally different story. The Dordogne is almost synonymous with Brits, it was the first area to be invaded by British second-home owners. The place is crawling with them.

*What does it cost?*
In the city of Bordeaux prices are rising as the major overhaul in the centre comes to an end. Wine-growing land is hugely expensive. In the Dordogne there isn't much left to buy and a tumble-down barn could cost you more than a *château* in Limousin.

*Why is it hot?*
A great quality of life if you can afford all the best the region has to offer. The wine industry

dominates, so it helps to be involved in that. Bordeaux itself is a major centre of commerce and communications, so travel almost anywhere is easy.

*Why is it not?*

Don't move to Bordeaux if you're not into wine, you'll find that's almost the only thing anyone talks about. Don't move to Biarritz if you can't surf.

## Auvergne

*Area*:
26,013 km²
*Population*:
Around 1,315,000
*Climate*:
Mountain/Continental
*Capital City*:
Clermont-Ferrand
*Departments*:
Allier, Cantal, Haute-Loire, Puy-de-Dôme
*Miles from V&A Museum in London to Clermont-Ferrand*:
517
*Estimated driving time*:
8 hours 40 minutes
*Cost of tolls*:
£33.08
*Where is it?*

In the middle of the country. Some might say in the middle of nowhere. Clermont-Ferrand is the half-way point of a drive from England to the south of France.

*History*:

Rebels. A tough people, historically opposed to the government. The Auvergne has been inhabited since the Celts in 400 BC. Was once an important wine region but phylloxera wiped out the industry in the 19th Century.

*What do they eat?*

Cheese. This is where Cantal and Salers come from, as well as Saint-Nectaire and Bleu d'Auvergne. Staple dishes include anything *à l'auvergnate* which means with cabbage, bacon and sausage. The *potée auvergnate* is a typical local dish, a hot pot of vegetables and pork.

*What do they drink?*

Anything to keep warm.

*What do you do there?*

Walk, hike, swim, hang glide and enjoy the dramatic landscape.

*Who lives there?*

Not a lot of people, as a lot of it is above 3,000 feet and largely uninhabited. The ones that are there are rugged, independent and quite poor.

*What does it cost?*

Cheap. The image is of a poverty-stricken region with dire housing. There really isn't a market in holiday homes, but you could start a trend. With £10,000 you could still buy a derelict place, and it's one of the few places in France where you can still do that.

*Why is it hot?*

The volcanoes. Apart from that, er, well, some French would describe it as a place to leave, not to go to. If you like countryside and lots of space, it's for you. Masses of outdoor activities including skiing, rafting, biking, hiking and hang-gliding. Also some wonderful Romanesque churches and medieval castles.

*Why is it not?*

Remote, cold. Apart from on top of the volcanoes of course.

## Brittany (Bretagne)

*Area*:

27,506 km²

*Population*:

Around 2,860,000

*Climate*:

Oceanic

*Capital City*:

Rennes

*Departments*:

Côtes d'Armor, Finistère, Ille-et-Vilaine, Morbihan

*Miles from V&A Museum in London to Rennes*:

124

*Estimated driving time*:

8 hours 41 minutes

*Cost of tolls*:

None

*Where is it?*

The far north-western corner.

*History*:

Brits have been emigrating here since the end of the Roman Empire. It became fully French in 1532, prior to that it was an independent dukedom that generally avoided the Anglo-French wars. If you speak Welsh or Cornish then you will understand a lot of the Breton language which is still spoken, although it has been suppressed by Paris. There is a move to resurrect this Celtic language, parents can now send their children to Breton schools.

*What do they eat?*

Legendary seafood (the official *plateau de fruits de mer* is expected to have at least six different shellfish), lamb and artichokes. For the French the region is symbolised by crêpes, every crêperie in France calls itself Bretonne.

*What do they drink?*

Cider. Brittany was once full of vineyards but they were torn up in the 16th century and replaced with orchards. Cider goes very well with crêpes.

*What do you do there?*

750 miles of coastline so lots of water activities. For history fans there are lots of megaliths, museums, *châteaux* and medieval towns. The Gulf of Morbihan on the southern shore is stunning, dotted with tiny islands and the Ile aux Moines with its fairy-tale woods. Further inland is the medieval forest where the Knights of the round table sought the holy grail.

*Who lives there?*

Lots of Brits with second homes. The locals are used to us by now. We even had the same name, Great Britain is *Grande Bretagne* and Brittany is *Petite Bretagne*. But Mark, one Breton friend of mine, says he is appalled by the fact that there are now totally British villages. 'We don't really like foreigners,' he says. 'And by that we mean people from other parts of France as well.' Watch out—there are some members of the Breton liberation front left, though it has almost died out now. They famously (accidentally) killed a McDonald's worker in 1999 when they bombed it.

*What does it cost?*

Around 20 per cent of homes are second homes but prices are still very reasonable.

*Why is it hot?*

Proximity to home, coastline, countryside.

*Why is it not?*

Rain. In the winter you might as well have stayed in England and saved yourself the crossing.

## Burgundy (Bourgogne)

*Area*:

31,582 km²

*Population*:

Around 1,624,000

*Climate*:

Continental

*Capital City*:

Dijon

*Departments*:

Côte d'Or, Nièvre, Saône-et-Loire, Yonne

*Miles from V&A Museum in London to Dijon*:

430

*Estimated driving time*:

7 hours 30 minutes

*Cost of tolls*:

£24.83

*Where is it?*

The northeast of France, a good place to stop off on your way to the ski slopes.

*History*:

An independent kingdom for 600 years, there is a wealth of historic towns and beautiful *châteaux*.

*What do they eat?*

*Boeuf Bourguignon*, in fact anything *à la bourguignonne* (cooked in red wine sauce with mushrooms, shallots and bacon bits), foie gras, coq au vin and extremely garlicky snails cooked for hours in Chardonnay. In fact anything likely to raise your cholesterol levels and give you bad breath. If you don't like the taste of anything you can just cover it with Dijon mustard.

*What do they drink?*

Wine, wine, wine. But the good stuff doesn't come cheap. Home to Chambertin, Pommard, Meursault, Chablis and Pouilly-Fuissé.

*What do you do there?*

The medieval city of Vézelay from where Richard Lionheart launched the Third Crusade. The Musée des Beaux-Arts in Dijon is sometimes called 'Le Petit Louvre' due to its extraordinary collections ranging from medieval art to Impressionist.

*Who lives there?*

My aunt and uncle. Winemakers. Mustard makers. Brits who like the countryside because it looks just like England. Rich Parisians with weekend cottages. Don't forget Burgundy was an independent kingdom for 600 years. They are very proud of their heritage, cuisine, wine and so on. But the locals I have met are friendly

*What does it cost?*

Not cheap, but you can find

bargains if you're prepared to live very rurally. Prices rise closer to Paris and the TGV

*Why is it hot?*

Gorgeous countryside. Easy trip to Paris with the TGV, also excellent motorways with easy access to Lyon and beyond. Lots of lovely rivers and canals. No real industry so very unspoiled.

*Why is it not?*

Can get very cold in the winter. Some parts are isolated.

### Champagne-Ardenne

*Area*:

26,605 km²

*Population*:

Around 1,352,000

*Climate*:

Continental

*Capital City*:

Reims

*Departments*:

Ardennes, Aube, Marne, Haute-Marne

*Miles from V&A Museum in London to Reims*:

245

*Estimated driving time*:

4 hours 51 minutes

*Cost of tolls*:

£11.58

*Where is it?*

Right up in the north east, borders Belgium.

*History*:

The founder of champagne, a 17th-century monk called Dom Perignon came from the region. He tried adding yeast to bottles of fermenting wine and ended up with champagne. However, it was not until the 19th century that large-scale production got under way. This was largely because they developed glass bottles strong enough to hold the exploding wine. Twenty-six of France's kings were crowned here.

*What do they eat?*

Not one of France's gastronomic regions, the most notable local dishes are pig's trotters and white sausage. There are some fine cheeses such as Grand Condé and Rocroi.

*What do they drink?*

Champagne, the wine of kings and the king of wine.

*What do you do there?*

Celebrate. Make, sell, drink, grow champagne. If you're not into champagne you would go walking or boating. There are 650 kilometres of waterways and lakes.

*Who lives there?*

Champagne makers. Heidsieck, Moët et Chandon, Taittinger, Veuve-Clicquot. This isn't really a tourist destination so not many second home owners.

*What does it cost?*

Not much at all, as long as you're not trying to buy wine-growing land.

*Why is it hot?*

Close to the Channel, cheap houses, lovely countryside and lots of champagne.

*Why is it not?*

Champagne can give you a hangover. The *Climate* is wet and humid.

## Corsica

*Area*:
8,681 km²
*Population*:
Around 260,700
*Climate*:
Mediterranean
*Capital City*:
Ajaccio
*Departments*:
Corse-du-Sud, Haute-Corse
*Miles from V&A Museum in London to Ajaccio*:
Don't even think about it, get on a plane. Or, if you happen to be in the south of France, a ferry from Nice, Toulon or Marseille.

*Where is it?*
In the middle of the sea, 100 miles south of the French Riviera, 50 miles from the Italian coastline and eight miles from Sardinia.

*History*:
Has not been independent since Roman times. France bought the island in 1768 from the Italians. Napoleon Bonaparte was born in Ajacco in 1769. Christopher Columbus was also Corsican.

*What do they eat?*
All kinds of fruit. The local cuisine is strongly flavoured with wild herbs. The national dish is stewed goat but all sorts of game is popular as well. Sea fish and shell fish, a must.

*What do they drink?*
A white muscat aperitif from Cap Corse. The island also produces some wines: Santa Barba and Fiumicicoli, to name two. Also a strong liquor made out of myrtles.

*What do you do there?*
There is no industry, the only income comes from the tourist trade. If you're on holiday you swim, walk, eat and pick fruit.

*Who lives there?*
Corsicans, who speak a dialect that is more similar to Italian than French. Lots of Italians with summer homes, they are generally more welcome than the French.

*What does it cost?*
Expensive. Anything by the sea is sold at a huge premium. The cost of living is much higher than mainland France.

*Why is it hot?*
A stunning island. Nicknamed Island of Beauty. 600 miles of coastline. People's hospitality (as long as they're not members of the FLNC, the Corsican liberation movement).

*Why is it not?*
Corsicans are prone to using dynamite to blow up non-Corsican residents' houses. It is also quite inaccessible.

## Franche Comté

*Area*:
16,202 km²
*Population*:
Around 1,084,000
*Climate*:
Continental
*Capital City*:
Besançon
*Departments*:
Haute-Saône, Doubs, Jura, Territoire de Belfort
*Miles from V&A Museum in*

*London to Besançon*:
451
*Estimated driving time*:
8 hours 31 minutes
*Cost of tolls*:
£22.82
*Where is it?*
Good question. My French friend Alex didn't even know, neither did Caroline, another French friend. On the eastern border with Switzerland.

*History*:
Became part of France in 1678 when Louis XIV annexed it. The city of Belfort has a rich history: it was part of the Habsburg empire in the 14th century, later on it was ruled by the princes of Monaco, then became part of Alsace under German rule in 1871.

*What do they eat?*
Meat – Franche-Comté is known for its charcuterie, particularly smoked beef, sausages and hams. The local cheese, Comté, is said to be the most popular in France.

*What do they drink?*
Wine, mainly white, there are four AOC areas in Jura.

*What do you do there?*
In Besançon they make clocks. You are next door to Switzerland, there is lots of skiing, fishing, walking and white-water rafting.

*Who lives there?*
Not many foreigners, as it is very remote. Clockmakers and people who like the Swiss influence. Also pipe-makers.

*What does it cost?*
Building land is very cheap and there are plenty of timber-framed farmhouses for not much money.

*Why is it hot?*
Good if you don't ever want to see another English person and you like lederhosen. Also wonderful countryside, more than half the region is covered with forest.

*Why is it not?*
No TGV or plane links, very tough to get to. Freezing in the winter. My friend Caroline calls it *'une region paumée'*, a godforsaken place.

## Languedoc-Roussillon

*Area*:
27,447 km²
*Population*:
Around 2,445,000
*Climate*:
Mediterranean
*Capital City*:
Montpellier
*Departments*:
Aude, Gard, Hérault, Lozère, Pyrénées-Orientales
*Miles from V&A Museum in London to Montpellier*:
729
*Estimated driving time*:
11 hours 30 minutes
*Cost of tolls*:
£44.39
*Where is it?*
Down south, between Provence and the Spanish border.
*History*:
Greeks. Romans. Cathar massacres. The region is full of castles, abbeys and cathedrals to

visit. Canal du Midi, one of the world's first great engineering projects. One of Europe's most famous 'medieval' towns is Carcassonne, where crusaders slew heretics. Spanish refugees fled here after the civil war.

*Who lives there?*
Local wine making population and *pied noir* refugees from Algeria. Other immigrants from North Africa (accused World Trade Center conspirator Mohammed Moussawi is from Montpellier.) Recently invaded by northern Europeans seeking sunshine and cheaper houses than in next door Provence.

*What do they eat?*
Mediterranean food – fish, seafood, fresh fruit and vegetables, olive oil, anchovies, olives.

*What do they drink?*
Fantastic wines – this is the world's largest vineyard. My favourites are wines from Domaines Paul Mas, Canteperdrix (in my village), St Martin de la Garrigue Domaine Sainte Rose and Seigneurie de Peyrat.

*What does it cost?*
Has been one of the best values in Europe; prices rocketing in past three years. The brave willing to take on rehab projects can still find bargains. £150,000—two to three bedroom village or town house. £350,000—isolated farmhouse that needs renovating. £1 million—*château*, vineyard.

*Why is it hot?*
Location, it is easy to get anywhere. Montpellier, one of the fastest-growing cities in Europe, is being run by a visionary socialist dictator. Many successful, young, dynamic types are leaving the north to move down. Not just Brits but Swedes, Germans, Dutch and so on. There is a vibrant social and working scene that didn't exist five years ago. *L'Express* rates it as the best place to live in France. Furthermore, Spanish influence such as bullfighting and obligatory siestas in the summer. Cap d'Agde is Europe's largest nudist colony. A must-see.

*Why is it not?*
Worst drivers in France with highest fatal accident rate. Savage dogs, vicious wild pigs, scorpions, killer wasps. And my daughters. Scary.

### Limousin
*Area*:
16,942 km²
*Population*:
Around 717,600
*Climate*:
Cool
*Capital City*:
Limoges
*Departments*:
Corrèze, Creuse, Haute-Vienne
*Miles from V&A Museum in London to Limoges*:
499
*Estimated driving time*:
8 hours 30 minutes
*Cost of tolls*:
£23.10

*Where is it?*
The Massif Central, south west.
*History:*
Lots of museums in Limoges dedicated to the city's illustrious porcelain making past. Became part of France in 1607 under Henry IV. A stronghold in the Anglo-Angevin wars.
*What do they eat?*
The region is famous for its Limousin cows, some say they live better than the locals do. The local cuisine is often described as simple and filling. Lots of beef and chestnuts.
*What do they drink?*
Wine, Ricard, Pernod, the usual.
*What do you do there?*
Lots of outdoor activities. Limoges is world-famous for its porcelain, but even that can get boring after a few visits. This is France at its most rural and remote. Seen as a gateway between the industrialised north and laid-back south. Some cultural and gastronomic festivals during the tourist season. The painter Auguste Renoir came from Limoges, but other than that the region is rather lacking in the cultural tradition of the rest of the country. Jacques Chirac is from Sarran in Corrèze.
*Who lives there?*
Lots of tough, dour farmers. Walking into a bar can sometimes feel like wandering into a pub in deepest, darkest Yorkshire where everyone stares at you but no one talks to you.
*What does it cost?*
About the lowest in France.

*Why is it hot?*
Looks just like rural England did 50 years ago, stunning countryside, rolling hills. Lakes, rivers, chestnut forests and wide open spaces. This is a place for those who love a rural life. Sparsely populated.
*Why is it not?*
Slightly removed from the rest of the world, let alone the rest of France. A bit of a cultural desert. And personally I am not remotely interested in porcelain. During World War I, Marshal Joffre sent an incompetent general to Limoges. As a result there is a French verb—*limoger*—which literally means demoted or sent to some god-forsaken post.

### Centre/Val de Loire
*Area:*
39,151 km²
*Population:*
Around 2,443,000
*Climate:*
Continental
*Capital City:*
Orléans
*Departments:*
Cher, Eure-et-Loire, Indre, Indre-et-Loire, Loiret, Loir-et-Cher
*Miles from V&A Museum in London to Orléans:*
338
*Estimated driving time:*
6 hours 18 minutes
*Cost of tolls:*
£17.89
*Where is it?*
Near the middle, slightly to the west of Paris.

*History*:

Known to the Brits as the Loire Valley, evidence of the struggle to get rid of the English in the 15th century is everywhere in the form of fortresses and castles. It was known as the playground for the aristocracy and the result is hordes of splendid *châteaux* to visit.

*Who lives there?*

Lots of fruit farmers and wine-makers. Lots of Parisians with second homes.

*What do they eat?*

A fertile region which produces more cereal than anywhere else in France. Also big soft fruit producers. Home to the most popular French pudding, the Tarte Tatin, invented by the Tatin sisters in Lamotte-Beuvron.

*What do they drink?*

No fewer than 22 AOC wines including Sancerre, Vouvray and Valençay.

*What do you do there?*

Visit *châteaux* and cathedrals. The cathedral at Chartres is a world heritage site.

*What does it cost?*

Expensive as the regional capital is only an hour from Paris. Almost 20 per cent of properties are second homes, but prices are not unreasonable.

*Why is it hot?*

Lots of culture, *châteaux* and rivers.

*Why is it not?*

Flat landscape. And after visiting 10 *châteaux*, you'll probably have had enough.

## Pays de la Loire

*Area*:

23,081 km²

*Population*:

Around 3,155,000

*Climate*:

Oceanic

*Capital City*:

Nantes

*Departments*:

Loire-Antlantique, Maine-et-Loire, Mayenne, Sarthe, Vendée

*Miles from V&A Museum in London to Nantes*:

306

*Estimated driving time*:

9 hours

*Cost of tolls*:

None

*History*:

Always popular with kings and noblemen. Nantes was the traditional seat of the Dukes of Brittany. In fact, it was part of Brittany until 1962. Traditionally royalist, they defended the king during the revolution.

*Who lives there?*

Lots of young dynamic people in Nantes, as well as students. Lots of culture vultures – this is the home to several celebrated theatre companies including the Royal de Luxe.

*What do they eat?*

*Mogette* – white *haricot verts* basically. According to my friend Alex who comes from here they eat them in sandwiches. Fish, seafood (lots of baby eels), Port Salut from the Mayenne.

*What do they drink?*

Muscadet wines, Saumur Brut, a white sparkling wine, pudding wines from the Côteaux du Layon, wines from the Fiefs Vendéens.

*What do you do there?*

Alex tells me that Vendée is the second most visited region in France after Provence. There are fine sandy beaches and two beautiful islands off the coast; the Ile d'Yeu and the Ile de Noirmoutier. Lots of water sports, as well as golf and walking. Also, lots of castles to visit: the Mayenne is reputed to have more *châteaux* per square mile than anywhere else outside Paris. Nantes is a very popular and dynamic city.

*What does it cost?*

Along the coast about 20 per cent of properties are second homes. Prices vary. Nantes, one of the most popular cities in France, can be quite expensive. The Mayenne is much cheaper.

*Why is it hot?*

According to my friend Jacques Kuhnlé, the locals are very friendly. 'In Angers, one driver saw I was looking for my way around and spontaneously showed me the way. One lady I asked about a good not too expensive restaurant went out of her way to take me to one.' Alex says the locals can be cold at first but are very loyal once they get to know you. Parts of the region (Nantes and Vendée) are often voted the best place to live in France.

*Why is it not?*

The Mayenne is not reputed to be the most welcoming region in France, as you will have gathered from stories in this book. Very agricultural, more closed.

**Lorraine**

*Area*:

23,547 km²

*Population*:

Around 2,311,700

*Climate*:

Continental

*Capital City*:

Metz

*Departments*:

Meurthe-et-Moselle, Meuse, Moselle, Vosges

*Miles from V&A Museum in London to Metz*:

361

*Estimated driving time*:

6 hours 26 minutes

*Cost of tolls*:

Nothing if you go from Calais to Lille and then into Belgium through Charleroi, Namur then south to Luxemburg where petrol is much cheaper. Otherwise £19.35.

*Where is it?*

North east, next to Germany.

*History* :

Traditionally a coal exporting region but the coal mines are now closed.

*Who lives there?*

Farmers, ex miners. Has a fairly grim image.

*What do they drink?*

Moselle white wine, Gris de Toul

*What do they eat?*
quiche lorraine, tarte aux mirabelles, Munster cheese. This is dairy-farming country so lots of dairy products.

*What do you do there?*
Go to Metz and Nancy where there is plenty going on. There is a *'festival du film italien'* in Villerupt where the greatest film directors meet. First world war monuments in and around Verdun. You can visit the ligne Maginot fortifications.

*What does it cost?*
Going up because of Germans, Belgians and Dutch buying houses.

*Why is it hot?*
Both rural countryside and mountains, skiing in the Vosges.

*Why is it not?*
Cold wet Climate. Locals rather cold too, but reliable. More friendly in the industrial areas where the first waves of immigrants settled.

### Nord/Pas-de-Calais
*Area*:
12,414 km²
*Population*:
Around 4,000,000
*Climate*:
Oceanic/Rainy
*Capital City*:
Lille
*Departments*:
Nord, Pas-de-Calais
*Miles from V&A Museum in London to Lille*:
145

*Estimated driving time*:
3 hours 37 minutes
*Cost of tolls*:
None
*Where is it?*
The very north, next to Belgium
*History*:
Came under French rule in 1668. Prior to that, a borderland between Flanders and France.

*Who lives there?*
Big drinkers and party animals. 'These people are renowned for liking the good life,' says my Breton friend Mark. 'They love to party and are always very welcoming.'

*What do they eat?*
Distinctly Flemish: *moules frites*, fried chicory, meat in aspic.

*What do they drink?*
Beer, beer and more beer.

*What do you do there?*
Play golf at Le Touquet, one of the best courses in France. If you're looking for a job, this is where all the home shopping catalogues have their headquarters, a huge industry in France. The locals also have a reputation for partying and enjoying bar life.

*What does it cost?*
Quite reasonable prices, has been largely overlooked by people getting off the boats at Calais and driving through it. On the coast prices go up.

*Why is it hot?*
Very easy to get to from London, only two hours by trains to Lille. Lille is a fantastically dynamic city with lots going on. Also very close

to Paris and Brussels. The Carnival of Dunkirk. Very nice people with a reputation for being calmer than your average French person due to the Flemish influence.

*Why is it not?*
Cold in the winter. One of France's most industrialised regions. Also very flat.

## Lower Normandy
*Area*:
17,589 km²
*Population*:
Around 1,416,000
*Climate*:
Oceanic, like southern England really, but with more reliable summers.
*Capital City*:
Caen
*Departments*:
Calvados, Manche, Orne
*Miles from V&A Museum in London to Caen*:
86
*Estimated driving time*:
6 hours 50 minutes
*Cost of tolls*:
None
*History*:
Strong ties with Britain and North America. The resorts of Trouville and Deauville made famous by the Emperor Napoleon in the 19th century. Still frequented by rich Parisians. The birthplace of William the Conqueror.
*Who lives there?*
See below
*What do they eat?*
Fresh fish, duck, fruit,

Camembert, Livarot and Pont l'Evêque cheeses. Lots of cream and butter with everything. Sea food.

*What do they drink?*
Calvados. Strong, dangerous and far too easy to drink.

*What do you do there?*
Visit the Bayeux Tapestry. Mont Saint Michel, one of the seven wonders of the world.

*What does it cost?*
Not bad at all, although the coastal properties sell at a premium.

*Why is it hot?*
Close to England if you're only planning to come for holidays. Combined with Upper Normandy it has almost 400 miles of seaside with cliffs, pebbly and sandy beaches. Inland wonderful forests and streams. Lots of beautiful orchards to lie and dream in.

*Why is it not?*
Cold in the winter.

## Upper Normandy
*Area*:
12,258 km²
*Population*:
Around 1,781,5000
*Climate*:
Oceanic
*Capital City*:
Rouen
*Departments*:
Eure, Seine-Maritime
*Miles from V&A Museum in London to Rouen*:
114
*Estimated driving time*:
4 hours 30 minutes

*Cost of tolls*:
None
*History*:
Rich history with links to England. Big connection with writers and artists inspired by its countryside while still being close to Paris. Monet grew up at Le Havre.

*Who lives there?*
Mainly Parisians with second homes. But the locals at least have a reputation for being friendly.

*What do they eat?*
As above.

*What do they drink?*
More Calvados.

*What do you do there?*
Visit Claude Monet's garden at Giverny.

*What does it cost?*
As above.

*Why is it hot?*
Seriously close to London and Paris. Rolling pastures and half-timbered houses.

*Why is it not?*
Cold in the winter. Not a good place for a bored housewife. Look what happened to Emma Bovary.

## Paris and Ile de France

*Area*:
12,072km²
*Population*:
Around 11,028,000
*Climate*:
Temperate
*Capital City*:
Paris
*Departments*:
Paris, Essonne, Hauts-de-Seine, Seine-et-Marne, Seine-Saint-Denis, Val-de-Marne, Val-d'Oise, Yvelines
*Miles from V&A Museum in London to Paris*:
254 Miles
*Estimated driving time*:
2 hours 34 minutes
*Cost of tolls*:
£12.14
*Where is it?*
North, in the middle.
*History*:
Paris became significant in 987 AD. It became the centre of the French state when Hugues Capet crowned himself king in the 10th century, because it was the only region under his control.

*Who lives there?*
People from all over the world. And of course from all over France, although my French friend Mark says you go to Paris 'as a last resort if you can't get a job anywhere else'. Mind you, he lives in Exeter, so can we trust his judgement?

*What do they eat?*
Steak and frites. Eat them in a brasserie on a leafy boulevard.

*What do they drink?*
Anything you like, you can enjoy the best of France here.

*What do you do there?*
Where do I start?
Notre Dame, the Eiffel Tower, you know it all by now. If it's your first visit take a walk though the elegant streets and soak up the atmosphere. Outside the city you have splendid countryside and of course Versailles.

*What does it cost?*
Very expensive in the centre of town and houses rarely come on the market. The best you could hope for would be an apartment.

*Why is it hot?*
Only the most beautiful city in the world, and one of the most pleasant to live in according to polls in newspapers. The surrounding area is beautiful as well.

*Why is it not?*
Parisians have a reputation for being incredibly unfriendly. I once overheard a foreigner asking saying to a chic Parisian lady: 'I'm looking for the rue d'Anjou.' 'Well, I hope you find it,' was her response.

## Picardy
*Area*:
19,399km²
*Population*:
Around 1,863,500
*Climate*:
Continental
*Capital City*:
Amiens
*Departments*:
Aisne, Oise, Somme
*Miles from V&A Museum in London to Amiens*:
172
*Estimated driving time*:
3 hours 55 minutes
*Cost of tolls*:
£6.59
*Where is it?*
Between Calais and Paris.
*History*:

The Battle of the Somme, one of the most poignant names in history. Around 1,353,000 died trying to win some land from the Germans. Also the birthplace of France in 486 when Clovis made Soissons the first capital of the Franks. Later, in 987, Hugues Capet was crowned King of France at Noyon. Amiens has an amazing architectural heritage.

*Who lives there?*
Who knows? Certainly none of the French people I asked. None of them had ever been there, although they all said Amiens was a nice city.

*What do they eat?*
Fresh food from market gardens, smoked river eel, cheese, waterfowl and lamb.

*What do they drink?*
Cider and beer.

*What do you do there?*
Amiens is known as the Venice of the North (along with Amsterdam) due to its lakes, watergardens and rivers which you can explore in punts. Major literary festivals. There are also 70 kilometres of dunes, cliffs and beaches.

*What does it cost?*
Not too much, it has been largely ignored by foreign home owners.

*Why is it hot?*
Very close to England and Paris, lovely countryside, marvellous Gothic cathedrals.

*Why is it not?*
Wet and flat.

## Poitou and Charentes
*Area*:
25,810 km²
*Population*:
Around 1,622,800
*Climate*:
Continental
*Capital City*:
Poitiers
*Departments*:
Charente-Maritime, Deux-Sèvres, Vienne.
*Miles from V&A Museum in London to Poitiers*:
341
*Estimated driving time*:
8 hours 54 minutes
*Cost of tolls*:
£7.56
*Where is it?*
West, between the Loire Valley and Bordeaux.
*History*:
Scene of a great English victory in the 100 Years' War in 1356. Also the seat of the Dukes of Aquitaine. Parthenay was on one of the main routes of the pilgrimage to Santiago de Compostela so has a lot of Romanesque churches.
*Who lives there?*
Insurance brokers. Farmers. This is the middle of nowhere. Not much else to report.
*What do they eat?*
Fish, lots of oysters, seafood.
*What do they drink?*
Cognac. This is the centre of the brandy industry.
*What do you do there?*
Visit Futuroscope, a virtual reality theme park. Also the largest national park and wetland on the western side of France, the Marais Poitevin. If you work in insurance, you could easily get a job in Niort which is the centre of the French insurance industry. Or you could make slippers, a product the region is famous for. Lively resorts such as La Rochelle, Royan and the islands of Oléron, Aix and Ré. Music festival at La Rochelle.
*What does it cost?*
Getting expensive, especially the area bordering the Dordogne.
*Why is it hot?*
Supposedly as sunny as Provence on the coast, 2250 hours a year, according to the tourist office. Good place to live if you like Cognac. Not much rain at all.
*Why is it not?*
The marshlands, to be avoided.

## Provence Alpes/Côte d'Azur
*Area*:
31,400 km²
*Population*:
Around 4,452,000
*Climate*:
Mediterranean in some parts, dry summers overall, humid winters further inland.
*Capital City*:
Marseille
*Departments*:
Alpes-de-Haute-Provence, Hautes-Alpes, Vaucluse, Bouches-du-Rhône, Var, Alpes-Maritimes.
*Miles from V&A Museum in London to Marseille*:
734

*Estimated driving time*:
11 hours 39 minutes
*Cost of tolls*:
£44.11
*Where is it?*
Down in the south, between the sea and the Alps, pretty convenient.
*History*:
Marseille is France's oldest city, founded by the Greeks in the 5th Century BC. It was Roman from 49 BC and then under the counts and kings of Provence in the Middle Ages. It became French in 1481. A gateway to North Africa, it has become home to large numbers of immigrants. It has nothing at all in common with the expensive resorts of the Côte d'Azur, which were so popular with the Victorians, the first tourists to visit the region.
*What do they eat?*
Lots of extremely healthy food; olive oil, fresh vegetables and fruit, fish, *aioli* (garlic mayonnaise), Salade Niçoise, and fish soup (*bouillabaisse*). The Camargue, wild horse and cowboy country, is France's rice-growing region.
*What do they drink?*
Rosé de Provence, pastis (especially in Marseille), lots of excellent Rhône wines like those made by Jean-Luc Colombo.
*What do you do there?*
Depending on where you are; pose, eat, drink, chat to celebrities.
*Who lives there?*
George Michael, Michael Schumacher, Posh and Becks,
Elton John, lots of other foreigners as well as some locals although they are becoming a rarity.
*What does it cost?*
A lot, the prices are equivalent to Paris. Expect to pay €145,000 for a 2 bedroom flat in an old village house in the Var.
*Why is it hot?*
The place to be. International hotspots like Nikki Beach in St Tropez make this coast the one to be seen on. The rich and famous have been coming here for years. The landscape is stunning, a mix of mountains and coastline.
*Why is it not?*
Very expensive and built up. Terribly crowded in the summer, it can take you half an hour to get two kilometres in a car. 'Lazy noisy people' according to an anonymous French friend. Danger of running into Elton John.

### Midi-Pyrenees
*Area*:
45,348 km²
*Population*:
Around 2,505,900
*Climate*:
Continental hot
*Capital City*:
Toulouse
*Departments*:
Ariège, Aveyron, Gers, Haute-Garonne, Lot, Hautes-Pyrenees, Tarn, Tarn-et-Garonne
*Miles from V&A Museum in London to Toulouse*:
677

*Estimated driving time*:
10 hours 50 minutes
*Cost of tolls*:
£31.56
*What do they eat?*
Celebrated cuisine including foie gras, roquefort cheese and the infamous cassoulet which my husband says is a little bit like running across a ploughed field. You start well, but get bogged down towards the end.

*What do they drink?*
Great local wines including the wonderfully robust Cahors, Fronton and Gaillac. Armagnac is made here.

*What do you do there?*
Toulouse is a fantastic city with lots going on. It is renowned for its Asian cuisine, something Brits often miss over here. The region is one of the largest in the country and has a landscape of ancient towns, villages, castles, Romanesque churches and colourful history.

*Who lives there?*
This is *La France Profonde* and expats are not around every corner. Locals have a reputation for being laid-back and good fun. Lots of industry in and around Toulouse, especially in the aerospace sector.

*Prices*:
The last five years have seen increases. There are still bargains to be had in rural areas.

*Why is it hot?*
A truly French experience. Easy access to the rest of the world and France via the TGV or airport at Toulouse. An IKEA that is easy to find just outside the city, delivery of Swedish meatballs every Tuesday.

*Why is it not?*
Bloody cold in the winter. In fact, I was there in April one year and it hailed.

### Rhône-Alpes
*Area*:
43,798 km²
*Population*:
Around 5,608,200
*Climate*:
Continental
*Capital City*:
Lyon
*Departments*:
Ain, Ardèche, Drôme, Isère, Loire, Rhône, Savoie, Haute-Savoie
*Miles from V&A Museum in London to Lyon*:
540
*Estimated driving time*:
8 hours 58 minutes
*Cost of tolls*:
£30.52
*Where is it?*
South east, just above Provence.
*History*:
Gallo-Roman remains, Romanesque art, Renaissance and Medieval sites.
*Who lives there?*
People with serious jobs in industry, gastronomical enthusiasts and wine makers. The locals are said to be welcoming and full of nice people.

*What do they eat?*
Anything you want, Lyon has more restaurants per capita than anywhere else in France. Local

food predominantly dairy and meat based. Specialities include *quenelles*, fish or meat dumplings. Lyon is also known for its calf's and sheep's feet. Bresse chicken is a must, patriotic chickens with blue legs, white feathers and red crests.

*What do they drink?*
Beaujolais, Côte du Rhône and rather more expensive Châteauneuf du Pape.

*What do you do there?*
This is a vast region with much to offer. Lyon is very industrialised, over 80 per cent of the population is involved in some kind of industry. In terms of holidays, you eat, drink, eat some more then maybe visit one of the famous sites like the Gorges de l'Ardèche.

*What does it cost?*
The prices vary enormously. The Ardèche is particularly popular with Brits but there are still some bargains to be had.

*Why is it hot?*
So much to do, so much variety, Lyon is now France's second largest city. The countryside is marvellous, endless lavender fields, lakes, and Mont Blanc, Europe's highest peak.

*Why is it not?*
The spaghetti junction around Lyon. You haven't lived until you've got lost there. Also the industry. Lyon is not a place to come to live the French rural idyll.

# Contacts

*Here are contact details of some of the people in the book.*

## Places to stay

Peter and Lizie Wildman www.holiday-rentals.com/index.cfm/property/10037.cfm

Jill Allcroft www.holiday-rentals.com/index.cfm/property/7257, www.esbayles.com

Alan and Penny Hastings-Jones tel: +33 (0) 4 67 24 78 99

Fiona and Bruno De Wulf, Château de Créancey, www.creancey.com

Gavin and Angela Quinney, Château Bauduc, www.bauduc.com

Fiona Cantwell and Tony Archibold, Château de Marcenac, www.chateaumarcenac.com, fiona@chateaumarcenac.com

## Advice and Professionals

Dawn Alderson, solicitor and avocat, partner with Russell Cooke Solicitors, aldersond@russell-cooke.co.uk, tel: +44 (0) 20 8789 9111

Bill Blevins, Blevins Franks International, www.blevins-franks.com, tel: +44 (0) 20 7336 1116

Tony Tidswell, www.frenchpropertydigest.com www.1stvacations.com

Marcelle Speller, www.Holiday-Rentals.com, marcelle@holiday-rentals.com, tel: +44 (0) 20 8743 5577, fax: +44 (0) 20 8740 3863

Richaed Allcroft allcroftrchrd@aol.com (builder)

Kris Misselbrook www.french-property.com/aurignac, tel: +33 (0) 5 61 98 86 92

Paul Beaufils, www.buyahouseinfrance.com

Jeffrey Quirk, JQ International, tel: +33 (0) 6 87 83 07 58

John Siddall Financial Services Ltd, www.siddalls.net, tel: 01329 288 641, fax: 01329 281 157, jenny@johnsiddalls.co.uk

Pat Bellis, patbellis@wanadoo.fr

## Wine contacts and makers

Charles & Ruth Simpson,
  tel: +33 (0) 4 67 39 07 54,
  crsimpson@sainte-rose.com,
  www.sainte-rose.com
Ruth de Latude,
  www.baronnie-de-
  bourgade.com (Ruth now does
  wine courses as well)
Jean-Claude Mas,
  www.paulmas.com
Helen Genevier and Julie
  Statham,
  www.picwines.co.uk,
  info@picwines.co.uk,
  tel: +33 (0) 4 99 62 09 27
Nerida Abbott
  www.abbottswine.com
Gregory Guida, Saint Martin de
  la Garrigue,
  www.stmartingarrigue.com

## Miscellaneous

Alistair Norman,
  www.uprighttours.co.uk
Helen Goossens
  merton@dircon.co.uk
Stephanie Godwin (dog breeder),
  tel/fax: +33 (0) 2 43 03 20 94,
  godwinsj-
  aron@netcourrier.com
www.parsonrussellterrier.com
Teddy Hutton and Nicola
  Russell, La Maison Verte,
  www.lamaisonverte.co.uk,
  tel: +33 (0) 4 67 24 88 52,
  fax: +33 (0) 4 67 24 69 98

## Schools

*A list of International Schools in
France and contact details (with
thanks to www.frenchentree.com)*

Bordeaux International School
53 rue de Laseppe, 33000,
Bordeaux, France
Tel: +33 (0) 5 57 87 02 11
bis@bordeaux-school.com
www.bordeaux-school.com

CIV International School of
Sophia Antipolis
BP 097, 06902, Sophia Antipolis,
France
Tel: +33 (0) 4 92 96 52 24
secretary@civissa.org
www.civissa.org

Mougins School
615 Avenue Dr Maurice Donat,
Font de l'Orme, BP 401 Cedex,
06250, Mougins, France
Tel: +33 (0) 4 93 90 15 47
information@mougins-
school.com
www.mougins-school.com

British School of Paris
38 Quai de l'Ecluse, 78290,
Croissy-sur-Seine, France
Tel: +33 (0) 1 34 80 45 94
bspprincipal@wanadoo.fr
www.ecis.org/bsp

College International De
Fontainebleau
Anglophone Section, 48 rue
Guerin, 77300, Fontainebleau,
France

# CONTACTS

Tel: +33 (0) 1 64 22 11 77
admin@anglophonesection-
fontainebleau.com
www.anglophonesection-
fontainebleau.com

Ecole Active Bilingue Jeannine
Manuel - Ecole Internationale de
Lille Métropole
418 bis rue Albert Bailly, 59700,
Marcq-en-Baroeul, France
Tel: +33 (0) 3 20 65 90 50
v.leroy@eabjm.com

Ecole Bilingue Greenfield
14 rue da la Mairie, 69660,
Collonges-au-Mont-d'Or, France
Tel: +33 (0) 4 72 27 87 80
greenfield@wanadoo.fr
www.greenfield.fr

Cité Scolaire Internationale Lyon
Section Anglophone, 2 Place de
Montréal, 69361, Lyon, Cedex
07, France
Tel: +33 (0) 4 78 69 60 06
donnamp@wanadoo.fr
www2.ac-lyon.fr/etab/lycees/lyc-
69/csi/accueil.html

The American School of Lyon
80 chemin du Grand Roule,
69110 Ste Foy les Lyon, Lyon,
France
Tel: +33 (0) 4 78 50 44 00
info@tasol.org
www.tasol.org

International School of Bearn
Rue des Fougeres, Quartier
Berlanne, 64160, Morlaas, France

Tel: +33 (0) 6 12 56 68 67
isbearn@wanadoo.fr
site.voila.fr/isbearn

The International School of Nice
15 Avenue Claude Debussy,
06200, Nice, France
Tel: +33 (0) 4 93 21 04 00
dorothy.foster@cote-azur.cci.fr

American School of Paris
41 rue Pasteur, 92210, Saint
Cloud, France
Tel: +33 (0) 1 41 12 82 82
mcalon@asparis.org
www.asparis.org

Ecole Active Bilingue
Boulevard Malesherbes 117,
75008, Paris, France
Tel: +33 (0) 1 45 00 11 57
infovh@eab.fr
www.eab.fr

Ecole Active Bilingue Jeannine
Manuel
70 rue du Théâtre, 75015, Paris,
France
Tel: +33 (0) 1 44 37 00 80
reception@eabjm.com
www.eabjm.com

Eurécole
5 rue de Lübeck, 75116, Paris,
France
Tel: +33 (0) 1 40 70 12 81
direction@eurecole.com
www.eurecole.com

International School of Paris
6 rue Beethoven, 75016, Paris,

# CONTACTS

France
Tel: +33 (0) 1 42 24 09 54
info@isparis.edu
www.isparis.edu

Lycée de Sevres, International
Sections
7 rue Lecocq, 92310, Sevres,
France
Tel: +33 (0) 1 46 23 96 35
association.sis@wanadoo.fr
www.sis-sevres.net

Marymount School
72 bd de la Saussaye, 92200,
Neuilly sur Seine, France
Tel: +33 (0) 1 46 24 10 51
school@ecole-marymount.fr
www.ecole-marymount.fr

United Nations Nursery School
40 rue Pierre Guerin, 75016,
Paris, France
Tel: +33 (0)1 45 27 20 24
unns@noos.fr
www.unns.net

Lycée International of St
Germain-en-Laye (American
Section)
Rue du Fer a Cheval BP 5230,
78175, St Germain-en-Laye,
France
Tel: +33 (0) 1 34 51 74 85
american.intl@wanadoo.fr
www.lycee-intl-american.org

Strasbourg International School
Château de Pourtales, 161 rue
Mélanie, Robertsau, 67000,
Strasbourg, France
Tel: +33 (0) 3 88 31 50 77
info@strasbourgis.org
www.strasbourgis.org

International School of Toulouse
S.A.
Route de Pibrac, 31770,
Colomiers, France
Tel: +33 (0) 5 62 74 26 74
ist@intst.net
www.intst.net

# Index